Beyond Our Means

How the Brethren Service Center Dared To Embrace the World

R. Jan and Roma Jo Thompson

Frank & Jennie.
Friends from Belise & Guatemalia
And other ministries. Enjoy your
books -
    Thanks for The fine Book
Review in messenger!
            Shalom
        R. Jan & Roma Jo

Brethren Press

Beyond Our Means: How the Brethren Service Center Dared To Embrace the World
R. Jan and Roma Jo Thompson

© 2009 Brethren Press

Published by Brethren Press®. Brethren Press is a trademark of the Church of the Brethren, 1451 Dundee Avenue, Elgin, Illinois 60120.

Library of Congress Cataloging-in-Publication Data

Thompson, R. Jan, 1935-
  Beyond our means : how the Brethren Service Center dared to embrace the world / R. Jan Thompson, Roma Jo Thompson.
    p. cm.
  Includes bibliographical references and index.
  ISBN 978-0-87178-100-0
 1. Brethren Service Center. 2. Church work--Church of the Brethren. I. Thompson, Roma Jo, 1936- II. Title.

  BX7827.3.T46 2009
  267'.1865--dc22

                                                                2009002050

13 12 11 10 09   1 2 3 4 5

Printed in the United States of America

This book is one of several Brethren Press publications displaying the mark of the 300th Anniversary of the Brethren (1708-2008). It represents the theme "Surrendered to God, Transformed by Christ, Empowered by the Spirit."

*To the thousands who have worked in ministries
and education on this campus
and to the millions who have benefited.*

*Because of their labors,
we dedicate this book.*

Contents

Husbands and wives met here. Refugees from around the world passed through here on their way to starting over. Children scraped together beloved coins to send here for relief. Youth groups bundled piles of school supplies and health kits for kids like them in other parts of the world. Housewives sent cooking grease here to make soap for relief, and men wrangled cows onto trains and ships from this spot. We would be nostalgic about the Brethren Service Center at New Windsor, Maryland, but there isn't time before the next natural disaster, the next call for medicines and supplies for people displaced by war and famine, or the next group of volunteers that shows up to help with shipments.

Beyond Our Means is a chronicle of the Brethren Service Center and the central part it has played in the life of the Church of the Brethren in the twentieth and twenty-first centuries. As an educational institution, Blue Ridge College, and its predecessors for that matter, struggled endlessly to make ends meet and finally declared bankruptcy. But as a service center, the campus flourished, getting extraordinary results from very modest amounts of money. Members of the Brethren Service Committee took a chance borrowing funds from Bridgewater College to purchase the campus for about $32,000, not knowing if it would be viable in the end. But in a very few years, the programs and partnerships of the Center yielded results far beyond anyone's predictions.

Service work has changed over time. When the Brethren started this work, we and other church organizations supplied much of the war relief in Europe after World War II. Now numerous private and governmental agencies have been spawned to address issues of hunger, health, and homelessness around the world. Relief agencies now purchase and ship supplies from places geographically close to the need instead of wasting enormous amounts of money on shipping and warehousing.

The need for service, however, has not changed. Regional wars, genocide, famine, epidemics, and natural disasters plague the world still. And New Windsor is our hatchery for creative solutions that, in theory, are beyond our means as a small denomination. Our greatest resource is people power. Our members and partners help magnify the efforts to feed the hungry, clothe the naked, give a drink to the thirsty, and visit the prisoner.

The Center has lived—and thrived—beyond its means. The world would not believe that so much has come from one little rail stop, one small post office, one bankrupt little college in rural Maryland. Roy Winter, director of the Center, testifies to this disbelief when he tells the story of a member of the Sierra Leone parliament who entered for a visit to the United States through the airport in Baltimore. Many times the MP had seen boxes of relief supplies in his country with the "Brethren Service Center, New Windsor, Maryland" stencil on them. When he landed in Baltimore, he began asking around about New Windsor, but he was surprised to find that nobody seemed to know of it. Surely, he thought, everyone in America would know of this important place. But it is perhaps more well known abroad than at home.

It is not the place but the work. It is not the work but the love of neighbor. It is not the love of neighbor but the glory of God that buttresses the work of the Center. God is the one who makes something from nothing, sending us out to live beyond our means. As disciples we don't always know how we will feed the world's hungry, but with some loaves of bread and a few little fish, God feeds the multitudes.

R. Jan and Roma Jo Thompson gave enormous energy to this project. They, being one of the couples who met at the Center and married, know first hand the power of the Center to change people and deepen their faith. They convinced the Center and Brethren Press of the need for a history and made themselves available to do the hard work. In the course of preparing the manuscript, they traveled the country in their motor home to talk with veteran volunteers. They dispelled some of the folklore surrounding the purchase of the Center and lifted up little-known stories about its past. Then, after the book was "finished," they worked patiently with the editors, returning to the archives over and over to check facts and search for photographs. They are giving their lives to the work of the Center, unable to retire without numerous requests for their help from the church. Without their vision and energy, this book would not have come to be.

The Thompsons supplied the elbow grease, and the Brethren Service Center gave financial support to underwrite the production of this book by Brethren Press. When the Center expends money, it usually has dramatic results—changing lives and saving lives. No lives were saved in the creation of this book, but the record is preserved, and with it the commitment and devotion to service. Every once in a while, we have to take a sabbath break from our work and survey what we've done and know that it is good.

Julie Garber
Editor

We had never visited the Center until the day we arrived for Brethren Volunteer Service training with Unit 25, December 1954. From that time on, the Brethren Service Center has been an important part of our lives. The fact that Jan loves history and Roma Jo works at being interested started the project of researching this place that has had schools and service ministries throughout its existence. Because many of the Civilian Public Service (CPS) volunteers who had been assigned to work at New Windsor in the fall of 1944 were getting older, we thought there should be a record of their experiences. We also believed they would provide us with information about the birth of the Relief Center.

In the summer of 2000, we approached Stan Noffsinger, director of the Brethren Service Center at the time, with our idea. He was supportive and offered to pay our mileage if we would do the actual interviews. Encouraged by his support, we made appointments for personal visits and had wonderful and inspiring conversations with the men and women as they shared their memories. Journals, photos, personal letters, the excitement in their voices, and emotions of "those times" filled our recordings and notes. During the next three summers, we spent many hours in the Carroll County Historical Library where the staff was most helpful. Our visits with Julia Cairns, the local historian in New Windsor, were informative, and we heard stories like none we had read or heard from anyone else. Julia, a Brethren and resident of the New Windsor area for more than ninety years and a founding member of the New Windsor Heritage Committee, provided us with a treasure trove of news clippings and other articles about Blue Ridge College and Carroll County.

As we researched the history of higher education at the New Windsor campus, we learned that, despite the desire and need for education, it was a struggle for those in charge of the colleges to keep the finances in line. We also learned that most of those on the school boards or in direct administrative responsibility maintained a strong Christian focus. The Church of the Brethren (German Baptist Brethren) members knew if they ran the school, it would measure up to the expectations of most of the area church members.

We learned that even before the Church of the Brethren purchased the campus in September 1944 the campus was used for gathering and packing relief goods for Europe's war victims in the spring. The condition of the buildings had been neglected, and repairs and upgrading needed to be done. It was then that the CPS men were moved from their camps to the Center to work on repairs, bringing with them plumbing, heating, and carpentry skills. With innovative leadership and ecumenical involvement, the Brethren Service Center developed into a bigger and more productive place than anyone had ever imagined it would.

We would review all the information that we gathered and discover that we needed more information on a particular time period or situation. Back to the Carroll County Historical Society and the public library we would go. Or we would e-mail or call Ken Shaffer, director of the Brethren Historical Library and Archives in Elgin for more information. We learned how to search for certain information and welcomed the suggestions of those who referred us to people who had lived at that time. We checked the works of authors who had written on topics that might shed light on particular issues.

Finally, we felt we had as much information as we needed, and we set aside time for writing. We divided up the topics, and each wrote on the areas in which we had interest. In the summer of 2006, with access to an office at the Brethren Service Center, we rented an apartment and read and typed five days a week, usually six to seven hours a day, for eight weeks. We went to NOAC (National Older Adult Conference) where we sought out people who might be able to answer some of our questions.

Then we went home to Mesa, Arizona, and followed up on our new leads, spending the next several months working on the final details. By Thanksgiving we were able to send copies of the manuscript to friends who volunteered to read it. The Reverend Jim Benedict, Jim Davis, Doris Dunham, and Howard Royer gave us excellent feedback.

We would not have started this project without encouragement from Stan Noffsinger. We are grateful for his encouragement and the follow-up support from Roy Winter, the present director of the Brethren Service Center. We thank the CPS men and their wives who told their stories and the early volunteers and staff who also shared stories and files. We are grateful for the beginning of the relief work and the example it set for all of us to this day. This was a time when leaders had visions and put them to work.

We express deep gratitude to the staff at our denominational archives, Ken Shaffer and his intern, Logan Condon. They worked diligently to find the missing links to several parts of the story. Special thanks to Julie Garber, our editor, and to Nancy Klemm, copy editor, who took our written words and presented them in a "readable" form. Both current and past staff of ministries on the New Windsor campus were very helpful, too. We extend a special word of thanks to the staff of Wheeler Chrysler of Westminster for the information they shared from their wonderful historical exhibit in the lower level of the dealership. They permitted us access to documents that we had not found in any other location. Thanks to Dale Harter, librarian and archivist at the Alexander Mack Memorial Library, Bridgewater College, for his assistance in providing access to the Blue Ridge College records located in that archive. A big thank you to all who have encouraged us along the way.

As we worked on this project, we gained new insights and appreciation for the leaders who, in times of difficulty, continued to hold true to the teachings of Jesus, ministering to people in need around the world. It seems that God has called forth ordinary people to do extraordinary tasks all throughout history. God is good!

Part I

---⊚---

The White Building on the Hill

Courtesy of Alexander Mack Memorial Library, Special Collections, Bridgewater College.

I

Calvert College, 1848–1870

Long before the wooded hilltop in New Windsor, Maryland, became the Brethren Service Center campus that we know today, it was the setting for a succession of educational institutions.

In the mid-1830s Andrew Hull Baker, a local farm boy from the New Windsor area, enrolled at Mount Saint Mary's College, a Catholic institution in nearby Emmittsburg. Although he had been reared in a Protestant home, he returned to New Windsor after graduation as a professing Catholic. In 1846 Baker converted an abandoned church in New Windsor into a schoolhouse and hired teachers. Soon so many students enrolled in his school that he opened a boardinghouse for them. After two years of teaching at the secondary level, Mr. Baker perceived the need for a college where his students could continue their education. With support from other Catholics in the area, he was able to purchase a piece of land from Josiah Hibberd in 1848 called "the Woods on the Hill." There Baker built Old Main, as it's still called today. The footprint of the building was 100' x 75' and consisted of a basement and three floors with a tin roof. It was built as a classroom and dormitory building. A second building was constructed to house a kitchen, dining rooms, laundry, and housing for male students. The construction of the buildings was completed in 1850 for a cost of approximately $60,000.[1]

The general contractor for the construction was Amos Caylor, a German Baptist man who, at age twenty-one, was already well known in the area as a carpenter and farmer. Some years later, in 1872, Caylor was called into the free ministry and in 1887 was elected elder of the Pipe

Creek German Baptist Church (later known as the Pipe Creek Church of the Brethren).

Mr. Baker was able to secure recognition and a charter from the Maryland Department of Education for the new school he called Calvert College. The school was named after Lord Calvert, one of the early settlers in the state of Maryland and an important person in Maryland government and the Catholic Church. Since Mr. Baker was a practicing Catholic as well, the institution was known by reputation as a Catholic college, but in reality Calvert College was never owned or controlled by the Catholic Church.[2]

The first classes were held in Old Main on October 21, 1850. The school year was divided into two semesters, and the course offerings were mathematics, natural and moral philosophy, chemistry, astronomy, French, German, Spanish, and study of the classics. The winter semester ran twenty-six weeks and cost $75; the summer session ran eighteen weeks and cost $50. These fees included tuition, board, laundry, and "attention to clothing." For an additional fee of $30 per year, one could receive music instruction. Books and writing materials were extra.[3]

Mr. Baker was an excellent headmaster as well as a strict disciplinarian, though he had some strange methods of enforcing his rules. The catalog of 1852 states that all mail sent or received by students, except to parents and guardians, was under the direct supervision of the president. Students also were strictly forbidden to read novels and other immoral books. In the oral tradition of the school, a darkened room located on the top floor of Old Main was used for imprisoning those who had committed misdeeds, and if the offense was grave enough, one of the possible punishments was to be confined in a coffin provided for that purpose.[4]

Timbers in the attic floor still show evidence of a fire. In 1860, while most students were attending a talent show, it's reported that the wood-burning stove in "Irish" Mike's room in the attic of Old Main overheated and the upper floor caught fire because the student who was assigned to monitor the fires and keep the rooms warm was inattentive. By the time the fire was extinguished, the top floor was heavily damaged, as was the tin roof. Since major repairs were necessary, school officials decided to take advantage of the circumstances to add a fourth floor and a slate roof to the building. An architect named Short from Emmittsburg was hired to draw plans for the repair work, and once again Amos Caylor was the general contractor for the rebuilding.[5]

Calvert College had an excellent reputation and was considered one of the finest classical schools in the state. Many leaders of the county and the state from that period were graduates of the college. Dr. Robert Bartholow of the Jefferson Medical Center in Philadelphia and Frederick Dielman, creator of the mosaic "Law" and "History" panels in the Congressional Library and other distinguished works, graduated from Calvert.

The college was a sound investment for Mr. Baker until the beginning of the War Between the States. When the war broke out in 1861, the majority of the male students, who were from states below the Mason-Dixon Line, left the college and enlisted in the Confederate forces. Those who did not leave at the beginning of the war left in the summer of 1864 with the Confederate cavalry of Colonel Gilmar when his men came to New Windsor seeking supplies.

What Happened to the Chapel?

It was also in 1861 that the Catholic Church was given access to a plot of land next to Old Main on which to build a chapel. The Reverend Thomas O'Neill served as pastor under the administration of St. Joseph's Catholic Church in Taneytown. The cemetery associated with the chapel was located to the east on what is now Springdale Road on the property of the Yellow Turtle Inn. A photo taken in 1896 shows the chapel next to Old Main; however, soon after the picture was taken, the building, which cost $5,000 to build, was sold at public auction for $100 to John C. Buckey with the understanding that he would remove it from the school property. He used some of these materials to build a stable, which was located at the intersection of High and Church Streets just across the street from the Presbyterian Church. The building is now a garage for "horseless carriages." Mr. Buckey apparently enlisted help from others in the community to tear down the chapel (*Nathan Baile diary; Edward Crill History; Julia Cairns interview*).

Charles Spielman purchased the stained glass windows and a large chandelier from the original chapel. The stained glass windows remained in his family for three generations and were stored on a farm just outside New Windsor until 2005 when the widow of the grandson of Mr. Spielman sold the family farm (*Betty Warren, phone interview, summer 2006*).

The windows were sold to an antique dealer in New Market, Maryland, who commented, "The stained glass windows from the Catholic Chapel were very nice. I sold them as soon as I had them." The oil chandelier was sold at auction in the community of Marston.

We have scant information about the social activities of the students attending Calvert College; however, a short note in a history of Carroll County tells of college students playing baseball: "When the Olympian Club of Westminster played the 'Calvert Club' of Calvert College in New Windsor in 1866, a special train provided transportation to the game and back for fifty cents."[6]

When the majority of students left for the war, the school declined financially and in reputation. By the end of the 1860s, Calvert College was without students and had incurred large debts to various creditors. In 1870 when investors took over the college, Mr. Baker left Calvert and moved to a farm near Germantown, Maryland, where he spent the remainder of his life. He was able to repay $37,000 of his $62,000 debt prior to his death; several creditors never recovered from their lost investment.[7]

When Mr. Baker left the school in the hands of his creditors,[8] they tried to continue a school on the location by renting the buildings to a man named George H. Birnie, who maintained a school for several years. When Birnie left, he became a banker in the nearby community of Taneytown.[9]

1872–1894

The Presbytery of Baltimore appointed a committee in 1872 to study the possibility of establishing a college at New Windsor using the vacant Calvert College campus. In 1873, the Reverend L. B. Shryock, with the backing of the Calvert College Educational Society of Carroll County, purchased the land and buildings with the intent of establishing a Presbyterian college. The name of the new college was New Windsor College.[1]

Rev. Shryock was able to obtain credit to remodel some of the buildings. He built a porch on the rear of Old Main, remodeled the two dormitories into small classrooms, and moved the kitchen and dining hall to the basement.

New Windsor College opened in September 1874 as two separate and independent schools: the Ladies Seminary and a classical and mathematical academy for young men. "All the students were brought together every day in the dining hall, and once a month in the parlors, always in the presence of the faculty. At all other times, night and day, the girls were in the presence of a female faculty member."[2]

George Birnie returned from the bank in Taneytown to replace Rev. Shryock in 1876 as headmaster, but he served for only one year. In 1877 the Reverend A. M. Jelly, minister of the 12th Street Presbyterian Church in Baltimore, left his position to become headmaster of New Windsor College. Then, in 1878, Rev. and Mrs. Jelly purchased the college campus.

The school flourished under his leadership, growing to include more than one hundred male and female boarders. The Jellys also purchased additional land surrounding the college and bought cows and pigs to provide meat for the dining hall program. They hired a farmer to care for the animals and a gardener to plant and grow vegetables.

In 1876 the college received a new charter making provisions for New Windsor College (for the boys) and Windsor Female College (for the girls). The college granted A. B. degrees for the men and Mistress of Polite Literature for the ladies until 1892, when they changed their system of giving degrees. It was then possible for the college to award Bachelor of Arts, Bachelor of Science, Bachelor of Letters, Master of Arts, Master of Science, Doctor of Philosophy, and Doctor of Science degrees. Honorary degrees were given for Doctor of Philosophy, Doctor of Divinity, Doctor of Law, as well as Masters Degrees.[3]

Even in those days, the school became the site of meetings and gatherings, foreshadowing what it would become fifty years later:

During the absence of students [on] vacation, the college is much patronized as a charming summer resort, and is usually filled to its utmost capacity with boarders. Tourists find New Windsor a charming place to spend the heated term and the College offers them all the comforts of home, with the freedom and luxury of a good hotel.[4]

Manners and Morals

A newspaper clipping from 1885 describes the school and its philosophy:

The Colleges are two separate Institutions located adjacent to each other under the same general management. Parents and guardians are thus enabled to educate sons and daughters and wards of both sexes, without separation, save what the necessities of the case require. Where too, their minds, manners and morals are cultivated with all the care of high class educational

Institutions, mingled with the social and elevating influences of a genial and refined home.

Though conducted under the general auspices of the Presbyterian Church, the college is not under church control. The tenor of its religious influence being safe and healthful, but entirely free from bigoted bias. While students are required to attend religious worship, either at the college chapel, or elsewhere, no denominational preference is ever permitted to be disturbed. Students enjoy the advantage of a large and well-selected library, and also of the "William Andrews" Cabinet of Geology, which contains over 20,000 specimens.

Jay Graybeal, Carroll County Times *[Westminster, Md.]* **9 December 1996.**

1894–1912

After seventeen years as president, Dr. Jelly was forced to resign because of poor health. His wife, unable to continue the administration of the school, sold the campus to the New Windsor College Company, a group of Presbyterian men who had high hopes that the Baltimore Presbytery would assume control of the college.[5]

The new trustees asked the Reverend William H. Purnell, principal of the Frederick Female Seminary in Frederick, to accept the duties of president of the New Windsor colleges. Then two years later, in 1896, the Reverend Charles Ramsdell assumed the presidency of New Windsor College. In another two years, the Reverend James M. Nourse became president.

The presidency changed again in 1901 when Dr. James Frazier, LLD, became the owner and president. He came well prepared for the position. He was a world traveler, held degrees from both Toronto University and Syracuse University, and had both earned and honorary doctoral degrees. Dr. Frazier served on the faculty for some years in the department of languages. While teaching at New Windsor College, Dr. Frazier also served for eight years as pastor of the Presbyterian Church of New Windsor.[6] In all these years, however, the Baltimore Presbytery declined to take on the administration of the colleges.

During Dr. Frazier's tenure, the college buildings were upgraded with an addition of a "wind wheel" and a hot water boiler to provide heat and hot water to all the buildings. According to the *Democratic Advocate Supplement* (Westminster, Md.),

The comfortable buildings and ample grounds with the pure water for which Carroll County is noted and the mineral springs of New Windsor must appeal strongly to those who would have their children retain the bloom of youth while acquiring the mental charms that have delighted all ages. The dangers to health are often given no consideration when institutions are chosen and many pay the price of wrecked nervous systems in cities "where wealth accumulates and men decay." (13 October 1910)

3

Blue Ridge College

MARYLAND COLLEGIATE INSTITUTE, 1899–1912 (UNION BRIDGE)

At the time when New Windsor College was in full operation, plans for another institution of higher learning were afoot in the county. On April 18, 1899, the Sam's Creek congregation of the German Baptist Brethren petitioned the Eastern District of Maryland to make an immediate study to ascertain the advisability of starting a Brethren school. A committee, consisting of John E. Senseney, Ephraim Stouffer, Amos Wampler, John S. Weybright, and William E. Roop, was appointed to make this investigation. A special meeting of the district was called in August to hear the report of this committee.[1]

The committee reported that (1) in addition to the apparent need for this school, there was great enthusiasm to get started, (2) the teachers were procurable, (3) the money would be available, and (4) a temporary location for the school to operate had been found. The report was accepted by the District Meeting, and the plan for the proposed school was under way.

On September 25, 1899, Maryland Collegiate Institute came into being, though some reports indicate the school opened November 1, 1899. Trustees rented the second floor of the Union Bridge Banking and Trust Company for $125 for the school year. J. Maurice Henry wrote: "The session was to run twenty-four weeks of two equal terms. . . . with twenty-four students and four teachers and officers—W. E. Roop, president; William Wine, principal; Samuel D. Zigler and Emery

Crumpacker."[2] Once the school was thoroughly organized, the trustees set a goal of offering commercial and academic courses, as well as music, art, and Bible. It was to be a coeducational, nonsectarian, and Christian school. The school board members were Amos Wampler of Medford, W. E. Roop of Westminster (president), Ephraim Stouffer of New Windsor, John S. Weybright of Double Pipe Creek, and John E. Senseney of Linwood.[3]

The desire of a few spirited Christian minds to establish an institute of learning where young men and women could fit themselves for life in every worthwhile way became a successful endeavor. All worthy young people were welcomed. Parents were assured that both sons and daughters attending the same institution would have all possible safeguards. Training in religion and morality received as much attention as intellectual training.

On January 31, 1900, the trustees met to make plans for a permanent location of the school. They agreed to form a stock company by selling 1,000 shares of stock at $25 each, thereby establishing a capital fund of $25,000 for the corporation. Five acres of maple-shaded land with a magnificent view of the Blue Ridge Mountains were purchased at the south end of Union Bridge. In every direction lay the slopes and valleys of a prosperous agricultural region dotted with farmhouses and woodlands.

Plans moved forward with local builders Joseph Wolf and John Rakestraw hired to construct two buildings on the scenic property. The cost of the two buildings was estimated at $11,500, to include men's and women's dormitories with additional space for classrooms, offices, kitchen, dining room, and chapel. The buildings were completed by September 1, 1900, as agreed, and the second year of operation began with eighty-five students and six teachers. William M. Wine was elected president and continued in this position for the next eleven years. The following year a third building was erected.

Mackalean Hall held the president's office and commercial classroom. The treasurer's office, bookstore, and recitation rooms were on the second floor. The chemical laboratory was in the basement. The third floor provided twenty-two sleeping rooms for the male students and teachers.

The Ladies' Home provided tastefully arranged rooms for the female boarding students, teachers, and a matron. The first floor had a well-furnished parlor. There was a frame structure attached to the rear of this building primarily for the use of the president's family. The kitchen, dining room for students and teachers, and a boiler room were in the basement. There were six bedrooms and a bath on the second floor, with four more bedrooms on the third floor.

Adelphian Hall provided space for the library, recitation rooms, and a chapel. The third floor was reserved as a dormitory for men.[4]

Morality and religion were recognized as the foundation of education. Prayer meetings were held every Wednesday evening in the college chapel; there was preaching every Sunday evening and Sunday school each Sunday morning, after which students had the privilege of attending preaching services at any one of the five churches of different denominations in town.

The college year was thirty-eight weeks, divided into three terms. School officials kept careful records of attendance, scholarship, and conduct for each student; they also sent a general statement of progress to parents or guardians at the close of each term. Expectations for students were laid out clearly in the college brochure:

> Students entering this school are put under the supervision and control of the Faculty, and will be expected to comply with all regulations. They will be received as ladies and gentlemen, and expected to deport themselves as such. All excuses must be obtained from the Principal, or someone authorized by him. Any student failing to comply with the requirements will be informed of his or her misconduct, and given an opportunity for explanation or defense. If it be impossible to render satisfaction, such person will be required to withdraw. The discipline will be mild, but firm; its aim is, the true development of young ladies and gentlemen.

Generous donations have largely made possible the rapid progress of the College. From the start it found a welcome in the hearts of those who knew that if a College is not worth having for the money they can make out of it, it is for the good they can do through it. And the gifts are not all in the past; the advances made each year to meet increasing demands are mainly due to them. It is the aim of the Institution to make every contributor feel that it is worthy of the interest manifested in its behalf. The recommendations it has to offer are the young men and women, who, during the half decade of its existence, have been by it better fitted for a nobler life.

An Endowment Scholarship Fund has been started by the Alumni and Alumnae of '04. It is an accepted fact that a large proportion of the best students in any institution is found to consist of those who are in financial straits while in school. Our graduates realize this to the extent that they have decided to start a fund, of which the interest only will be used, to assist worthy young people in getting an education.[5]

From 1901 to 1906, the school experienced slow but steady growth, requiring a few additions to the faculty, some coming from Bridgewater College, a Brethren college in Virginia.

In 1907 there were several human relations conflicts to be resolved. Also at this time, some stock fell into the hands of non-Brethren, which proved awkward for officials who were trying to run the school according to Brethren practice. Meanwhile, the school officials were preparing to seek accreditation, which meant that faculty members were required to have advanced degrees. The student body would have to be increased, and additional equipment and buildings would be needed. Financial records showed a deficit instead of a surplus for the period from 1900 to 1906.

A New Name: Blue Ridge College

For the first ten years, the curriculum included Bible, art, music, and commercial subjects. On March 11, 1907, the trustees voted to enlarge the curriculum to include a liberal arts program, but this increased costs that exceeded the school's income. When the liberal arts program was added, the charter was amended and a discussion ensued about changing the name of the school. Blue Ridge College was chosen from among the many submissions. The school was rechartered under the new name in 1910, giving the trustees full power to hold property, elect a faculty, and confer degrees in any sciences, arts, and the professions that colleges commonly provided.

As enrollment and income began to decline, church leaders began to consider the welfare of the school. Some felt the time was right to consolidate Blue Ridge College with either Bridgewater College or Elizabethtown College, two of seven Brethren schools. Many opinions were voiced and the communities of Hagerstown, Waynesboro, and Myersville asked that the college be relocated in one of their towns. Though the stresses of the decision-making process caused some board members to resign, the board pressed on to find a place to offer young men and women a college education in a Christian surrounding.

Meanwhile, the Tidewater Portland Cement Company had begun construction in 1909 directly behind the college buildings in Union Bridge. The dust and noise of the cement factory was no environment for a school. After much negotiation, the college land and buildings were sold in 1912 to the cement company. (See Appendix 1.)

A proposal to join Blue Ridge College with Bridgewater College at its Virginia location nearly came to pass. The movement for consolidation in 1912 had resulted from the firm conviction of some leaders that the Church of the Brethren was attempting to support too many schools and would show wisdom by concentrating its energies and resources on "half the number." A "deliberate or forced thinning out" of the schools was certain to occur "in the course of time, unless we experience a sudden phenomenal growth," some churchmen predicted.[6]

In January, 1912, when Blue Ridge College (formerly Maryland Collegiate Institute), a Church of the Brethren school then at Union Bridge, Maryland, was seeking a new location, the Bridgewater College Board of Trustees considered the advisability of inviting Bridgewater's sister school to unite with her.

... On February 1, the Bridgewater trustees decided unanimously to extend such an invitation. ... On March 25, the Bridgewater trustees, with William M. Wine, Uriah Bixler and Charles D. Bonsack, trustees of Blue Ridge College, present and participating, discussed further the combination of the two colleges, and adopted the following proposal for approval by the trustees of the two institutions: That Bridgewater College, of Virginia, and Blue Ridge College, of Maryland, "should be considered consolidated"; that the name of the "consolidated institution be 'Blue Ridge College' and its president be John S. Flory; that Uriah Bixler, Hiram G. Miller, and John S. Flory . . . nominate the first faculty members; that the Blue Ridge College trustees, for the time being, should continue to manage the funds in their care, but that the income from their investment should go for the benefit of the consolidated college. This proposal, already adopted by Bridgewater's trustees, received the approval of Blue Ridge's trustees on March 30."[7]

More of the story indicates there was a celebration at Bridgewater the evening of March 30, 1912, with ringing of the college bell and a parade of students with a periodic "rah, rah, rah" for Dr. Flory. The celebration culminated in a huge bonfire on the college athletic field the evening of April 2, after the college boys collected debris and brush for the fire. More than three hundred people witnessed this bonfire and heard speeches by faculty, alumni, students, and a representative of the town of Bridgewater.

The celebration, however, was premature. The Blue Ridge College trustees, meeting in special session on April 10, 1912, reconsidered their previous action and, responding to pressure from the college's alumni, annulled their approval of the consolidation.[8]

It seems that one of the major reasons (in addition to objections from Blue Ridge alumni) that this agreement failed was because the stocks sold to establish Blue Ridge College had been issued in the state of Maryland. A serious problem arose when the college announced plans to move out of the state while still being financed through these stocks.

A committee of A. P. Snader, John Jay John, C. D. Bonsack, J. Walter Englar, and John E. Senseney was then appointed to find a suitable location for the college in Maryland and a sale bill of college equipment was circulated. Then, two days before the sale, the committee had an option to buy the New Windsor College property from Dr. James Frazier of the Baltimore Presbytery. The sale of school equipment was cancelled.

In August 1912, Blue Ridge College moved to the campus at New Windsor. The information sent out from Blue Ridge College announced that the fourteenth session of the school would open at New Windsor on September 17, 1912. With only seven weeks to move all the equipment and have everything ready for the school opening, farmers and friends of the community volunteered their wagons, teams, and willing hands. The school year began on September 17 as announced.

A Prime Location

Blue Ridge College is located on the summit of a hill overlooking the picturesque town of New Windsor. New Windsor is a beautiful little residential town of about six hundred inhabitants, and is located on the Western Maryland Railroad about midway between Baltimore and Hagerstown. The town, which is situated in the midst of one of the best farming sections of the state, is easily reached from any point of the Western Maryland Railroad, and good connections can be made in Hagerstown or Baltimore, with other railroads. Frederick can be reached in a short time either by trolley or rail. Also York is within easy reach.

A beautiful view of many miles of surrounding country may be had from any side of the College. On a clear day, from the cupola, may be seen Western Maryland College, at Westminster, seven miles away. The most beautiful view is that to the west, where hill and dale, covered with the fertile soil of Maryland, stretches away eighteen miles to the Blue Ridge Mountains, from which the College takes it name.

Both town and college are supplied with an abundance of sparkling, pure, clear water from a never failing spring, about three miles distant. The town and college are lighted by electricity.

Stories of Union Bridge—Yesterday and Today, *Centennial Celebration Committee, 1974. Wheeler Automotive Museum, Westminster, Md.*

Blue Ridge College, 1913–1927

Without support from the Baltimore Presbytery, President Frazier of New Windsor College had been seeking to relieve himself of the financial and administrative tasks of the college. Until a sale of the property could be arranged, he rented the campus to the trustees of Blue Ridge College, operated by the Eastern Maryland District of the Church of the Brethren. The following year, 1913, the buildings and grounds were sold to the Church of the Brethren.

Blue Ridge College trustees soon began remodeling Old Main. New classrooms, dormitories, and equipment were added. In 1913 Windsor Hall, a ladies dormitory with accommodations for forty-eight women, also housed a chapel, two parlors, a dining hall, and kitchen. A gymnasium-auditorium, with seating for six hundred people, was constructed in 1914 with a floor suitable for basketball and other sports. In 1919 a building near Old Main, once used for housing students, was demolished, and Becker Memorial Hall, a residence hall for boys, was built to take its place. This building had rooms for sixty-six men, with classrooms and social rooms on the first floor and several large rooms in the basement. As recently as 2006, there was a large painting of a brain on a wall in the basement hallway that, one can assume, was likely on the wall of a science classroom. For decades the maintenance staff at New Windsor painted around this drawing to preserve a small bit of history. However, in the spring of 2007, the picture was painted over to cover the original lead-based paint. A small library housed 4,500 volumes, but the students also had access to the Washington County Free Library of 30,000 volumes.

The school operated primarily as a liberal arts college and, secondly, as a business college. Courses in music, the arts, and the Bible were offered as well. Soon Blue Ridge College also had a major for those interested in receiving a certificate to teach in public schools in Maryland.

With the move to New Windsor, Blue Ridge College had renewed life and vigor. One of its former teachers, John Jay John, served as interim president. In 1913 trustees asked C. D. Bonsack, chairman of the board, to serve as acting president until a permanent president could be found. He served for two years before being replaced by Paul H. Bowman, who resigned two years later to accept a position at Bridgewater College. The board of trustees then named F. F. Holsopple to the office of president in 1917. The college was by this time a four-year college.

Blue Ridge College board members were required by the charter to be members of the Church of the Brethren, as were all administrative staff, professors, and teachers. Students attending Blue Ridge College were largely members of the Church of the Brethren, though some were from other denominations.

When Blue Ridge College moved from Union Bridge to New Windsor, it's interesting to note that the German Baptist meetinghouse at 111 Church Street was converted to a private residence after the congregation left the building to worship with the college community in the chapel in Windsor Hall.[9]

From a Student's Perspective . . .

The standards of behavior at Blue Ridge College were in accordance with the cultural standards of the day, as well as the expectations of the Church of the Brethren. Some of these expectations can be seen in letters from students. Following are excerpts from correspondence between Bertha Fike, a student at Blue Ridge College, and Joe Whitacre prior to his arrival on campus. When he arrived on campus, Bertha worked elsewhere until their marriage.

September 22, 1917 [*Bertha writing to Joe*]:
The war certainly is doing its work. I tell you there are not many teachers left or boys either. Our physiology teacher has to go. He has been in school fourteen years, just ready to go out and do something with his education. I pity him so. Bro. Bonsack's boy has to go too, and David Dotterer. Some of the students took a walk out to see the gypsy's tent today. I suppose it must be two miles long. They certainly are strict here, and I'm glad. The girls can go to town every other day, and the boys ditto, but not at the

same time. A boy can take a girl out walking after quiet time Sunday afternoon, if they get permission.

October 6, 1917 [*Bertha writing to Joe*]:
You misunderstood me about keeping company. We are allowed after Society on Friday nights, and we are allowed to go out walking Sundays between 3:30 and 5:00.

October 13, 1918 [*Bertha writing*]:
Bro. Mallott and Bro. Kinsey are wearing the plain clothing in class and everywhere. Prof. Stump doesn't wear the plain clothing, but I understand that he and his wife are applicants for China when the war is over. Bro. Holsopple still sticks to his tie, Miss Fogelsanger to her hat. Maybe if we pray a little more, we will get them to come over. I have dining room work which pays all my expenses with the Stover Scholarship. The only thing I need money for is my books, car fare, etc.

October 20, 1918 [*Bertha writing about the flu epidemic*]:
The flu isn't bad if you go to bed as soon as you feel the least bit sick, stay there until you feel able to be up, and don't eat any solid food at all. They have had at least twelve girls in bed for the last few days. They are all out today, except seven, and they will be out tomorrow. The boys have Dr. Brown, and he isn't an extra good Doctor. One boy has been in bed two weeks. Mrs. Schue took a backset. She stays over in the boys' dorm with Mr. Schue. The school is closed now for one week, but I can't go home because it is too far. Mama says there were seventy-five people died in Oakland in one night. Homer (her brother-in-law) had it. Use onion fried in lard, put them on your chest as hot as can be borne. For the fever, tie cold raw onion on your wrists and bottoms of your feet. Use Vicks VapoRub salve according to directions. You can get it at the store. Drink plenty of lemonade, eat lemon juice with sugar. *DON'T EAT PICKLES!* The Doctor told me to eat all my bread toasted and drink hot cocoa, and plenty of soft-boiled eggs and roasted potatoes.

November 3, 1918 [*Bertha writing*]:
John Biddinger died with the flu. His wife and children had to carry him downstairs and wash him after death.

January 16, 1919 [*Joe writing to his mother after arriving at Blue Ridge College*]:
Send me a great big box of good things to eat. We hardly ever get any meat. I have only had meat about three times since I came here, but, we have plenty of other things to eat. Kill one of those old big chickens and send it down here and it won't last long. Bible term is next week. Tell Daddy, I said he should come. It will only cost him $2.50 for meals and he can stay right here in the room with us and it won't cost him a cent!

September 1920 [*Joe writing to Bertha*]:
If you were here on campus now, we could be out there with them. I miss you so much. They are going to give couples two hours outside on campus now instead of an hour and a half. . . . Murphy told us this morning that it was up to the student ministers and the deacons of the town to care for the members of the church here at school. . . . We started morning watch last Thursday morning, and it has been well attended so far. . . . My subjects are: Caesar, French, Algebra, Modern History, English, Literature, and Solfeggio [An exercise for the voice in which the Solfa musical syllables are used]. I could not get out of History because Biology comes in the second year of Prep now.

November 21, 1920 [*Joe writing*]:
I preached out at Edgewood this morning, and after I was through, Brother Green came to me and gave me a dollar. He certainly is a good man. I wish we had more in the church like him.

Personal collection of the authors.

Like most other colleges, Blue Ridge College was affected by World War I. The drain of the war and strict enrollment requirements limited the pool of possible students in 1917. The college soon began to have problems with enrollment, and financial support generated by tuition and fees declined. On November 26, 1917, the trustees set a goal of raising $200,000 to establish an endowed fund to "receive, procure, create, invest and manage a permanent endowment fund, the income only therefrom to be used for sustaining and extending the educational work of said corporation, all as provided by a resolution of the Board of Trustees of said corporation passed and adopted on the twenty-sixth day of November, 1917."[10] It was further stated that if Blue Ridge College ceased to exist as an educational institution under the control of the Church of the Brethren, "The permanent endowment fund" should be delivered to the "General Educational Board of the Church of the Brethren."[11]

The college announced to the general public that it had received donations of $86,000 for the endowment fund; however, it is difficult to account for this amount of money. Ultimately, the funds that were received were used by the college to pay off debts incurred in the construction of new buildings, contrary to the published purpose of the endowment fund.

Students and professors alike were drafted into the military, and the U.S. commissioner of education requested that the campus be used for military training. The following resolution by the board of trustees was passed on September 14, 1918:

> Resolved: 1) That in view of the doctrine and practice of the Church of the Brethren in regard to militarism and war, that we, the trustees of Blue Ridge College, do not introduce military training into Blue Ridge College.
>
> 2) That we place ourselves on record as supporting the government in every possible way consistent with our religious practices and belief.[12]

Ross Murphy was elected to succeed F. F. Holsopple as president of the college. President Murphy was an able administrator and the college breathed with new life. Again, the raising of school standards for accreditation brought new challenges for the trustees. How could the college attract additional students and meet the financial obligations that would be incurred in upgrading the college to meet the requirements for accreditation? Thus, in 1922 the board of trustees attempted to drop these ambitious goals and change Blue Ridge College from a four-year college to a two-year junior college. This decision was "recalled," however, when the students learned of the decision and made it known that they wanted the college to continue as a four-year-degree program.

The board of trustees renewed their efforts to support a four-year program. Two members of the board were assigned to contact J. Maurice Henry, pastor of the Washington, D.C., Church of the Brethren, to see if he would be open to a call to the presidency of the college. After prayerful consideration and the support of his congregation, Henry accepted the position in the fall of 1922.[13]

To make better use of the campus, the college made arrangements with the Carroll County Board of Education for all New Windsor High School classes to be held on the college campus since there was no high school building in the community. These high school classes met on the college campus from 1922 to 1936. The gym was used for both high school and college athletic events. The high school sported both a boys' and a girls' basketball team. The girls' team won the Carroll County championship in the mid-'30s.

Even younger children attended school at Blue Ridge College. Helen Albaugh Fritz recalls her fifth grade year in the basement of the gym. She remembers that the students could go to the dining hall in the basement of Windsor Hall and buy two ice cream cones for a nickel. This way she could share the treat with a friend, and the next day the friend would buy the two cones and share them. And Edith (Bowman) McDowell remembers that students could go to the Bonsack house across the street from the college to buy a bowl of soup for lunch.

The college also generated income by renting space for conferences. At the District Meeting of Eastern Maryland held at the Monocacy Church of the Brethren in April 1923, delegates decided to hold a Young People's Conference at Blue Ridge College in New Windsor from July

26-31.[14] This first of a series of youth conference was attended by 87 youth and leaders. The following year attendance increased to 126. At this second youth conference, held in 1924, it was decided to form a Brethren Young People's Department cabinet. The following were elected: president, Mary Grace Martin, Baltimore, Eastern Maryland District; vice president, Grace Speicher, Accident, Western Maryland District; secretary, Alfreda Wallace, Hagerstown, Middle Maryland District; treasurer, James Blough, Denton, Eastern Shore. J. M. Henry and Earl Flohr were appointed adult advisers.

The conferences were held annually with registration on Monday and closing on Saturday. A visitors' day was held near the middle of the week for parents and siblings. Leadership for the youth conferences included national Church of the Brethren leaders as well as people from the district: Earl Flohr, McKinley Coffman, Perry Rohrer, Al Brightbill, Dan West, Stover Kulp, C. D. Bonsack, I. S. Long, Edward Frantz, H. K. Ober, Tobias Henry, Kermit Eby, Mark Shellhaas, Chauncey Shamberger, and many more.

Topics for the youth conferences followed a three-year cycle and included devotional life, vocational guidance, Bible study, "Materials and Methods for Young People's Work," race relations, church history, music and hymn singing, "Discovering Myself," "What We Believe," foreign missions, the Christian family, and nature study. For many years the cost for the New Windsor Young People's Conference remained at $9.50 per person, which included registration, board, and lodging. Each person brought bedding, notebook, flashlight, a Bible, and other personal items.

The success of the youth conferences held on the campus of Blue Ridge College led to the beginning of the camping movement for the district. Eventually the dream of a more rustic setting in which youth could draw "closer to nature and God's outdoors" was realized when Samuel Weybright donated land for the camp that was named Camp Peniel, located near Camp David, the presidential retreat near Thurmont, Maryland.[15] The 1931 Young People's Conference was the last to be held at Blue Ridge College with the first meeting held at Camp Peniel in 1932.

Sports at Blue Ridge College

Basketball. On Wednesday, July 22, 2006, the *Carroll County Times* published a picture of the Blue Ridge basketball team from 1926-27. The photo shows a twelve-person team, including Coach Wolfgang and Manager Duffy Speicher, eight young men dressed in basketball uniforms and two young men in street clothing. One wonders why the two were not in uniform. Were they not members of the team, or was there a shortage of uniforms?

Football. The football team did not do well in 1927. Sixty-three years later John Steadman wrote in the *Times* about an interview with Ralph Johnson, a member of the 1927 football team. The game was played on October 1, 1927. The team stayed at the Majestic Hotel in Philadelphia the night before their game with Temple University. Blue Ridge, by then a junior college, was trampled 110-0. So many Blue Ridge players were carried off the field that the Temple coach, Henry "Heinie" Miller, lent some members of his squad to Blue Ridge so the game could continue. The game did not last the allotted sixty minutes. At half time, the score was 78-0. The officials decided as an act of mercy to cut the second half to ten minutes, which allowed Temple to add "just" 32 more points.

A check of the records for 1927 indicates that the football team did not score once all season. Johnson explained that he was the extra-point kicker and "I never got a chance to kick for the simple reason we didn't score a touchdown all season long." The season record was Gallaudet, 21-0; Shippensburg, 25-0; Bridgewater, 9-0; American University, 38-0; and Shepherd, 19-0. Johnson went on to say that Coach J. Walter "Duffy" Speicher became so disgusted during the long season that he put himself in the game at fullback, even though he wasn't enrolled at Blue Ridge. The coach allowed Speigle Benedict, a high school student, to travel with the team and, on occasion, put him in the lineup as well. One redeeming factor in the Temple "event" was that Blue Ridge College received $1,500 from the host school for being on the schedule. At a time when the college was having financial problems, this might have softened the loss a small bit for the administration.

> *John Steadman*, Carroll County Times, *[Westminster, Md.] n.d. Julia Cairns collection. New Windsor Historical Society.*

Despite efforts to make the college more viable, the trustees were plagued with two recurring problems: low enrollment and insufficient income. First, in order to survive, enrollment needed to be increased to two hundred students or more, and, secondly, the endowment needed sufficient income to run the college. By the fall of 1923, enrollment was increased to more than two hundred and remained above that level for the next four years. The additional tuition dollars helped stabilize the endowment, but at least one problem remained: the school did not have bona fide certification as a teacher college. In 1926 the State Department of Education of Maryland was asked to evaluate the college for certification, whereupon it agreed to certify education graduates if they would take a six-week summer program in a "standard institution." After careful examination of the concerns of the student body and the education department's recommendation, President Henry offered his resignation to the board of trustees. The president felt he had completed his work. As his last official act, he recommended that Blue Ridge College take steps to organize as a junior college.[16]

The board of trustees sent a questionnaire to all alumni for a vote on the proposal to reorganize as a junior college. The results indicated that eighty percent favored the recommendation along with an affiliation with Bridgewater College. Summer sessions were held at Bridgewater for a few years, allowing Blue Ridge College graduates the opportunity to meet requirements for a teaching certificate.

BLUE RIDGE JUNIOR COLLEGE, 1927–1937

In 1927 Blue Ridge College became a junior college. E. C. Bixler was appointed president of the reorganized school and remained in the position for the next ten years, a period of major transition. During his tenure, Blue Ridge students studied for two years in New Windsor and then finished the bachelor's degree at either Bridgewater College, Juniata College, or Elizabethtown College, all four-year colleges associated with the Church of the Brethren. There were no formal agreements with any of the three colleges, however, until 1929.

On January 5, 1929, the board of trustees of Blue Ridge College called for a meeting with representatives of Bridgewater-Daleville College to discuss "uniting with Bridgewater College under some plan so as not to affect the state appropriations." This meeting was held at the George Washington Hotel in Winchester, Virginia, on January 23, 1929, "to confer on the problem of the relationship of our two schools."

The recommendations coming out of this meeting were that the two schools be merged into one educational unit but with two separate campuses. There would be representation from each campus on the other's trustee board. Each campus would be separate in administration and financial operation, and each campus would undertake its own financial campaigns. The students in their first two years of study would attend their respective colleges, but students of junior and senior rank would attend Bridgewater. Classes taken at either campus would be acceptable to fulfill prerequisite requirements for the junior and senior years at the Bridgewater campus. The school records for students from Blue Ridge College who completed their junior and senior years at Bridgewater would be transferred to Bridgewater for permanent preservation and certification. Transfer students from Blue Ridge would be granted all alumni privileges as Bridgewater graduates. (See Appendix 2.)

On February 11, 1929, the trustees of Blue Ridge College received and adopted the committee's report with the instructions that the recommendations be presented to the General Educational Board of the Church of the Brethren, as well as to the district conferences in the supporting states. The General Educational Board approved the recommendations on April 4, 1929, and encouraged the district assemblies to approve the cooperative agreement between the two schools. The Middle District of Maryland was the last district to approve the affiliation between the two schools in April 1930.

Following approval from all parties, President Bixler began the process of accrediting Blue Ridge College as a junior college by the State of Maryland. A survey was made by the Maryland State Board of Education and by the Association of Colleges and Secondary Schools of the

Middle States and Maryland, and approval was given for the college to move from a four-year college to a junior college.

Blue Ridge College began to promote the concept of a junior college to her constituents and the surrounding communities, hoping that options for both a short program and a long program would spur enrollment. The short track offered a two-year liberal arts program with the option of transferring to a recognized four-year college. The two-year options included commercial subjects (such as secretarial studies, bookkeeping, and accounting) and music and the arts. There was also a general two-year "completion" course for people who were unsure of their direction in life but wanted a college experience. Another program was preprofessional, preparing students to enter schools for the study of medicine, law, or dentistry. (See Appendix 3.)

Good and Faithful Servants

The college, like any other business, needed faithful workers behind the scenes. Cornelius Daniel Bowman, a farmer in Virginia, moved his family to a farm just west of Union Bridge, Maryland, in 1922. The Maryland property was small and productive but not especially prosperous, so when George W. Hull, the grounds supervisor at Blue Ridge College, suddenly died, Bowman "accepted the call" to become caretaker of the campus. The Bowman family moved from their farm near Union Bridge to the Bonsack house, one of the off-campus houses owned by the college.

Bowman's assistant, Weldon Brown, and his wife, Susie, lived in the small caretaker's house on Springdale Road at the "back" entrance to the campus. The Browns were often referred to as "Free Whites," a name given to former black slaves following the Civil War. Most other black families who worked in the community lived on the outskirts of New Windsor, but the Browns were able to live at the edge of town since they were living on college property. While Weldon worked for the college, Susie worked at the Dielman Inn in New Windsor. Julia Cairns, a student at the college in 1931-32, remembers that people commonly greeted Weldon, saying, "Well done, our good and faithful servant."

Weldon Brown was a well-liked figure on campus and was recognized for his excellent work. No record has been found that tells his length of service.

To draw more students and offer a less expensive option for education, the college admitted "day students" who lived nearby and commuted to campus. But income from day students and fees from the rental of the gym to New Windsor High School still did not eliminate the constant struggle to be solvent. During the 1932-33 school year, Dr. Robert L. Kelly, executive secretary of the Association of American Colleges, made an evaluation of Blue Ridge Junior College. His report pointed out serious flaws in the program. For instance, none of the twelve faculty members belonged to a professional association even though they had professional academic credentials. Kelly's report also criticized the president's overinvolvement in the day-to-day operation of the school. Not only did President Bixler have oversight of the program, he served as director of educational activities, curriculum, and course offerings. He also supervised entrance exams, approved all applications for admission, and interviewed each candidate. When necessary the president also acted as counselor and mediator between parents and students. Six of the twelve teaching faculty also carried administrative duties, including treasurer, dean of men, dean of women, practical nurse, and coaches.

Yearbook "Snapshots"

The Whispering Pine, the college yearbook, was first published in 1930. This first annual was dedicated to President Bixler for his seventeen years of devoted service to the school. Tucked in a copy of the yearbook was the school's alma mater, "To Thee, Blue Ridge," written by Nevin W. Fisher, instructor of piano and voice and a graduate of the college in 1920. Professor Fisher went on to write several hymns well known to Church of the Brethren members, such as "O Loving Father" and "Bless, O Lord, This Church of Thine." The yearbook also has pictures of the men's basketball and soccer teams as well as the women's basketball team. In the same issue, twelve faculty members are pictured, seventeen "seniors" (second-year students) and forty-one freshmen. Included in the list of freshmen were three students from Cuba: Roberto Parajon, Havana; Luis Martinez, Santiago de Cuba; and Luis Grimany, Santiago de Cuba.

The report was also critical of the location of the small library, which was housed in a room that not only served as a social center, but was a "passage room" for students going from one location to another. At the time of the review, no teacher was present in the library. On the positive side, the number of volumes was considered adequate for a junior college, but it was noted that there was no budget for the library.

The report also noted that the salary range for full-time staff was a very modest $1,450 to $2,100. The State of Maryland provided $7,000 for scholarship funds and another $4,750 for rental of classrooms and the gym for local high school classes and programs; scholarships were worth $100 per year; and the total cost for an average student did not exceed $375 annually, which included board, lodging, tuition, incidental fees, and books.[17]

Dr. Kelly, in his report, also spoke to the issue of the permanent endowment fund:

Pledges and various other items of uncertain value are frequently placed in the productive endowment fund, but as a matter of fact, do not belong there. In this connection it should be said that the investment of endowment in buildings, even though those buildings be service buildings such as dormitories, is not approved by the best authority. It is too much like a case of lending one's money to oneself. Neither is the use of money from the endowment fund for buildings or for current operations considered good practice. In general, it is irregular and causes deep concern, if not distrust, to the friends of the institution to take any funds from endowment funds.[18]

The board of trustees had "borrowed" from the endowment fund, writing an IOU for an amount to be repaid six months in the future. Usually, when the note came due, the trustees would "borrow" additional funds in order to "repay" the note and have funds to continue the operations of the college. Dr. Bixler, as president of the college, explained that this was a legitimate use of the funds since "the money was invested in the college plant."[19]

Dr. Bixler would later testify in a court case that the amount invested in the college buildings was $29,722, but he could only produce notes and receipts for $19,140.[20] He reasoned that "sustaining and extending the educational work of a college" could include erecting buildings for housing students and providing classrooms for their education. Thus, the college trustees "borrowed" money from the endowment fund they had established, as well as from an endowment fund established by the alumni association.

Overall, the credentialing report was not highly favorable to the college. President Bixler reported to the board of trustees on May 26, 1934, that "the College lacked a stable income of sufficient volume, that the library and laboratories were deficient, that teachers' salaries were too low, and that the plant in general needed repair and renovation to satisfy the accrediting authorities."[21]

Searching for a way to continue the educational opportunities at the New Windsor location, Blue Ridge College trustees in 1936 offered the college campus to Bethany Biblical Seminary of Chicago (the Church of the Brethren seminary), if they would consider relocating to New Windsor. The trustees of the seminary agreed to inspect the New Windsor location; however, there is no record that they made the visit or had any further conversation.[22]

A bequest helped sustain the school a while longer. On November 29, 1915, Annie Stoner, a member of the Board of Trustees of Blue Ridge College, had written her will instructing her heirs to "devise unto Blue Ridge College, its successors and assigns, my two farms lying contiguous to each other in Uniontown and in New Windsor Districts, containing two hundred and seventy-five acres of land more or less, which I obtained from my father, the late Upton Roop; and also a lot of land, improved by a tenant house, adjoining the said lands or farms, which I obtained from Lucy Snyder by deed dated April 2, 1904."

When Annie Stoner died and her will was probated on June 27, 1933, the farms became assets for Blue Ridge College. One of the purposes of the farm was to provide food to the dining hall, and for a projected agriculture department at the college. But on February 24, 1937, the college trustees passed a resolution that gave the title for the two farms to the Eastern Maryland District Meeting of the Church of the Brethren. This action would become one of the main issues in the court case brought against Blue Ridge College and the Eastern Maryland District Meeting of the Church of the Brethren by the Union Bridge Banking and Trust Company and other creditors of the Blue Ridge College in 1943.

The thirty-seventh annual commencement of Blue Ridge College, while under the administration of the Church of the Brethren, took place on May 31, 1937. Twenty-three graduates received diplomas. (See Appendix 4.) For thirty-eight years, Maryland Collegiate Institute and Blue Ridge College had offered higher education.

4.

Outside Investors in Blue Ridge College

THE RIDGE FOUNDATION, 1937–1938

As noted earlier, to establish the Maryland Collegiate Institute (the Brethren school in Union Bridge that became Blue Ridge College and eventually moved to New Windsor), Church of the Brethren members bought a total of 1,000 shares of stock at $25 each. By March 6, 1917, the Eastern Maryland District Meeting had acquired 771 shares of these college stocks, becoming the major stockholder for the college, but in 1927 the District Meeting was discussing ways to dispose of the college, which was becoming a financial burden.

According to a court document, when Edward C. Bixler became president of the college in 1927, he had tried to sell the college plant for $150,000 less 15 percent. It didn't sell. By 1936, the asking price was $50,000, but trustees were "willing to discuss price if plant is used for good purposes."[1] Early in 1937, The National Bureau of Private Schools produced a New Jersey lawyer, Elvin H. Ullrich, who claimed to represent a group of investors who were interested in the property. They called themselves the Ridge Foundation and had ambitious plans to recreate the school as a southern "ivy league" institution.

The trustees of the Eastern Maryland District Meeting of the Church of the Brethren voted February 24, 1937, to sell the college for $50,000 to Judge Ullrich, who was acting on behalf of the Ridge Foundation. The district would assume the college debt of approximately $14,500, in addition to holding the mortgage for the college campus.[2] Then the new board of trustees had some "undoing" to do. Meeting May 29, 1937, they passed a resolution to rescind the action of February 11, 1929, that affiliated Blue Ridge College with Bridgewater-Daleville College. They also had to undo the action of January 8, 1927, in which they accepted junior college status. Having done this, the college officially could be declared a four-year institution.[3]

At the same meeting, the college board of trustees executed a deed conveying to the District Meeting the two Stoner farms and the tenant house, as well as three improved properties in New Windsor. The consideration (payments) expressed in this deed is "five dollars and other good and valuable consideration, the receipt of which is hereby acknowledged," and "Federal Revenue stamps in the amount of $21.50 and State Recordation Stamps in like amount are attached." The deed was not recorded until October 7, 1937.[4]

On the surface it appears that the new college trustees, appointed by the Ridge Foundation, would sign a note and mortgage for $50,000 payable to the District Meeting trustees for a term of ten years, bearing an interest rate of six percent per annum. This note, along with a deposit of $1,000, turned over control of the college to the Ridge Foundation. This new group elected to keep the name Blue Ridge College, but many things would change. The college went from a two-year junior college to a four-year college, plans were pursued to make Blue Ridge College a southern "ivy league-type" college, and sororities and fraternities were permitted. A 1937 edition of the campus newspaper stated, "The doors of the institution have been flung open to the members of all religious denominations, and bans on dancing and such lighter forms of activities in a co-educational institution have been lifted."[5]

The summer of 1937 was a busy time for the new administration. Most notably they spent funds they did not have on laboratory equipment, remodeling the buildings, and buying several houses near campus. They "purchased" the houses with only minimal down payments and mortgages taken out at different lending banks in the area. The college's assets were used as collateral for the loans.[6] The administration also

New Leadership and Vision

The speaker for the May 31, 1937, commencement, Dr. James Lough, would become the new president of a reorganized Blue Ridge College. In fact, a *Times* newspaper article (n.d.) about commencement that year also announced the reorganization of Blue Ridge College as a four-year college once again (Julia Cairns collection). Judge Elvin Ullrich was named chairman of the new board of trustees, as well as financial manager. Dr. Bixler announced his resignation as president of Blue Ridge Junior College though he would remain on the faculty of the new four-year Blue Ridge College where he would teach Latin and Greek. He was given the title president emeritus. One other member of the faculty, Harold N. Eaton, formerly head of the chemistry and biology department, also was asked to remain in his position.

Oddly, the announcement in May listed Lough as president, but the fall announcement listed Dr. William York Critchley as president of the reorganized college. The educational achievements and backgrounds of the new administration and faculty spoke well for the new beginning. Dr. Lough had been associated with New York University as a professor and dean since 1901 and was a member of the American Psychological Association as well as Phi Beta Kappa. Dr. Critchley received his doctorate from the University of London and had been a teacher at Syracuse University, London University, and Columbia University. He also served as president of St. Francis College in Brooklyn. Other members of the new faculty were:

- Dr. Walter. L Nathan, holding degrees from the universities of Dublin and Bonn, who has taught at Princeton, will head the department of German.

- Dr. Peter Hans Olden, who holds degrees from the universities of Munich and of Chicago will teach social science and economics.

- Dr. D. Bonawitz, who has been associated with the State Department of Education of Pennsylvania, will teach English.

- Dr. E. H. Saltzman, who has been associated with the faculty of Columbia University, will teach mathematics.

> • Dr. A. C. Westerhof, who took his Ph.D. from Duke University and who was lately associated with Mercer University in Georgia, will teach philosophy and psychology.
>
> • Dr. Harold Rollins will teach the practical aspects of optometry, that is, the grinding of lenses.
>
> Steve Grenda, football star and coach of Columbia University, has been engaged as director of athletics for both men and women. The college is planning on fielding a football team, which has not had one since 1917.
>
> Pilot *[Union Bridge, Md.] 17 September 1937.*

initiated new programs, such as a school of foreign affairs, the first of its kind to be offered in the United States, and a program in collaboration with the Rollins Technical School of Applied Optics of New Jersey. Dr. James Lough, who was first appointed president, instead joined the faculty to begin a training school for kindergarten and primary teachers. Dr. Lough would also be responsible for the Schudder School to train students in secretarial arts and crafts, social welfare, and community service.[7] And Judge Ullrich planned to add a department of housing to teach about construction materials, an up-and-coming subject at the college level.[8]

In August the Baltimore *Sun* announced that Blue Ridge College had received between fifty and sixty new scholarships from anonymous donors; an article in the *Hanover Evening Sun* told of a scholarship fund of $20,400 established in the name of J. David Baile, a Maryland state senator and chair of the advisory board at Blue Ridge College. This scholarship fund was placed in the hands of the state senators of Maryland who would appoint one scholarship recipient from each legislative district. Each year $5,400 was shared between twenty-nine students.[9] Another scholarship fund of $20,400, called the Governor Harold G. Hoffman Scholarship Fund, was specifically for newsboys. According to the *Hanover Evening Sun,* "All the metropolitan newspapers in the

East have written favorably concerning their participation in the scholarship fund with responses as far west as Chicago."[10] These scholarships did not include room and board, but several newspapers whose employees received the scholarships indicated they would pay the board and room costs.[11]

In the flurry of changes, the state of Maryland granted the school $5,000 to be used for erecting a "colonial" fence around the campus.[12] This wooden fence can be seen in several college bulletins that were published after this date.

In August, the administration announced in the *Evening Sun* that the enrollment capacity of 175 students had been filled and "a number of persons had been rejected due to not meeting the high standards required to enter this college as a student."[13] The "new" Blue Ridge College opened on Monday, September 20, 1937, with the announcement that Dr. W. S. Y. Critchley was president.

A long article appearing in the *Pilot* a few days later, written by President Critchley, announced the gift to the college of the Dielman Inn, the local hotel in New Windsor, which was to be renamed the Blue Ridge College Inn. Oddly, no record exists of a transfer of the mortgage of this property by Dr. Dielman to Blue Ridge College.[14] Furthermore, the hotel was not listed among the properties sold at public auction during the bankruptcy proceedings in 1944. In fact, Dr. Dielman's will, dated July 22, 1948, bequeaths this property to Julia Roop Cairns. It appears that the hotel was never given to Blue Ridge College as President Critchley had announced.[15]

By October, just five months after the school had been purchased, it became clear that the administration was in financial trouble. On November 12, 1937, a man came into the New Windsor Bank and identified himself as an FBI agent. He asked for the house of Dr. Critchley and revealed to the teller that the college was approaching bankruptcy. Dr. Critchley announced his resignation and left town with his family on the train the next day.[16]

W. Roscoe Slack, a New York real estate agent, was named to replace President Critchley. Slack was left with many unpaid accounts and creditors asking for payment. The Eastern Maryland District Meeting of the Church of the Brethren, desiring that the new college venture become successful, continued to involve itself with loans and endorsements.

NEW WINDSOR EDUCATIONAL FOUNDATION, 1938–1939

The Ridge Foundation dissolved early in 1938, and a group from New York known as the New Windsor Educational Foundation formed a new corporation. In March of 1938, it assumed management of Blue Ridge College. It's clear that the New Windsor Educational Foundation continued in the effort to make a clean break from the traditions that were established when Blue Ridge College was under the oversight of the Church of the Brethren. This new administration claimed that Blue Ridge College was in the lineage of a school established by the Reverend J. P. Carter in 1839 in the back rooms of the Atlee Hotel, so 1939 was publicized as the "Centennial Year." A pictorial booklet titled "As the Students See Blue Ridge College" was published with the note "Centennial 1839-1939" clearly listed on the front of the booklet.

Pictures in the centennial booklet demonstrate just how far the school was drifting from its Brethren heritage. The commemorative book shows a dance band and students dressed for formal dances on campus, field trip excursions to department stores, horseback riding, a two-rank pipe organ, and a kindergarten class for practice teaching.[17] Considering that pianos and organs were not used in many Church of the Brethren congregations, the college pipe organ was one of many "new improvements." After the school closed, several members of Civilian Public Service (CPS) carried out a large pool table from the fourth floor of Old Main. Even in the mid-1940s, Brethren considered billiards immoral and prohibited CPS fellows from playing the game.[18]

Ultimately, the changes in philosophy and the activities permitted at the college didn't keep the alumni association from supporting the college. The active alumni, many of them Brethren, worked to acquire new endowments for the school just two years into its new administration.[19]

By 1940 Homer E. Cooper was president of the college. According to a local paper, his wife "sponsored a young women's fellowship, whose purpose was to unite the young women of the three faiths present in the student body, Protestant, Catholic, and Jewish." This group attended the National Conference of Christians and Jews in Washington, D.C., where Mrs. Franklin Delano Roosevelt was the principal speaker.[20]

Although the college administration was making a clean break from the Church of the Brethren influence, there remained a strong religious presence on the campus. College chapel services were held three times each week, as well as vesper services. A special room was constructed for the forty Catholic students so they could attend Mass every Sunday, led by the Reverend William E. Kelley of St. John's Catholic Church, Westminster. The Reverend Miles S. Reifsnyder, associate dean of the college, conducted a Sunday afternoon vesper service. And on alternate Sundays a vesper service was led by the Reverend John Ross Hays, pastor of the New Windsor Presbyterian Church.[21]

5.

Effects of World War II on Blue Ridge College

Just as the War Between the States caused the decline of Calvert College in the 1860s and World War I siphoned professors and students away from Blue Ridge College in 1917-1918, clouds of war hovered over the campus again in the mid-twentieth century. The effects of World War II were forcing the college down a slope to nonexistence as fewer and fewer students enrolled. The college had innovative ideas and talented students, most of whom, it appears, came from well-to-do homes.

Beatrice Schroeder, a Rising Star

Blue Ridge College was able to attract strong students, such as Miss Beatrice Schroeder. As a member of the freshman class of Blue Ridge, she gave a harp recital at the Waldorf-Astoria in New York City. At age eighteen, she had already given more than sixty-five recitals. She performed at the New York World's Fair and appeared on the Music Appreciation Hour, broadcast coast to coast and rebroadcast by shortwave to Canada and Europe. Prior to enrolling at Blue Ridge College, she performed for the Duke and Duchess of Windsor at their official residence in Nassau. Miss Schroeder was the youngest harpist to hold a contract with a symphony orchestra, the Teaneck Symphony Orchestra, where she continued as their first harpist.

Blue Ridge Collegian, *Blue Ridge College Collection (BCSC-3), Special Collections and Archives, Alexander Mack Memorial Library, Bridgewater College.*

The ability of the college to host a Christmas dance at a hotel in New York City indicates that students and contributors were financially able to support the school, but Blue Ridge was failing primarily because of the war.

In the spring of 1940, the Young Republicans was still a vital organization. The Blue Ridge College chapter organized a mock convention on May 1, 1940, at the Armory in Westminster. The colleges of Western Maryland, Hood College, Blue Ridge College, and others sent delegates to the convention. The principal speaker was Charles Hamilton, president of the Young Republicans Association of New York and a delegate to the National Republican Convention. Raymond Graber, chairman of the Blue Ridge College chapter was in charge of the arrangements for the mock convention.[1]

Athletics Struggle to Survive

Athletic events continued in the early war years. "The cheerleaders managed to get to every game but one—under all kinds of queer conditions. The oddest was their means of transportation to the Albright game: Their last hope lay in the trunk of Westerhof's Chrysler. It was a tight squeeze, making rather an embarrassing arrival, for they were a motley crew who climbed out of the trunk that day. Their lungs were still able to produce the Vulture Yell even without many enthusiasts, and for days after this game, four drooping, limping lassies stumbled to classes unable to speak above a whisper" (*The Collegian Diary*, 1942, booklet written for the students by the students of Blue Ridge College).

Blue Ridge College announced in the local papers early in 1942 that they were "abandoning the intercollegiate athletic program for the duration of the war. An intramural program would be organized to replace the abandoned programs" (*Pilot* [Union Bridge, Md.] 23 January 1942). Presumably the male student population was dwindling due to the military draft; moreover, rationing of tires and gasoline made intercollegiate travel difficult.

According to the *Pilot* in 1942, despite dropping enrollment, the college drew students from as far away as White Bear Lake (Minnesota), New York, Seattle, and New Jersey.[2]

As finances became tighter and tighter, the college pursued new sources of funding for scholarships. In the summer of 1941, the trustees announced the creation of 120 special legislative scholarships to be distributed by the members of the Maryland House of Representatives. These came in addition to the Maryland Senate scholarships already in existence and helped defray the annual price tag of $430 per student.[3]

THE WAR EFFORT

As the school struggled to survive, it joined the war effort, perhaps believing it had landed on a new mission. In September of 1942, Dr. Miles S. Reifsnyder, a captain of the Minutemen of Taneytown, a Civilian Air Patrol radio operator, and rector of the Baptist church, was appointed dean of the college. At the same time, an American flag began to fly over the "temporary Administration Building" after an absence of three years. At the beginning of the 1942-43 school year, the college made arrangements with the military to serve in several ways.

> To forward war efforts the Blue Ridge College is instituting night courses in Accounting, Bookkeeping, and Typing, open to residents of Carroll and nearby counties. It is proposed to add groundwork in aviation to the courses later in the year. This groundwork will also be open to local residents.
>
> It will prepare men for service with the armed forces. This course, which will also be open to women, is designed to prepare students for air service during the war and to take their part in the great expansion expected to come with peace.
>
> The night courses in Accounting and Bookkeeping will be taught by Paul R. Kuhns, treasurer of Carroll County. The Typing will be taught by Herbert F. Wooden, the new head of the Department of Business and Administration and Accounting, who will be in charge of the Night School.

The government is in great need of typists for war service. The course of instruction will prepare students for this type of war service and will also give them a basic training for business life later.

The course in Bookkeeping and Accounting will be based on practical experience and will fit students to handle this type of work for Government and Business life.[4]

In the spring of 1942, the college contributed to the war effort by practicing blackouts and organizing civilian patrols. One day in February the college was completely "blacked out" during a trial run conducted by the community of New Windsor. On that same day, the Union Bridge newspaper reported that Dr. A. C. Westerhof of the Blue Ridge Air Raid Precautions (ARP) addressed the student body in the college chapel on air raid precautions in the event of an enemy air raid.[5]

The school also administered the test for the V-12 Program, a program to produce naval officers of young men between the ages of seventeen and nineteen while they were taking college classes.[6] None of these programs was enough to keep the school open and solvent.

Not Without a Lawsuit

As the school struggled under the burden of war, several new members were elected to the board of trustees in the summer of 1942, including Arthur E. Hungerford, who was elected chair of the executive committee and comptroller.[7]

A letter from a number of trustees, including E. C. Bixler and Jesse P. Weybright, to Mr. Hungerford stated that the executive committee had been created to collect all funds due the college and to protect the interests of the same, and that Mr. Hungerford should "do whatever is necessary for the best interest of Blue Ridge College and we do hereby agree to stand by and confirm the same."[8]

Mr. Hungerford evidently took his assignment seriously. He employed a lawyer on behalf of the college and brought a suit against the Eastern Maryland District Meeting of the Church of the Brethren, asking that the deed and mortgage for the college, held by the District Meeting, be annulled and that the District Meeting be required to provide an account of their expenses and payments made on behalf of Blue Ridge College.[9]

The lawsuit (*The Blue Ridge College v. The Eastern Maryland District Meeting of the Church of the Brethren*) was filed in the late summer of 1942. Mr. Hungerford, representing the college, alleged that the District "sold" the college (in 1937 to Judge Ullrich) but kept the assets of farms and houses as well as income from such properties that should have been transferred with the mortgage for the college campus.

The Eastern Maryland District responded that the properties, which had not been included when the New Windsor Educational Foundation negotiated for the college campus, were given to the college when it was under the administration of the Church of the Brethren and that if and when the college ceased to be administrated by the Church of the Brethren, the said endowment funds (including farms and houses) should revert to the General Education Board of the Church of the Brethren.

The District noted that it had assumed an indebtedness of $66,000 when it turned over the administration of the college. That amount included a payment of $34,000 to the endowment fund and $10,000 to pay off a lien against the value of the Stoner farms, because Mrs. Stoner, at the time of her death, did not have enough liquid assets to fulfill her pledge. Added to that was a $3,500 indebtedness to the Alumni Fund and outstanding charges due the college of $18,500.

The calling of witnesses was set for January 4, 1943. The charges and the defendant's answer is recorded in the court packet; however, the case was withdrawn prior to the judgment when the board of trustees of the college rescinded the letter that instructed Mr. Hungerford to do all that was necessary for the best interest of the college.[10]

Despite every effort to keep the college open, the inevitable happened. In a letter to Jacob F. Replogle, George Touwsma writes, "I attended Blue Ridge from September 1940 until I entered the service in February 1943. The school closed at the conclusion of that semester, June 1943, and never reopened as Blue Ridge College. When I left to go into service, there were approximately forty students registered."[11]

6

Blue Ridge College Closes Its Doors

Blue Ridge College finally closed its doors at the end of the spring se-mester, 1943, after many years of struggling to remain financially sound while providing quality education for the students enrolled in the college. However, the details about the closing are murky at best. First of all, it's difficult to tell from the record who led the college at the time of the closing. The Eastern District of Maryland was holding a large mortgage on the campus and had been trying to help the college stay afloat for several years. Several members of the Church of the Brethren continued to serve on the board of trustees, though it's not known if they served as representatives of the District Meeting, or if they served out of a personal interest in the college.

The *Times* for Friday, August 13, 1943, published a large sale bill taking up a half page and listing a mortgagee's sale of property known as the Blue Ridge College Property, September 4, 1943, at 1:30 p.m. The sale bill listed several houses and several empty lots as well as the main campus buildings for a total of 26 acres, 1 rod, and 35 square perches. The buildings listed for sale on the main campus included Old Main, Girls' Dormitory, Boys' Dormitory, Gymnasium, and Auditorium. The attorney named in the mortgage sale was Theodore F. Brown of Brown and Shipley, Solicitors. Sterling Blacksten was the auctioneer.

This same sale bill ran in two more editions of the *Times*. Then on Friday, September 3, just a day before the sale was to take place, a notice was printed in the *Times* that said the sale was postponed. (See Appendix 5.)

Interestingly, two months later, in November, the newspaper published a notice saying, "The fence along the College Campus is being torn down and the lumber will be used on the buildings at their farms."[1] The two farms that would be the center of another lawsuit were not listed as a part of the college campus in the aborted sale bill. Who was in charge of the vacant campus, and who had the authority to make the decision to tear down the fence? More importantly, who owned the farms? the college or the district? It was likely the legal counsel in the bankruptcy case who had posted the sale notice. A year later it was the legal counsel who rented the campus buildings to the Brethren Service Commission prior to the auction that was held in September 1944.

A Second Lawsuit and an Appeal

The complexity of court cases surrounding the Eastern Maryland District Board and Blue Ridge College goes back to 1936-37. At that time the board of trustees of the college, under the administration of the Church of the Brethren, transferred the college stock, the two Stoner farms, and a house that was "owned" by the college (but was being used as the parsonage of the Pipe Creek Church of the Brethren) to the Eastern Maryland District Board. The trustees also signed over to the district the three houses in New Windsor that were used by the college. The only record of any payment by the district to the college for these properties is listed as $5.00 "and other good and valuable consideration," which are not listed.[2]

In February 1937, the trustees of the district understood that the Ridge Foundation, represented by Judge Ullrich, would "buy" the college for $1,000 down and assume a mortgage of $50,000 payable at six percent interest over a ten-year period. For their part, the district trustees agreed to assume the college debt of approximately $14,500, subject to ratification by the District Meeting. Unfortunately, there is no record of such an action by the District Meeting.

College records show that on June 15, 1937, the Ridge Foundation said "they [trustees of the Foundation] were not interested in buying said plant." The college trustees did, however, agree to buy from the District Meeting trustees the "outstanding stock" for the sum of $50,000 payable by note and mortgage for a term of ten years and bearing interest at the rate of six percent per annum."[3]

These transactions left the college stripped of its assets and only a technical title to the property that was covered by a mortgage. The college was left to operate "upon the good reputation" but without capital. By November of 1937 the officers of the Ridge Foundation had resigned and President Critchley and his family had left town with the FBI on their heels. A meeting of the district trustees was held on November 11, 1937, at which time the trustees devised a plan to protect their mortgage and also to help the college's condition. The board of trustees agreed to borrow $5,000 and lend it to the college, but to assume no further obligation. In return the college was to turn over all of its income to the District Meeting and the District Meeting would provide for the payment of the current expenses out of this income. If this was insufficient, the District Meeting would supplement the funds to the extent of $5,000 and no more.[4]

The New Windsor Educational Foundation, Inc., was organized as a holding company early in 1939. In an agreement signed March 19, 1939, the district agreed to release the $50,000 mortgage and its loan of $5,000 by reducing the mortgage to $34,500 and the interest rate to five percent. This was to occur when the Foundation paid $500 in cash, as well as the costs for the summer work of $15,000, and half the cost of the athletic goods purchased for the 1937-38 school year.[5]

Then on November 6, 1939, the Foundation dissolved as a corporation without assets. Prior to their dissolution, however, they transferred 470 shares of college stock to W. R. Slack and 470 shares to Richard Hartze. Interestingly, W. R. Slack was associated with the National Bureau of Private Schools, the organization that had brought Judge Ullrich and the Ridge Foundation into the picture in 1937. These two men held the shares until May 18, 1940, when they transferred the shares of stock back to the college. Prior to its dissolution, the New Windsor

Educational Foundation paid off college debts to the amount of $15,313.96. It appears that they used college tuition income for the years 1938-39 and 1939-40 to pay these debts.[6]

A lawsuit was brought by Union Bridge Banking and Trust Company in the summer of 1943 against the district to foreclose on a mortgage on a house where the college property had been used as collateral. The argument was that when the Eastern Maryland District Meeting of the Church of the Brethren agreed to sell the college to the Ridge Foundation and hold the mortgage for the campus property, they sold the liabilities and kept the assets, that is, the Stoner properties. By allowing the district to maintain ownership of the houses and farms, the new administrators of the college were stripped of any ability to be successful in operating the college. The District Meeting countered that the will of Annie Stoner clearly stated that the farms were given for Church of the Brethren educational purposes and, if the college were to be removed from the administration of the church, the farms would revert to the "General Education Board of the Church of the Brethren."[7]

In the meantime, the Ridge Foundation had used the "assets" of the college, which they believed they were entitled to, to borrow money to purchase houses across the street from the campus. They borrowed from three different banks, using the Stoner farms as collateral. The charge against the District Meeting was that it willfully intended to defraud the creditors of the college.

Judge James Clark, Howard County associate judge of the Fifth Judicial Court, ruled on 6 July 1944,

> By taking to itself the property conveyed by the deed, the District Meeting deprived the Endowment Fund and the Alumni Association of the security afforded by those properties to those creditors. In doing this, it hindered, delayed and defrauded them; and so the conveyances must, by the terms of the statute, be considered "fraudulent as to both present and future creditors."[8]

Then, on September 15, 1944, contrary to the church's biblically based opposition to taking court action, the District Meeting filed an appeal of the court's ruling. The appeals court reversed the ruling on January 10, 1945. The presiding judge was Ogle Marbury, chief judge for the court.[9]

The last paragraph of the opinion praises the work of the church as follows: "From 1900 to 1937 this church through its members, in the operation of the academy and then the college, performed an admirable service. It did not seek profits, but conducted these educational institutions for the innate good, at the expenditure of much labor. We do not find that fraud has been shown. Decree reversed and bill of complaint dismissed with costs to appellants."[10]

When the college closed at the end of the spring semester 1943, no formal announcement was made, but neither faculty nor staff nor students returned in the fall. Citizens of New Windsor recall that the college buildings were left unlocked and that local citizens wandered through the buildings, especially the library, and "borrowed" books and other items from the campus.[11] Church of the Brethren staff who came to work at the Center in 1944 tell of finding tables in the dining room in Windsor Hall with dirty dishes still on them. One person said, "You could tell what was eaten for the last meal—scrambled eggs and link sausage!"[12] Another person remembers finding the remains of a piece of pie left on the fireplace mantle in the parlor room in Windsor Hall.[13] One person thought the city of New Windsor shut off the water to the campus due to a large, outstanding water bill that was owed by the college, and that without water the college was unable to operate. There is no record of a water shut-off, but bankruptcy court proceedings show that the outstanding water bill was $836.59 for meter readings from July 1, 1937, through July 1, 1943.[14]

———— ⑥ ————

Part II

---------⊚---------

War Relief

7.

A Ministry of Service

The Church of the Brethren, with its long tradition of responding to the needs of brothers and sisters without regard for race, religion, or nationality, cites Matthew 25:31-46 with the refrain: "Just as you did it to one of the least of these . . . you did it to me."

Following the War Between the States, the churches in the North collected money and relief materials for Brethren in the South. After World War I, the church raised funds to assist the Armenian and Syrian relief program. Responding to the initial goal of $250,000 set by Annual Meeting, church members contributed a total of $267,265. These funds supported orphanages and schools, the reconstruction of gardens, buildings, and homes, and the renewal of vineyards for the wine industry.[1]

The Gospel Messenger of January 14, 1939, called on the women of the church to send relief clothing. Until this time the church had sent only money for relief in China and Spain, but on the eve of World War II, the church asked the Brethren colleges to assist in the collection of material relief. The colleges and college churches became the storerooms for parcels of clothing collected by local congregations. Then the clothing was sent on to the Friends (Quaker) processing center at 1515 Cherry Street, Philadelphia. From there relief shipments went to Spain where four Church of the Brethren relief workers were on the receiving end to assist in the distribution of the goods to needy people.[2] The four Brethren relief workers in Spain were Dan West, David Blickenstaff, Paul Bowman, and Martha Rupel. *The Gospel Messenger* reports that they distributed 25,000 pounds of clothing by the beginning of 1940. And during 1940, no less than 50,000 pounds of clothing were collected; 25,000 pounds were shipped in 1941, 20,000 pounds in 1942, and more than 20,000 pounds in 1943.[3]

At the same time, the churches on the West Coast were collecting clothing at three storerooms—Seattle, Washington; Oakland, California; and La Verne, California—for shipment to Asia. In the eight-month period between September 1940 and April 1941, forty-seven cases of clothing were received and distributed in Shanghai, China. The possibility of more shipments to China ended with the bombing of Pearl Harbor on December 7, 1941. The storerooms in Portland and La Verne remained open, however, with the anticipation that one day they would be able to respond again to human need.[4]

Local churches were also supporting conscientious objectors in Civilian Public Service (CPS) camps who needed bedding, clothing, personal health kits, and other supplies. Alternative Service was an official program of Selective Service, but received no federal financial support.[5]

In the summer of 1943, Dr. Eldon Burke, a professor at Ball State University in Muncie, Indiana, and his wife, Cecile, left Indiana and traveled on behalf of the Brethren Service Committee (BSC) to Philadelphia to investigate the possibility of establishing a research and training center for relief workers who would be needed in Europe at the end of the war. On that same trip, and well before the Blue Ridge College property was securely in the hands of the BSC, the Burkes scouted out the defunct Blue Ridge College campus to see if this might be a more suitable location for the Church of the Brethren to establish a processing center for sending relief goods to the war-torn countries of Europe. The Church of the Brethren had already established collection centers in Nappanee, Indiana; La Verne, California; Portland, Oregon; and McPherson, Kansas. The Burkes believed the former Blue Ridge College facilities in Maryland would be an ideal location for a processing center since it was located close to the ports of Baltimore and the buildings could be converted easily into usable space for processing material aid.

Their recommendation to the BSC was approved, and the Burkes arrived in New Windsor on March 1, 1944, to open such a center. They were soon replaced by John and Margaret Metzler, who had earlier established the Nappanee Brethren Service Relief Center in Indiana.[6]

With the Blue Ridge College properties in bankruptcy court, court trustees administered rental agreements for the Stoner house across the street from the campus and the college gymnasium. Monthly rent was $30 for the house and $25 for the gym.[7] Right away the newly established relief center at New Windsor began receiving used clothing for shipment to Europe from neighboring churches, and the processing center was established in the college gym.

It is no surprise then that Church of the Brethren congregations readily supported the new venture opening at New Windsor on the campus of Blue Ridge College. Soon after John and Margaret Metzler arrived on campus in 1944 to replace the Burkes, they arranged for college students to work as volunteers at New Windsor during the summer to sort and pack used clothing and other relief goods. Marion Noll, from Pleasant Hill, Ohio, claims to have been the first volunteer to arrive at the newly opened Brethren Relief Center, arriving with the Metzlers.[8]

Virginia and Kenneth Crim served as volunteers at the relief center from June 1944 to June 1945. Kenneth was classified 4-F by Selective Service, which meant he was not eligible to be drafted, and was therefore ineligible for CPS. Devising his own volunteer service, he chose work at the New Windsor relief center. Dorothy Deaven from Hershey, Pennsylvania, also volunteered for a year. The Crims and Deaven, along with Noll, were likely the first volunteers to give a year of service to the Center.

Volunteers from local congregations also arrived to sort and bail clothing. Once the clothing was separated into men's and women's summer and winter clothing and children's clothing, it was pressed by a baler, bound with metal strapping, and covered with a waterproof cover. The bale was covered again with burlap-type sacking and stenciled on the outside with a label that identified the type of clothing and "Brethren

Service Committee, New Windsor, Maryland" as the source of the bale.

Even with the steady flow of used clothing, the need was greater than the supply. Giving birth to the cut-garment program described later in this book, the relief center invested in equipment and supplies to cut material into garment pieces, which were then sent to local churches where women, and some men, sewed the pieces together to make children's outfits. These newly made garments were then returned to New Windsor to be packed and shipped overseas.

Just before sending the first shipment to Greece, the volunteers held a dedication service for the baled clothing. The Reverend and Mrs. Clarence Heckman, missionaries to Nigeria; the Reverend and Mrs. Harper Will from Chicago; and the Reverend Earl Flohr, with twenty people from Virginia who were visiting the Center, participated in the dedication service on July 4, 1944. Earl Flohr presided, Clarence Heckman read the scripture, and Harper Will gave the address and prayer.[9] Following the service, Kenneth Crim and Marion Noll drove the cargo from New Windsor to New York, but not without some challenges. The state police stopped them several times to check their out-of-state plates—the truck was owned by denominational headquarters in Elgin, Illinois, and displayed Illinois plates. Because of gas rationing and the scarcity of tires, it was very unusual for a truck with Illinois plates to be seen as far east as Maryland. Then when Crim and Noll arrived at the piers, they were told they were not allowed on the docks without a special permit issued by the Coast Guard. Marion and Kenneth went to the Coast Guard office where they just happened to encounter Stanley Rutherford, a Coast Guard officer who had graduated from school with Crim. Rutherford was able to obtain the needed permit quickly, and the supplies were soon delivered to the waiting ship.[10] The shipment itself had special traveling privileges, courtesy of the International Red Cross:

> Because of the special arrangements with the German and Allied governments under which the International Red Cross administers relief in Greece, this clothing will be sent through the blockade. This will be

the first shipment of Brethren relief supplies to be sent through the blockade to the people of Europe.[11]

The Brethren Service Relief Center shipped the first fifty bales of clothing to France early in August 1944. Their value was set at $3,750. The shipment included nearly eight thousand garments, which were distributed in Normandy through the Committee on American Relief in France. The staff at New Windsor soon received a message saying, "All clothes received to date have been distributed and immensely appreciated as shown by the moving letters received from Normandy."[12]

8.

Fulfilling a Dream: Creation of a Relief Center

With the sudden departure of the New Windsor Educational Foundation in 1943, the property, assets, and debt of Blue Ridge College came back to the Eastern Maryland District of the Church of the Brethren, which faced a sizeable financial liability and a campus that had no future as an educational institution. However, the Brethren Service Committee (BSC) was already renting space at Blue Ridge College to stage war relief efforts, and Dr. Eldon Burke had been instrumental in locating a training program at New Windsor for relief workers.

Meeting in Elgin in May 1944, the Brethren Service Committee accepted the proposal of the Eastern District of Maryland to finance the settlement with creditors of Blue Ridge College on the basis of sixty percent payments. This settlement would be made with funds independent of the current giving of the Church. Upon payment to creditors, the Blue Ridge College Corporation would be dissolved and all assets transferred to the Brethren Service Committee.

The officers of the Brethren Service Committee also resolved to negotiate a loan with the trustees of Bridgewater College for $35,000, with installments of $1,000 annually, at four percent interest.[1]

While the Brethren Service Committee was working to find money to purchase the vacant campus, the elders of the Eastern Maryland District came together on August 23, 1944, to talk about the fate of the college campus. They and others in the denomination did not want to let the campus "slip through the hands of the wider church," but neither could they afford to bail the facility out of debt. Brother John Jay John, former president and faculty member of the college, stated, "If we let this property slip away from us, we have lost an opportunity of a century. We need this as a Relief Center, and who knows, it might be sometime a home for returning missionaries and retired ministers." Dr. Paul Bowman announced, "If we want this property, we ought to decide how much we have to pay for it. The Disciples of Christ, 1.5 million members, also the Congregational Christian churches, over a million members, have indicated that they will administer their relief programs through our center. The U.S. Government will set up a soil conservation unit here, about fifty men. They are now ready to send men and equipment." And John Metzler reminded the group of the advantages of being located near Baltimore and international shipping. He added that the New York Zoo had offered to raise a heifer for the Heifer Project. And the Methodists had expressed an interest in cooperating with the proposed relief center.

Eventually Brother Frank E. Williar of Mt. Airy, Maryland, recommended the formation of a five-member committee, two from the District and three from the elders body, to study the plan to purchase, determine a price, raise funds and make the effort to purchase the Blue Ridge College property jointly with the Service Committee of the Brotherhood. The motion passed. Members elected to represent the elders on the committee were Brother John Jay John, Brother Frank E. Williar, and Brother Berkley Bowman. Twenty-six elders and six visitors were present at the meeting.[2]

In their minutes of August 1944, the Brethren Service Committee noted that the Eastern Maryland District had scheduled an auction for September to sell the school—its contents, its assets, and the property itself. The committee revisited the decision made at their May meeting and set a maximum bid of just $25,000, and if the property could be purchased for this amount or less, the district would be asked to provide $5,000 toward expenses from the amount they had raised by a special solicitation. The Brethren Service Committee also appointed Paul H.

Bowman and John Metzler to represent the committee in the purchase of the equipment at New Windsor. And, in a third action regarding the college campus, the officers of the committee were authorized to "negotiate a loan of $25,000 from the trustees of Bridgewater College" with the understanding that "this may be a four percent loan for a period of six months, subject to renegotiation, and that the schedule of repayment shall be mutually agreed upon." The BSC requested that the amount be made available on or before September 6, 1944, in order to purchase the Blue Ridge College property as a cash transaction.[3]

TRUSTEE SALE, SEPTEMBER 6-9, 1944

The sale that was originally scheduled by the New Windsor Educational Foundation, for September 4, 1943, was rescheduled by the Eastern Maryland District Meeting for September 1944. (See Appendix 6.) This time, however, the Stoner farms were included in the sale. The real estate, consisting of the college campus and buildings, three dwelling houses, and two unimproved lots, was to be sold on Wednesday, September 6. The personal property and the contents of the buildings were to be sold over the next three days. The attorney sponsoring the sale asked John Jay John, former professor and president of the college, and his son George Bucher John, to survey the Stoner farms. Both men worked part time as surveyors. Together the project took the better part of one week.[4]

College trustees and their attorneys "deemed it to be of an advantage" for all concerned to sell all college furnishings in bulk at a private sale, so the furniture, kitchen equipment (including dishes, silverware, and glasses), classroom equipment and supplies were sold in large lots. The Brethren Service Committee bought items totaling $5,200; Elizabethtown College spent $428; Westminster Theological Seminary bought supplies for $139.50; the Board of Education of Carroll County invested $1,206.50 in school furniture and supplies; and Maurice Kroop spent $37. In all, the sale of personal property brought $7,011.[5]

Interestingly, the pipe organ was listed as "personal property" in the auction sale bill, but receipts do not show who bought the two-manual Mason & Hamlin instrument or whether it was among other bulk items in a lot.

The first real estate to be sold on September 6 included the campus and buildings known as Blue Ridge College. "Paul H. Bowman, chairman, and M. R. Zigler, executive secretary of the Brethren Service Committee, [headquartered] in Elgin Illinois, were present at the sale with instructions to purchase, if possible, the college plant for the Brethren."[6] M. R. Zigler acted as the spokesman and bidder. Oral history suggests another person by the name of Millar Richardson came to bid on the campus as well, but when a bystander informed him that the church was interested in buying the campus to be used as a relief center, Richardson withdrew in deference to the church. And so the campus was finally purchased by the Brethren Service Committee for an amount slightly over its limit—$31,300.

Oral history and even some written accounts claim that M. R. Zigler bought the college property on his own and then made a phone call to the BSC in Elgin to notify the committee of his actions. As the story goes, he notified the staff that they would now have to find the funds to pay for his purchase.[7] From the minutes of the Brethren Service Committee and Eastern Maryland District Meeting, it is clear that many people were interested and involved in the events leading up to the auction and the purchase of the Blue Ridge College campus. Much footwork had already been done to secure the agreements of various ministries and programs that would join in the endeavors at New Windsor. No single person acting on his or her own initiative circumvented the months of planning that preceded the purchase. The official minutes of the Brethren Service Committee of the Church of the Brethren stated in November 1944:

> The Brethren Service Committee purchased the Blue Ridge College plant at public auction on September 6, 1944. The purchase was made on the basis of substantial gifts from a group of Brethren of Eastern

and Middle Maryland and a loan from Bridgewater College. The cost was $31,300.[8] (See Appendix 7.)

The three houses were the next to be auctioned. The Stoner house on Blue Ridge Avenue went to Walter and Norma Harman for $5,350. The Bonsack house, also on Blue Ridge Avenue, was sold to Charles and Clara Harman for $4,000. And the Flora house, a two-story, red brick house on College Avenue, was sold to Alton A. T. and H. Ruth Williar for $5,060. A vacant lot of 12,521 square feet on Blue Ridge Avenue was sold to Lawson G. and Maude L. Glass for $375. A second vacant lot of 12,108 square feet was sold to Harvey and Jane C. Palmer for $420. The two farms totaling 318¼ acres were the last to be sold. They were purchased by George Bucher and Edna E. John for $21,600.[9]

Going Once, Going Twice . . . Sold!

John Jean John tells the story that his father, George Bucher John, stopped by the auction on his way home from Westminster just to see how the sale was progressing. He was interested in the sale of the farms since he had assisted in surveying them for the auction. Feeling that the properties were about to be sold way under their value, he made a bid to raise the price on the other bidders. To his amazement, the other bidders dropped out and he found himself the proud owner of two farms. He arrived at home that day with the announcement he had just bought two farms at the auction in New Windsor. Now he needed to find the money to pay for his purchase.

George John's own Union Bridge farm was "put up for sale" and sold within the first week, but there was still a difference in the amount that was needed to pay for the "new farms." Three sisters of the John family living in Westminster, who were all single school teachers, had some savings they loaned to George to complete the purchase of the two farms. John Jean John, a young man, married for several years with a small child, moved with his family to the smaller of the two farms. His father, George Bucher John, moved his family to the larger farm.

As an aside, John Jean John recalls that during World War II German prisoners of war came from the federal POW camp at Westminster to dig a hole for the foundation of a silo on his farm in 1945. The prisoners were paid eighty cents per day, plus a meal served by the "host" family. (Interestingly, American men who refused to serve in the military and were in CPS camps received no reimbursement from the government and were wholly supported by families and churches. R.J.T.)

Interview with John Jean John, summer 2005.

The total amount raised from the auction of all the properties totaled $75,145. The outstanding indebtedness as decreed by the bankruptcy court amounted to $30,284, so when all debts were covered, the remainder of the proceeds was transferred to the General Educational Board of the Church of the Brethren. The Educational Board in turn agreed that Bridgewater College should administer the funds since the Blue Ridge College records and remaining students had been "transferred" to Bridgewater. Bridgewater College used the money to establish two separate scholarship funds:

Maryland Education Fund: This fund honors the many friends of Christian education who founded and supported Blue Ridge College at Union Bridge, and later at New Windsor, Maryland, for nearly half a century in its ministry to the youth of the church. Value: $24,861.32.

Stoner-Roop Memorial Fund: This fund perpetuates the memory of Annie Roop Stoner and her husband, Jacob Stoner, both of whom gave generously of their time, talent, and substance to the cause of Christian education as benefactors of Blue Ridge College. Value: $20,000.

According to J. Vern Fairchilds, Jr., the director of financial aid at Bridgewater, the scholarships are still being used more than sixty years later to assist students from Maryland who attend Bridgewater College.[10]

9.

Establishing a Permanent Place for Service

The purchase of the Blue Ridge College campus by the Church of the Brethren and their plans to establish a relief center to send clothing, food, blankets, and other needed supplies to countries that were declared enemies in World War II were major news items in the local newspapers in 1944. "Permanent Relief Center Set Up by Church of the Brethren," proclaimed the *Times*.[1] "Blue Ridge College Becomes Center for Food and Clothing Distribution," declared the *Pilot*.[2]

The purchase of the Blue Ridge College campus was announced in the October 1944 issue of *The Gospel Messenger*. "Through the help of very substantial gifts of Brethren in Maryland given specifically for the purchase of the four college buildings, and through a loan, the Service Committee can now announce the purchase of a permanent location for its clothing center and various other activities." The article went on to explain that this economical purchase would allow the expanding relief ministry to grow and assured the readers that "Current gifts to the Brethren Service Committee have not been used for the purchase of the buildings."[3]

Charles C. Sutton, one of the first CPSers assigned to the New Windsor campus, said, "I will always remember one banquet meal we prepared. A number of Brethren in the surrounding area of central Maryland gave contributions for the purchase of the Blue Ridge College property. We cooked a meal of fried chicken, mashed potatoes, peas, lettuce salad, and apple pie with ice cream to thank them for their generosity."[4]

Now that the property clearly belonged to the Church of the Brethren, things began to move very quickly. A CPS unit of fifty men was approved by Selective Service to be located at the New Windsor "camp." The men were to work with the surrounding farmers in soil conservation and prevention of erosion. The first twelve men were re-assigned from a camp near Williamsport, Maryland, known as Hopewell Farm. These men were to prepare the buildings to house the full CPS crew. One of the first men to arrive on the scene reported,

> We drove right by the place and on into the middle of New Windsor. We could not see the buildings from the road because the weeds were so high. When we found the Center, it was a mess! When the students moved out they really tore the place up. Becker Hall, the men's dorm, was in bad shape. They [the students] made holes in the walls—seems like they did not go out into the hallways, they just went through the walls. You could walk from one end of the building to the other without ever going out into the hall. Other buildings were also damaged but not to the extent of Becker Hall."[5]

Virginia Crim indicated that the college students had been permitted to paint their dorm rooms any color and, indeed, they used many colors.[6] Charlie Sutton gives his first impressions:

> When our group of twelve CPS men arrived at New Windsor and made our first inspection, we could see that we had much work to do to make the buildings habitable. The college group who had previously owned the property vacated it without draining the heating and plumbing system. The freezing weather had cracked some of the boilers that heated the buildings, and the plumbing pipes and equipment had to be replaced. There were holes in the walls and some broken furniture, which looked like the work of vandals. The kitchen and dining room were extremely filthy. Since the kitchen in Windsor Hall was not usable at that time, we prepared all our food and dined in the Stoner house for approximately two weeks.[7]

Dedicated to Serve

First volunteers: Wayne and Wilma Buckle from Washington City Church were long-term volunteers in the early years of the New Windsor Service Center. Wayne worked in the Investigation Bureau for the United States Post Office. Classified 4-F, he was exempt from the draft. His supervisors put pressure on him to buy war bonds because they wanted one hundred percent participation from the employees in the program to support the war. As a member of a peace church, Wayne did not feel he could buy war bonds that would be used for the war effort. When the Brethren, Mennonites, and Quakers were able to make arrangements with a large bank in Philadelphia to purchase nonmilitary bonds, Wayne was able to buy bonds that supported CPS, and the post office was able to qualify for the 100% Club. Wayne took a six-month leave from the post office to volunteer at the Brethren Service Relief Center. Later, when he requested a six-month extension on his leave, the post office refused, so Wayne left his employment. The Buckles volunteered from January 1, 1945, to January 1, 1946. Both Wayne and Wilma were given a "Volunteer Service Certificate" issued by the Brethren Service Committee to all long-term volunteers. The certificate was signed by M. R. Zigler, executive secretary. (See Appendix 8.)

The Buckles extended their term of service for an additional six months when John Metzler asked Wayne to become his assistant. Wayne was sent to Dayton, Ohio, to assist in establishing a processing center there, which opened in January 1946. The Buckles stayed in the homes of Mrs. Kathryn Wallicks and the Reverend John and Inez Long while in Dayton. The center in Dayton was apparently open for only a short period of time since it does not appear in any other written history of CWS or Brethren relief.

Wayne also tells of traveling to Pennsylvania to meet with the president of the Ralston Purina Company in his personal railroad touring car to discuss arrangements for the Church of the Brethren to buy low-cost, high-energy bulk food for distribution in Europe.

Wayne and Wilma Buckle, personal interview, 18 July 2001.

First CPS volunteers: CPSer Enos Heisey remembered that "one Saturday a van load of CPS fellows accompanied by staffer Dan West drove to Philadelphia to donate blood for . . . Albert Ritchey, the father of Emma Grace Ritchey, a volunteer who worked at the Center. Mr. Ritchey recovered from his illness due to the supply of blood provided by the van load of donors." Emma later married Roscoe Switzer and they both served for a period of time doing relief work in Europe.

Enos and Jane Heisey, personal interview, 24 July 2001.

First staff: Joel Petry arrived at the Center from his CPS assignment in 1946 and was assigned to work in the kitchen because of his reputation as a cook in his CPS camp. Joel remained at the Center after his discharge and continued to serve thousands of volunteers and guests. Joel was also a skillful maintenance man. In 1954, along with his supervision of the kitchen, he began overseeing many modifications and remodeling projects on campus. Staff at New Windsor often dated changes at the Center "before Joel" (that is, 1954) or "after Joel." The ribbing is a tribute to his talents as a designer and supervisor of many projects and improvements.

In that same year, the first National Youth Conference was held at Anderson College in Anderson, Indiana. Since the Anderson College kitchen crew was on summer vacation, Joel was asked to do the cooking. Joel took two of the "regular" kitchen staff (Bea Thompson and David Eberly) and four BVSers (Glenn Brechbill, Paul Gomes, and LeRoy and Anita Lapp) and drove from New Windsor with supplies in the Center's International Carry-all Van. Taking over the kitchen at Anderson College, they provided three wonderful meals each day for the young conferencegoers. After thirty-eight years at the Center, Joel retired in 1984 to spend his time and talents remodeling "the home place" in Western Maryland.

Personal interviews with Ruby Bollinger, 24 August 2006; Paul and Helen Gomes, 18 September 2006; David Eberly, 9 November 2006; LeRoy and Anita Lapp, 25 August 2007.

* * *

W. Ray Kyle, another long-term staffer, arrived at New Windsor in 1948 after serving in the U.S. Army in Burma during World War II. At New Windsor he was responsible for overseeing the trucking and shipping of relief supplies. Later he was handed supervision for all nine Church World Service processing centers. Ray was involved in the earliest plans for SERRV (Sales Exchange for Refugee Rehabilitation Vocations) as well. In fact, he has been credited with choosing the name SERRV. Ray died of a heart attack in 1965 while attending a meeting in Washington, D.C.

Soon after the purchase of the campus, volunteers came from local churches to trim trees, remove the fence, and clean the inside. The *Times* reported, "The clean up day at the Brethren Relief Center was on Monday last (11th) and they made a very good job of it until the rain interfered, but on Tuesday they finished taking down the fence; a lot of trees have been trimmed and numerous things done. The ladies did their work on the inside; dish washing and general house cleaning. The folks at the Center expect to move to the girls' dormitory (Windsor Hall) next week."[8] Harry Peters, a CPSer from Union, Ohio, had experience as a plumber, so his first assignment was to replace the plumbing and the heating. Two cast-iron boilers were installed in Old Main, and a trench was dug to carry the heating pipes to the other buildings. The trench was lined with cement, and a ceiling was installed, creating a tunnel, which is still in use sixty years later. Harry remembered that "M. R. Zigler and Harold Row would come around and ask what we needed. We would tell them what was needed and we were told 'Go ahead and order the supplies you need.' The boilers and supplies were purchased from a plumbing supply warehouse in Baltimore."[9] The two new boilers required a new chimney, so the CPS men built the chimney at the back of Old Main. Gilbert Walbridge was responsible for constructing the scaffolding used to build the chimney.[10]

Civilian Public Service workers were required to work forty hours each week, either with the soil conservation unit or on plumbing and reconstructing the campus. In the evening hours and on weekends, they did "unofficial" jobs, such as cleaning and painting rooms in Windsor Hall in preparation for long-term volunteers. When CPS fellows moved into Becker Hall they were given paint and "permitted" to paint their own rooms.[11]

Before CPSers arrived, volunteers managed the dining hall located at the Stoner house, but the CPS men took over kitchen duties when they came to New Windsor—except on Sundays. Volunteers Charles and Bertha Kimmel filled in on Sunday to feed dozens of people without any help.[12] When the Windsor Hall kitchen was in shape, the cooking was moved to that location. The Windsor Hall kitchen was replete with a large mixer for making mashed potatoes and for coloring margarine, which in those days was sold with a packet of yellow coloring to be added to make it look like butter. The large stove made it possible for several to cook without getting in each other's way. Vegetables were grown in a garden plot near the caretaker's cottage. The garden plot is still used by Center staff and local families.

But most of the volunteers who gave time to the Center came from surrounding churches. The Union Bridge ladies' aid society of the Pipe Creek congregation of Eastern Maryland was the first group to volunteer in the clothing center.[13] (The Union Bridge congregation was a separate fellowship that was under the leadership of the mother church, Pipe Creek, until 1952, when they built their new church in Union Bridge.) The trees used to make the roof rafters for the new Union Bridge church were donated by George Bucher John. They came from the Stoner farm that John purchased when the Blue Ridge College properties were sold at auction.[14]

MINISTRIES AT THE BRETHREN RELIEF CENTER

With the full support of the Brethren Service Committee in Elgin, the New Windsor Brethren Service Relief Center quickly developed the many ministries that were to affect people all around the world. When the Church of the Brethren agreed to process used clothing at the Brethren Relief Center for Church World Service (the new relief and service arm of the Federal Council of Churches, the Foreign Mission Conference, and the American Committee of the World Council of Churches), John Metzler, the prime mover for the program, wrote a letter to all personnel at the Center, saying, "You are a part of a great movement." On the day the first train carload of good used clothing arrived, all the people working at the Center were invited to go to the depot for a dedication service and news conference.[15]

Processing material aid. John and Margaret Metzler had first established the clothing process on the basketball court in the gymnasium in March of 1944. When CPS fellows arrived in the fall of that year, they organized a basketball team and wanted to play their games in the gym, so at their request, processing moved to the basement of Old Main. In January 1945 it moved once again to the large auditorium on the first floor of Windsor Hall, though once the clothing was baled, it was moved to the gym and stored around the perimeter of the basketball court until it could be shipped. By the next year, however, the volume of clothing had grown so large that processing, as well, had to move back to the gym.[16] But even the gymnasium was not big enough to handle the project, and a second floor was constructed above the basketball court to expand the clothing and relief supplies process. Earl Flora supervised the construction of the second floor.[17]

Wilbur Mullen was working in a CPS camp near Tallahassee, Florida, on a famous hookworm project, but he wanted to be involved at the processing center, so he requested a transfer to the Soil Conservation Project, knowing he would be able to volunteer his time in the evenings and on weekends at the Center. His assignment was approved and he arrived in early fall of 1944. Once established in the soil conservation unit, he worked very few days before he was put in charge of scheduling volunteers to work at the clothing processing center and arranging their transportation from Pennsylvania, Maryland, Virginia, and Ohio.[18] An appeal went out to recruit workers:

> **Volunteers are needed** to sort, clean, mend, pack, bale, and ship clothing at the clothing department of the Brethren Service Center at New Windsor, Maryland. About twenty or twenty-five persons—men or women, old or young—are needed immediately to get clothing ready for pending shipments to foreign countries. Volunteers may stay several weeks, or they can give a year of service here. The Brethren Service Committee will provide maintenance and will pay transportation for those who stay as long as three months. Write to Brethren Service Center, Box 26, New Windsor, Maryland.[19]

Volunteers who stayed for a minimum of three months received "basic maintenance" (room and board) and $10 per month.

Cooking school. Blanche Spaulding, wife of CPSer J. Lloyd Spaulding, came to New Windsor to open a cooking school for CPS fellows. She had done the same for CPS camps in Magnolia, Arkansas, and at Manchester College in Indiana. She and her assistant, Bertha Kimmel, taught the men who were assigned to be CPS cooks at the camps to prepare food in a camp setting. They learned all the rudiments, even how to make the best use of a side of beef.[20]

Relief training. By Monday, September 25, 1944, less than three weeks after the purchase of the college campus, eight Brethren relief workers had already gathered at the Center for training for relief work. The eight volunteers were headed to China and Europe; their training consisted of studying "the most suitable techniques for our work today and . . . to develop the spiritual resources for the days when our units will face starving people whose spirits are seriously broken."[21] Attending the three-week training course were Eldon Burke, E. L. Eikenberry, Wendell Flory, Luther Harshbarger, Velma Ober, Martha Rupel, and Mary Schaeffer. The training class ended on October 13, 1944.[22]

Shoe repair. A shoe repair shop that had been located in the CPS camp in Wellston, Michigan, repairing shoes for the CPS men, was transferred to New Windsor in late 1944 or early 1945 to better address the expanded need for shoes in war-ravaged countries. Wilmer Garber, a member of the Washington City Church of the Brethren added $500 to his congregation's gift of $259, which enabled the relief center to purchase additional equipment for shoe repair.[23] The repair shop was first located under the stairs in Windsor Hall, but was moved to the basement of Old Main by January 1945. Charles Brashares was the lead worker, with Enos Heisey and Phil Trout working as his assistants. Old shoes were collected and fitted with new soles, heels, and stitching. Volunteers often had to sort through the collection to find mates for shoes, since pairs got separated during transport to the Center.[24] The shoe repair shop was transferred to the second floor of the gym by 1947 and closed altogether by 1949.

Soap. In war-torn countries, the absence of common commodities often makes the difference between life and death. Soap, for instance, becomes a vital medical need. Typhus fever, spread by lice, can be prevented by personal cleanliness, which only soap and water can provide. During World War II the ingredients of soap (fats from cooking grease and rendering animals) became scarce, and the amounts allotted to make soap were small. Soap production was cut to thirty percent in Belgium by 1941, and by 1944 soap was practically unobtainable in most parts of Europe. The same was true in China. Volunteers serving in Europe told many stories about homes that were demolished or so badly damaged they were not habitable. There was no electricity and people lost most of their personal belongings in bombings. Sitting in cold, wet bomb shelters with little or no food, many people, especially the elderly, suffered from disabilities, which affected them for the rest of their lives.[25]

As cooking grease accumulated in CPS camps, some CPSers started to make soap for their own use, but seeing the possibility of a war relief effort, they expanded the project until a ton and half of soap was shipped from one CPS camp to New Windsor for reshipment abroad. By 1945 Selective Service had assigned a man from the New Windsor CPS camp the task of making soap. Local churches and households were encouraged to save cooking grease and fat and were given thousands of five-gallon gasoline cans in which to ship the grease, sending it along with used clothes on trucks going to New Windsor and Nappanee, Indiana. "Grease for Peace" was stenciled on the cans.[26] Some of the early truck drivers for New Windsor tell about the difficulty of loading slippery cans of grease and how on hot days the grease became liquid and ran all over the floors of the trucks. Later on, local churches were encouraged to make their grease into soap *prior* to shipment to New Windsor.

Canned food. One of the most important projects of the relief program was collecting cans of food and preparing them for shipment. In 1945 Ralph Delk, a CPS worker in a mental hospital in Connecticut, was transferred to New Windsor where he was asked to assume the directorship of the canned food program. It was his responsibility to collect the food and prepare it for shipment. Only food in tin cans could be shipped overseas. Volunteers made wooden crates for the shipments of food. This program was located in the basement of the gym.

One Million Dollars for Christ. At the 1945 Annual Conference in North Manchester, Indiana, the Council of Boards of the Church of the Brethren called on the assembled Brethren to increase their giving so the needy people of the world might be clothed and fed. It was noted that the giving among members in 1944 represented only 1.33 cents per day per capita. It was requested that the challenge budget be raised from $807,000 to $1 million and be called the One Million Dollars for Christ Fund. Congregations were encouraged to canvass every member or use some other method to challenge more giving. It was not a small task. One million dollars then would have been the equivalent of $10,504,820 in today's economy (2006).[27] Annual Conference granted the request to raise the budget to $1 million.[28]

Annual Conference in 1946 was held at Wenatchee, Washington, and the financial report given to delegates:

Congregational giving for Brethren Service totaled, $1,055,797. This is an increase of 147 percent over the preceding year. This sum includes $292,480, the value given to contributed material goods—wheat, corn, heifers, etc. It does not include the value of contributed clothing. The clothing . . . had a value of $337,500. The per-capita giving for Brethren Service was $5.83. Many friends of the church have chosen Brethren Service as a channel for relief giving.[29]

Printing and publicity. In the early months of the Brethren Relief Center/Church World Service Center, someone located a mimeograph machine, and Center staff began producing a newspaper called the "Weekly Processor." Charles Webb, director of education and publicity, was editor of the weekly paper and assisted all the other offices in printing and publicity. In time, the mimeograph was replaced with a small offset printing press, giving brochures and other publicity a more professional look. The exact location of the first "print shop" is not known, but from 1954 through 1967, the print shop was located on the lower level of Old Main. A participant in Brethren Volunteer Service from the December 1954 unit, Philip Meek, was assigned to the print shop for his two years of alternative service. Denny Myers was working in the print shop in 1976.

In addition to all the work that was being done at the Center, the new community that sprang up on the defunct campus became a vital part of the area church community. Often local churches would ask for the CPS quartet to bring special music on Sunday morning. One such ensemble included Phil Trout, who later became professor of music at Bridgewater College; Chester Keller, who became professor of philosophy at Central Washington University; Gilbert Walbridge, who took over the family construction business in Easton, Maryland; and Leo Jarrells. Some of the CPS fellows or volunteers filled pulpits in local churches, and a "community choir" directed by Phil Trout would travel on the Center's bus to churches in the area to give programs. The Center became the life of the Brethren Service Committee, and, in many ways, the Brethren expression of a lived faith.

"Bear Ye One Another's Burdens"

On a hilltop that towers above this Western Maryland village, muffled voices and a sound of hammers break the quiet of a hazy spring day.

Within a labyrinth of old buildings, a cobbler repairs shoes. Women cut cloth into patterns. Men and women pack boxes. A truck pulls tortuously up a steep road. . . .

Down in the valley the town postmaster tugs wearily at so many parcels that it might have been Christmas.

On a railroad siding, a freight car is being loaded with strange haste, while the dispatcher looks at his watch and remarks that they'd better hurry—the fast freight'll be along in twenty minutes. . . .

The buildings on the hill housed generations of students at Blue Ridge College, which finally closed its doors in 1943 after 104 years. It's doubtful whether many people outside of this section of the country ever heard of the college or its little town of New Windsor. . . . But homeless Poles, destitute Czechs, hungry French, Germans, and Dutch are staring every week at boxes that bear in bold stencils, "From the United Church Service Center, New Windsor, Md, U.S.A."

There will be many thousands who will never forget New Windsor.

For here on this old campus, the Protestant churches, some thirty denominations, have united in a relief project, which is sending a steady stream of desperately needed things to Europe and Asia—clothing, food, seed, and dairy cattle.

At this headquarters, where you can look across a vast stretch of valley to the jagged haze of the Blue Ridge on the horizon, Christianity has become more than principle and precept. It has been translated into action.

These workers, young and old, men and women, boys and girls, are obeying the kindly mandate: "Bear ye one another's burdens." Nearly all of them are volunteers. . . .

The campus houses about 150 volunteer workers. They have come from more than twenty states, offering their services for a few days, for weeks or even months. Every weekend, boys from Western Maryland College at Westminster, only seven miles away, come to put in a day or two helping out. Church workers have come from Washington,

Baltimore, and many other places. But there's more than enough work for all, and more volunteers are needed, especially those who can stay awhile.

Members of the [Church of the Brethren], having started the project, still are the prime movers in carrying it forward. But many faiths are represented.

No one asks those who drop in to help exactly how they interpret the Book of Genesis or whether they believe in infant baptism or favor total immersion at a later age. They are asked only, "Can you help? How long can you stay?"

Selective Service has assigned about seventy-five conscientious objectors to the Center, and these youths are eager to serve here. Officials say they are invaluable.

The volunteers have included college professors, laborers, farmers, artisans of every type, ministers, lawyers, engineers.

. . . Sometimes a whole group will come from some community to stay a week or a month, sewing, sorting, baling up clothing, and otherwise lending their hands to whatever is needed.

Amish women in organdy caps give a colorful touch to the work rooms and the cafeteria. [Likely not Amish, but conservative Church of the Brethren women. R.J.T.]

There is Anna Karicofe, a missionary, who is working here while she awaits her return to North Africa. Rudy Sailor, a farmer from Illinois, looks, with his long chin whiskers, like a portrait of an old- time Dunkard, as the Brethren once were called. And Mr. Sailor, sorting shoes for victims of war, has given much else to the cause of his country. His son was killed in the Pacific.

One who has not inspected the Center might think that a group of workers [gathered] haphazardly would turn out that sort of work. The contrary is true. The project moves with quiet efficiency from start to finish. No wasted motion is apparent. The workers have been provided with the latest equipment, and they operate it so effectively that three to four carloads of clothing and a car of food move out every week. During one recent week, seven carloads left for the docks in Baltimore or New York, but that was a record week.

The clothing is sorted and baled in the school gymnasium. Under a torn basketball [net], a baling machine of the newest design pressed the garments into compact bundles, which are wrapped in paper and burlap automatically and sent down a chute to waiting trucks.

Efforts are made to obtain gifts of clothing in good repair. Repair work, except on shoes, no longer is done at the Center. If torn clothing does arrive, however, it is not discarded, but sewing kits are enclosed when it is shipped, so that the recipients can mend it.

Shoes are in a different category. If they are salvageable, they are welcome. The Center has as complete a repair shop as you'd find in any city. Shoes are soled, heeled, and mended until they come out looking new. Hundreds of pairs are renovated and boxed every week. . . .

Canned food of all sorts is donated and this is boxed and consigned to places abroad where it is needed most.

On the day this reporter visited the Center, 120 cases of seeds were ready to go out. These seeds are for vegetable gardens, to help those with a little land to grow their own food.

There were thirty-two varieties of seeds in the shipment. There are about sixty potential gardens in each case, and each garden is designed for six persons. The seeds are divided among the various countries needing relief, with due care taken to send to each only those varieties suited to its soil and preferred by the people. . . .

More than two hundred bales of clothing move out of the gymnasium every day. There are four hundred to the [truck]load. Each bale weighs one hundred pounds and costs $5.90 to make up. These expenses include labor, materials, transportation, office overhead, telegraph, and warehouse rental. . . .

The Center has its own carpentry and repair shops, where crates are made for shipping food and other materials and machinery is repaired. . . .

The freight agent has become one of the busiest on his whole line. Postmaster William D. Lovell handles 250 incoming sacks of parcel post every week. He used to take in around forty. There's talk of raising the rank of his post office from third to second class. . . .

The Federal Council of Churches hesitated at first when it was suggested that it sponsor a national relief program. Officials wondered whether they would be duplicating or overlapping the work of the United Nations Relief and Rehabilitation Administration [UNRRA]. Then they did some checking and decided all it could do and all their organization might do would only begin to meet the need, so they went ahead.

The relief shipments of the Protestant churches are made in close cooperation with UNRRA. Routes and destinations are worked out through UNRRA. . . .

Carter Brooke Jones, "New Windsor—Where 150 Men and Women Toil for the Suffering Millions," Sunday Star [Washington, D. C.] 17 March 1946.

In 1946, the Relief Center shipped 66,288 relief items. These goods weighed 4,844,538 pounds and were valued at $2,749,820.61. In 1947 there were 61,099 items shipped, weighing 4,555,853 pounds and valued at $2,378,865.96. The commodities included books, blankets, candles, Christmas toys, used clothing, dried milk, dry goods, egg powder, first aid supplies, flour, handbags, gloves, hospital supplies, "kiddie kits," new garments, rice, seeds, sewing kits, shoes, shoe box kits, shoe supplies, commercially made soap, homemade soap, sugar, tools, towel kits, toys, vegetable shortening, and wheat. The following countries were recipients: Africa, Austria, Belgium, Bulgaria, Burma, China, Czechoslovakia, Denmark, Ethiopia, Finland, France, Germany, Greece, Holland, Italy, Japan, Korea, India, Malaya, Norway, Pakistan, Philippines, Poland, Puerto Rico, Romania, Russia, Siam, Sweden, and Yugoslavia.[30]

Searching for the Lost "Treasure"

An interesting sidelight to the avalanche of relief goods arriving at New Windsor is told in the following story reported by John Metzler. "The New Windsor post office was upgraded several classes (because of the volume of shipments being made to the Service Center). The railroad had such a problem with schedules because of heavy express shipments that they began putting New Windsor express in cars that were simply uncoupled there for later unloading. One day there were

eleven express cars unhitched with packages for the Center. Shipments were unloaded and placed in the Quonset hut warehouse. One
day an express crew arrived from Baltimore; they were searching for a
lost trousseau that had been shipped to an individual in New Windsor,
but it had not been received by this person. The crew was faced with
the job of going through the Quonset hut to find the package—if it had
not already been processed and sent overseas! Fortunately, for the
express company and the bride, it was in the warehouse and it did not
take even a half day to find it!"

John Metzler, Sr., Brethren Service Center staff meeting minutes, 1945.
Brethren Service Center files. New Windsor, Md

10.

Partnership with Church World Service

When Eldon and Cecile Burke chose New Windsor over Philadelphia for a service center, they reported to the Brethren Service Committee that the buildings at New Windsor would be useful for storing relief supplies, but they were not yet certain how those relief items would be distributed. M. R. Zigler (the Burke's supervisor) and the committee encouraged Eldon to talk with other church-based groups in New York City to determine how they could work together to get the job done efficiently and ecumenically. When Eldon did manage to forge a number of partnerships, he sailed to Europe in 1945 to arrange for the distribution of relief supplies sent on behalf of these Protestant churches in America.

While the Burkes focused largely on the European end of the process, John and Margaret Metzler took charge of the Center and the processing operation for the partner churches and organizations.

CHURCH WORLD SERVICE ESTABLISHED

The growing network of church organizations involved in relief work finally took on a life of its own, and "On May 4, 1946, the Federal Council of Churches, the Foreign Missions Conference, and the American Committee of the World Council of Churches established Church World Service (CWS) to be the relief and service arm of the churches."[1] Participating denominations were invited to appoint a representative to this program. Seventeen groups, including the Church of the Brethren, did, and another twelve organizations who were new to the idea appointed provisional representatives. Church World Service became the partnership that the Church of the Brethren was looking for that could magnify its relief efforts. The Church of the Brethren has been an active member of CWS from the beginning and one of the leaders in its formation.

> Thus, the first inclusive, ecumenical, and coordinating instrument for overseas relief and reconstruction in the history of the Protestant churches in the United States came into being. The name "Church World Service" was in many ways an inspired choice as it brought together the three words that described the program on which it was about to embark: the Church in Service in the World. A. L. Warnshuis, Secretary of the International Missionary Council of the FCC, was named its first director.[2]

International relief was not a new idea, of course. "Long before 1946 . . . church groups had provided food and other essentials to thousands who suffered and perished from hunger in the great China famines of the nineteenth century." And "in 1939, the Federal Council of Churches (FCC) and the Foreign Missions Conference created a Committee on Foreign Relief Appeals in the Churches, while in 1944, they formed the Church Committee for Relief in Asia. Later, another organization, the Church Committee for Overseas Relief and Reconstruction (CCORR) served as an umbrella agency and included the YMCA, YWCA, the American Bible Society, the World Student Christian Federation, and the American Friends Service Committee."[3]

When Church World Service was formed, the representatives of the denominations and organizations, such as Church Women United, met to discuss which appeals would be addressed. "A *New York Times* article in late 1946 announced a CWS appeal with a goal of $12 million to be 'used for relief and reconstruction in both Europe and Asia.' The *Times* article described Church World Service as 'the largest private agency distributing foreign relief.' "[4]

There were several material aid centers across the United States that were operated by individual church denominations. With the formation of CWS, these centers agreed to come in under its umbrella. The New Windsor facility was one of these centers and became the major processing site for CWS. "In the first few months of its existence, CWS shipped forty-eight [freight] carloads of food and four million pounds of clothing to people overseas. In 1946, CWS provided eighty percent of all relief goods shipped from U.S. voluntary agencies to Europe and Asia."[5]

When Church World Service became fully organized in 1946, it worked through Church Women United to gather personal health kits (soap, washcloth, comb, toothbrush and paste wrapped in a towel), which were collected at New Windsor. The response was much greater than anticipated and soon the Center was overwhelmed. The local post office in New Windsor was also overloaded. Sometimes the Postal Service stored arriving packages outside on the sidewalk because there was no room in the post office itself. Passenger trains running through New Windsor on their regular routes were often delayed by the time it took to unload health kits and clothing parcels from the mail coaches of the train. Frustrated passengers had to wait while relief supplies were loaded onto the Center's only means of transportation, a "broken down, half-ton pickup truck." The movement of supplies from the railroad and post office was very slow until additional vehicles could be obtained.[6]

Early on in the processing of relief materials for other denominations, the name of the Center changed to "Church World Service Center" to indicate to cooperating denominations that all ministries were being conducted under the overarching organization of Church World Service. The Church of the Brethren continued to provide administration of the Center as well as eight other centers that were soon established under the name of Church World Service.

As the relief effort grew among the churches, additional centers were established until there were nine centers scattered across the United States. Interestingly, the managers of the nine centers were mostly Church of the Brethren workers, with Brother W. Ray Kyle based in

New Windsor serving as manager over all the centers. The service centers were located in Modesto, California; Houston, Texas; Vancouver, Washington; Pasadena, California; St. Louis, Missouri; Denver, Colorado; New York City; Nappanee, Indiana; and New Windsor, Maryland. A short-term, temporary processing center was located at Dayton, Ohio. In addition to coordinating all centers, W. Ray Kyle managed the New Windsor Center staff for the Church of the Brethren, and Melvin B. Myers directed the services of Church World Service at New Windsor. This was a cooperative arrangement among denominations that created an even greater network of relief work and collection centers for used clothing known as "CWS depots." All the churches in a town used the depot for clothing donations, and trucks from each regional center made a monthly pickup. The trucks from the New Windsor Center went up and down the East Coast and as far west as western Ohio. Anywhere from two to six trucks would return with a full load each week. Volunteers and neighbors unloaded an average of 25,000 pounds of goods each day. Later, when the Brethren Service Center hosted the training and orientation of Brethren Volunteer Service volunteers, trainees unloaded trucks and reloaded them for shipping at the Baltimore piers.[7]

CUT-GARMENTS PROGRAM

Many of the Church World Service centers had a specialty of sorts. For example, thousands of gallons of cooking grease were collected and shipped to the Nappanee Center where they had facilities to manufacture soap from the grease. New Windsor was known for, among other things, its cut-garment operation. The cut-garment department was born when the Greek War Relief Association gave wholesale quantities of yard goods for relief.

> The Greek organization is to furnish 50,000 yards of cloth to Brethren people for manufacture into garments.
> This cloth (over twenty-eight miles of it) is now shipped to the Brethren Service relief center at New Windsor, Maryland, and

Nappanee, Indiana, where it will be cut into pattern sizes by recently installed cutting machines. . . .

Greece was one of the last countries to be occupied by German forces and, therefore, to be affected by the British blockade. . . .

Because of the special arrangements with the German and Allied governments under which the International Red Cross administers relief in Greece, this clothing will be sent through the blockade. This will be the first shipment of Brethren relief supplies to be sent through the blockade to the people of Europe.

. . . Under the direction of Miss Anetta Mow, the women of the church are organizing to do the sewing job. . . .

This is the first project of this kind which has been handled through the system of relief centers and Brethren Service trucks, which has been set up in preparation for the expected relief needs after the war.[8]

In 1945, John D. Metzler, Sr., wrote in more detail about the cut-garment program. This unbleached muslin was to be made into undergarments for Greek children. M. R. Zigler and John Metzler had confidence that Church of the Brethren women could stitch up the needed undergarments, but cutting thousands of pattern pieces could be a problem. "Totally inexperienced in commercial garment making, we agreed to try it. We walked in the garment district of New York, looking in the windows of shops until we found one that had the required supplies. We bought a commercial cutting machine and got some ideas from the shop personnel. Thus was 'born' the cut-garment program."[9]

Pauline Delk was in charge of the cut-garment department when it started; it was housed in the lower level of Old Main. Her helpers were Ruth Webb and Ella Flora. The women layered sheets of fabric in piles ten to twelve inches thick. Elsie Yohn was a cut-garment worker in the late 1950s and was expert in using the machine to cut out patterns with the cutting tool. Yards of flannel became baby layettes. Printed cottons became children's shirts and shorts sets. Church women from all over the denomination would pay a small price for the pieces of an outfit to sew on their machines at home and then return them to the Center for shipping. In the late 1970s and early '80s, Marilyn Rice and Harry Gray-bill did much of the work in the cut-garment program.

Our Young People paper, dated October 20, 1945, printed "the first letter to be written by anyone who has received our gifts of clothing abroad . . . from Greece."

> Dearest Friend:
> We all are in good health, wishing for you the same. Today I received the clothes, one dress, and I am very glad because I have a dress to wear. We all are without any clothes. The Bulgarians took all from us. They burned all the houses and we all walk without shoes. When I put on the dress I pray to God to give you all the happiness. I want to write you how much we suffer from the Germans and the Bulgarians, but I don't know where to start from. We thank God that we are alive. I have a family of four children, two boys and two girls, my husband and myself. My husband and children send you a lot of appreciation.
>
> With love,
> Kyriake Nymbrog

By the 1960s, the Brethren Service Center, CWS, and CROP were all conducting major operations out of New Windsor, Maryland, and were running together as a well-oiled machine. In the Blue Ridge Building, staff from each organization displayed relief items so visiting church members could see how their contributions were used. The display included tied comforters, knitted baby blankets and sweater sets, sewn shorts and shirt sets, each accompanied by a story. Bimmy Little gave tours to visitors on a regular basis. She estimated that between 6,000 and 8,000 people toured the Center in the early years. As she told the story of the Service Center, she told not only about the recipients of relief but about the people who contributed items for those less fortunate, such as the gentleman in a nursing home who sent 1,200 knotted comforters in one year. She told of a group of widowed women from Pennsylvania who nicknamed their knitting group the "Unclaimed Jewels." And when Bimmy told visitors to the Center how unwed girls from Jamaica took their babies home from birthing centers wrapped in newspaper, an on-slaught of Remsen baby blankets began arriving from tour groups.[10]

Many service ministries came and went through the Brethren Service Center, some sponsored by the Church of the Brethren and some by Church World Service. CWS/CROP responded to droughts, famines, wars, and natural disasters all over the world. Thousands of tons of clothing, blankets, tents, plastic sheeting, garden tools and seeds, medicines, and mechanics and equipment for digging water wells were sent when requested by individuals and organizations in crucial times. In 1979, a document called "The Nature of Church World Service" made clear that "the common goal of all that CWS does is based on the belief that human well-being depends on the interplay of the spiritual, social, and material aspects of life." The working paper added two functions that it saw as "integral to its ability to fulfill its primary role of enhancing the quality of life: constituency (now global) education and public policy advocacy."[11]

Most Brethren have participated in Blanket Sunday or the Gifts of the Heart projects (school kits, health kits, baby layettes, sewing kits, tools, and seeds), which are all Church World Service projects. Used clothing is no longer collected to be sent overseas, though Church World Service still uses financial contributions to provide help to thousands of people who have material needs, often purchasing items nearer to the source of the need rather than shipping them from the United States. As the need for collection sites waned, Church World Service had less need for space at the Brethren Service Center in New Windsor, but the Brethren are still deeply involved in CWS ministries. The need for shipping material aid has changed, but the efficiencies and fellowship of working together for relief with member denominations of CWS thrives.

———————— ⑥ ————————

Part III

---------- ❦ ----------

Post-War Relief Ministries

Brethren Service Center collection, New Windsor, Md.

II.

CROP
Christian Rural Overseas Program
Community Response to Overcome Poverty

In 1946 Great Britain had to reinstate the bread lines of the war years because there was a shortage of wheat. Ironically, the United States had a record crop of wheat that year—1,123,000,000 bushels. Upon learning of the shortage, Church World Service (CWS) staff called a meeting of midwestern wheat growers, "who voted unanimously that 'the Protestant churches of the wheat belt should engage in a "Wheat for Relief Project" at the time of the 1947 wheat harvest.' " Wheat growers in Oklahoma, Colorado, Kansas, North and South Dakota, and Nebraska took the lead on this project, organizing commitments to fill the cars of a train with grain as it traversed the center of the country. This enormous undertaking received lots of publicity, thanks to Drew Pearson, popular journalist and member of the American Friends Service Committee (Quaker). Charles Luckman of the Citizens Food Committee at the White House suggested the name "Friendship Train" for the freight train. As the train chugged across the United States, CWS staff representatives in each state encouraged all people who were able to contribute a bag of flour or a bushel of wheat to the cargo on the Friendship Train for the people of Europe.[1]

The wheat appeal was so successful that M. R. Zigler suggested to Church World Service that a new food aid organization be established to take advantage of the generosity of rural Christians in the United States. The new effort was called Christian Rural Overseas Program, or CROP for short, and functioned as a program of CWS. John Metzler, Sr., director of the New Windsor Service Center, was appointed the national director of CROP, and funds were supplied by the Brethren Service Commission and the Evangelical and Reformed World Service Commission. Metzler opened the first CROP office at Bethany Theological Seminary in Chicago in a men's dormitory room. Ruth Milner was the field officer. The staff set up CROP offices in Kansas, Illinois, Iowa, and Oklahoma where coordination of the commodities was handled. Ken McDowell, a student at Bethany Seminary, became the first business manager. Eventually Bill Cline became the public relations director and was instrumental in publicizing the project in the midwestern and western states.

Efforts for other CROP grain trains were very successful, and by the end of 1948 at least twenty-three states participated in a Christmas Train, loading 2,000 to 2,500 freight cars with beans, rice, wheat, cotton, meat, and other products of U.S. farmlands. The train split and cars headed to ten different U.S. ports. A dedication service was held at each port on Christmas day at exactly the same time.[2]

CROP was a work in progress. In 1952, Albert Farmer, a former Iowa regional director of CROP, became the national director. Under his leadership, fundraising and promotion became more diversified and included vacation Bible school materials to educate children about human needs around the world and how they could respond. "Ralph Taylor, one of the senior CROP staff, was made responsible for introducing CROP to churches and communities on the East Coast." His office was located at the New Windsor Service Center with his "region" stretching from Maine to below the nation's capital. "CROP was no longer just a 'rural' commodity collection program."[3]

In 1952 CWS/CROP began to supply more than just grain. They also shipped small farm implements to help farmers around the world improve their techniques and their yields. But there was much to learn about appropriate technology in those days. One year, CROP received a plea from African farmers for shovels; however, the shipment was soon sent back to the United States with a request to remake the shovels. The farmers who would use them didn't wear shoes and needed a flat step at the top of the shovel head on which to plant their feet. So welders added a flat piece of metal to the top of the shovels for the barefoot farmers.

John Metzler, Jr., staff member for CROP in the 1970s, remembers that the idea of the "CROP Walk" was introduced in 1972 by Roger Burtner, then Mid-Atlantic regional director, almost against National Office wishes because it was such a different idea for raising funds. But Burtner gives credit for the walk idea to George Sturgeon, CROP director for the Dakotas at the time. According to Ronald Stenning, a former CROP director, "Wherever the first CROP Walk was held, there is no question that the walk has become a major activity of CWS/CROP, and that it has now been used by dozens of other organizations."[4]

The CROP program of Church World Service became independent in 1952 and moved to Elkhart, Indiana, from its original offices in Chicago. The CWS/CROP eastern regional office that was established at the Brethren Service Center in 1969 was moved to Columbia, Maryland, in 1981. This move came at the request of the newly hired regional CWS/CROP director, who shifted the emphasis of the organization to work more with metropolitan populations. Today the letters in CROP stand for Community Response to Overcome Poverty, reflecting shifts in the organization's mission.

CROP Directors at the Brethren Service Center

Ralph Taylor
Helen Herr
Phyllis Metzger
Jean Armstrong
Roger Burtner
Marietta Yarnell
Kathy Petty
Stan Noffsinger
Roma Jo Thompson
Timothy Speicher
Bimmy Little, secretary

12.

Heifer Project

Heifer Project was one of the earliest Brethren Service Commission ministries in the history of the Brethren Relief Center. In addition to serving as an animal collection site, this office also recruited "seagoing cowboys" to feed and care for the animals while in transit from ports in America to ports in war-ravaged countries around the world. Originally called Heifers for Relief, it was begun by Dan West, a farmer from northern Indiana who was one of four Church of the Brethren members assisting in relief work in Spain during the Spanish Civil War (1936-1939). As he distributed meager food relief, this dairy farmer began to dream of handing out fresh milk instead of powdered milk to hungry children. Why not send bred heifers to these needy countries? When the calves were born, the mothers would give fresh milk and the calves could be given to other families, who in turn would raise them and breed them and give their offspring away so that the original gift could continue to assist others.

On his return from Spain in 1938, West proposed his idea to a group of his northern Indiana neighbors, and a volunteer committee was formed to promote "Heifers for Relief." In May of 1942, the committee and the program received official recognition by the Northern Indiana Brethren Men's Group, and in June of that year it was approved as an official program of the Brethren Service Committee. The concept caught on throughout the denomination; soon farmers, churches, and church camps were either raising calves or money to buy animals for this program. The response was great in the beginning, but since there was no possibility of shipping animals to Europe at the height of World War II, some heifers were given to sharecroppers in the southern United States and some were shipped to Mexico.[1]

The first shipment of heifers "across the waters" went to Puerto Rico in 1944. Twenty heifers were gathered with the Brethren Service Committee's oversight and held at the county fairgrounds in York, Pennsylvania, until shipping arrangements could be completed for their departure from the port in Baltimore. Roger and Olive Roop from Union Bridge, Maryland, drove to York to see the heifers and to talk with those responsible for the care of the animals. As they drove home to their farm, they discussed the location of the collection center and decided their small farm, only seven miles from the Relief Center, might be more convenient as a collection center. Soon after, Olive and Roger went to the Brethren Relief Center and discussed their idea with John Metzler, the director. They told him they could make about fifteen acres of good grazing land available and proposed that CPS fellows at the Center assist in caring for the animals. Later M. R. Zigler, executive secretary for the Brethren Service Commission, came to visit the Roop farm. By the time he left, he had reached an oral agreement with the Roops. If shipments could be limited to the summer months when pasture and water were available to feed the animals, the Roop farm could serve as a collection site.

Roger noted in his diary that nothing was decided in that meeting about who was to care for the animals. Several weeks later, Harvey Kline from Manassas, Virginia, drove into the farm lane with a load of Guernsey heifers and asked, "Is this farm where the heifers are to be collected?" Roger replied, "I guess so, but do you know who is coming to care for them and keep records?" Neither man had the answer, but since the animals were there and Mr. Kline had the proper health papers and a record of the donors, the two men decided they should be unloaded.

When news reached the Brethren Relief Center that a truckload of heifers had arrived at the Roop farm, a group of CPS fellows went to the farm and began to build fences to keep the heifers corralled until they were ready for shipment. As word got around and support for Heifer Project continued to build, animals began to arrive by the truckload, in trailers pulled behind cars, in small trucks, and by railroad to the Union Bridge train station. It became clear in short order that Roop's fifteen acres would not be enough pasture for the four hundred to five hundred animals that would graze at the "holding center" at any given time. Arrangements were made for Roger to rent his entire farm to Heifer Project and become a full-time employee of the organization. He sold his own herd to make room for the donated animals. The first shipment of 350 heifers from this collection farm went to France.[2]

The animals most often were shipped via railroad from Union Bridge to the port in Baltimore. For every shipment, eleven or twelve cattle cars would be placed on the railroad siding the day before loading. Local volunteers and men from the CPS unit would cover the floors of the cattle cars with crushed corn cobs donated by a local grain elevator. Then some 350 or so animals were transported to the railroad yard via small cattle trucks, a process that would usually take three hours. The evening freight train would haul the cars to Baltimore, with Roger Roop accompanying each group to the docks. Vernon Gladhill was also a faithful assistant. He volunteered his truck to assist in unloading the cattle when they arrived at the Roop farm and again when they were to be moved to the train yard for transport to the port in Baltimore. He never charged for his time or the use of his truck. He would always say, "This is my contribution to Heifer Project."[3]

Not all people in the community understood the reasons for shipping good animals to the people they had called "enemies" just a few months and years earlier. In fact, local opponents of the program removed the signs directing deliveries to the Heifer Project farm or turned the signs to point another direction. The three Roop girls were often teased at school by their classmates because they "were helping the enemy." This feeling was not true for the entire community, however.

Dr. Edward, a local veterinarian, volunteered his time and expertise working with the cattle.

On one occasion, a blizzard arrived at the same time a shipment of cattle was expected at the Roop farm. D. D. Funderburg, center manager, allowed the cattle to be unloaded at New Windsor into the Quonset building where used clothing was being stored prior to processing. CPS fellows and other volunteers built a temporary fence to separate the cows from the donated clothing. Once the storm passed and it was possible to "host" the cows on the farm, they were quickly transferred to Union Bridge and the "Roop Ranch."[4]

In 1948, Roger Roop contracted undulant fever through an open sore on his hand and had to quit working for Heifer Project and using his farm for a collection site. The Roops did not have insurance at the time, so Heifer Project assisted them with some of the hospital costs. The collection center was moved to Berkley Bowman's farm, a neighboring property. There Kenneth West was put in charge of caring for the animals and keeping the records. In his journal, Roger Roop reported that 3,600 animals, more or less, passed through the Roop farm from 1944 to 1948.

Collecting the animals and getting them to the Baltimore ports may have been the easier part of the project. The more difficult question was who was going to pay for the shipment of the animals to designated countries? The United Nations Relief and Rehabilitation Administration (UNRRA) was also sending animals to war-ravaged countries, but they did not have people to tend the animals in shipment. Coincidentally, Ben G. Bushong, director of Heifer Project, had animals to ship but no money for their transportation. Bushong was able to arrange with UNRRA that he would provide people to care for "their cattle" if UNRRA would provide the transportation for "his cattle." An agreement was reached. The Brethren would "rustle up seagoing hustlers to herd the UNRRA animals. UNRRA was delighted and agreed to pay volunteers $75 monthly expenses, [and] token salaries of 1 cent daily."[5] The cowboys were not permitted to be a part of the ship until they joined the Maritime Union. Ivan Patterson remembers that the dues were a dollar for each cowboy. Years later, in 2001, he still had his "Union Card" when he visited the Brethren Service Center.

Bob Zigler, Jr., son of M. R. Zigler, was in charge of the UNRRA office at New Windsor and was responsible for recruiting volunteer "seagoing cowboys." During 1945 and 1946, Fran Clemens (Nyce) spent her summers between semesters at Juniata College working with Mr. Zigler. Her assignment was to contact people who might be willing to serve as attendants of the animals on ships going to Europe and making arrangements for them to travel to the Center prior to their assignment and departure.[6]

One of the first shipments of animals to Europe left for Poland in November of 1945, but by 1948 the United States government would no longer provide transportation costs for shipment of animals to Poland because of increased political tensions of the "Cold War." Realizing, however, the continuing need for animals in countries allied with the Soviet Union, the Heifer Project office in New Windsor secured $40,000 to purchase cattle in Denmark, which were then sent on to Poland by local transportation, skirting the problem of U.S.-Soviet relations.

No cattle were sent to Germany until early 1949, because food for animals was scarce. All available grain there had to be used for human consumption. Finally, in February 1949, the German authorities, in collaboration with the American Occupation Forces and the United Nations Food and Agriculture Organization, agreed that recovery had reached the point where they could receive livestock. Thus, Heifer Project began to send heifers to Germany, and John Eberly became the organization's representative in Germany.[7]

The first Heifer Project logo was designed at New Windsor by Dick Underwood, a commercial artist from Chickasha, Oklahoma. He designed the logo on the small offset press that was part of the print shop located on the campus.

"Killer Kittens"

Apparently Heifer Project's innovative idea of giving goats, rabbits, ducks, bees, camels, and many other animals to the hungry almost included cats. In "community meetings" at the Brethren Relief Center, staff and workers recorded an interesting conversation in their February 9, 1948, meeting minutes about a "kitten training unit." Apparently several relief workers in Europe had shared about the great problem of rats eating relief supplies and the meager food supplies in the homes of people recovering from war. Since there was a shortage of cats following the war, the rat population had grown so large that families had health and storage problems. The minutes mention establishing a committee at the Brethren Relief Center to "train kittens to kill rats" and, according to the plan, send these "Killer Kittens" along on cattle transports to assist in controlling the rat population. No evidence exists that this project ever came to be, but it was a creative idea for solving a problem that plagued the devastated countries of Europe.

To illustrate only a few Heifer Project shipments, a shipment to Quito, Ecuador, sponsored by the Foreign Mission Board of the Church of the Brethren, included five Brown Swiss cattle, five Toggenburg goats, and six Corriedale sheep. These animals were destined for several mission stations in Ecuador. Also, a total of two thousand goats had been shipped to Japan by November 1948. And heifers were sent to Venezuela to assist in the European refugee resettlement program in that country.[8]

In addition to serving as a collection site for animals, the Brethren Relief Center served as a "collection location" for the hundreds of men, pastors, teachers, students, farmers, family men, and others who cared for the animals in shipment. Depending upon the availability of ships and transportation schedules, some of the seagoing cowboys would be at the Center for a few days, a few weeks, and, in some unusual cases, several months. While awaiting their departures, these fellows volunteered in the various ministries conducted at the Center. Primarily, they would process clothing, sometimes load or unload trucks, assist in building the wood crates for shipment of food and soap, or even assist in caring for the cattle on the collection farm.

In 1953 the central office of Heifer Project moved from New Windsor to North Manchester, Indiana, near the home of the director, Thurl Metzger, though the shipping and publicity operations remained at New Windsor. In the early 1960s, the New Windsor offices of Heifer Project were moved to Upper Darby, Pennsylvania, while Metzger's office remained in North Manchester. In 1969 the national headquarters moved again, this time to St. Louis, Missouri. Finally, in 1971, the headquarters moved to Little Rock, Arkansas, where they are located presently.[9]

Thurl Metzger served as a seagoing cowboy and then director of Heifer Project for a major portion of its existence. He was director from 1951, when the organization operated entirely from New Windsor, through 1981, when the organization settled in Little Rock, Arkansas. He was awarded an honorary doctorate from Manchester College in 1972 for his lifelong ministry to the less fortunate. Thurl Metzger died in July of 2006 at his home in Little Rock where he lived following his retirement from Heifer International, as it is called today.

Another key employee of Heifer Project was Joe Dell, who was transferred from Church World Service in New York to New Windsor in September 1948. Joe later transferred to Modesto to become the director of the clothing processing and relief program there. He was a lifelong employee of the Brethren Service Committee, first with Heifer Project and later as the director at the Modesto Service Center until his retirement in the early '80s.

R. Jan Thompson attended junior high church camp at Camp Sugar Grove in Southern Ohio in 1946 or 1947 where the goal for campers was to "buy" a heifer for Heifer Project. When campers had given enough of their spending money to purchase a quarter of a cow, someone colored in a portion of a large drawing of a cow on the wall, representing the portion that had been purchased so far. Enthusiastic campers gave up ice cream treats in order to give more toward the cow and the relief of hungry people in Europe. Many readers will remember assisting in similar projects.

As is the practice of the Brethren, the church has hatched many seminal ideas and then invited other denominations to join in to increase the effect. This was the case for Heifer Project as many other denominations supported the Church of the Brethren in sending animals to poor and devastated countries. With such broad ecumenical support, Heifer Project made the decision in April 1953 to formally leave the Church of the Brethren to become an independent organization. However, Heifer Project reappeared at the Brethren Service Center in 1980 for a brief period when John Dieterly opened the southeastern regional office in the Blue Ridge Building. In addition to establishing this administrative office, volunteers built holding pens at New Windsor for a petting zoo to promote Heifer Project. The work was conducted under the supervision of Roger Roop, older by this time but still very interested in the ministries of Heifer Project. The regional office closed April 10, 1998, when John Dieterly resigned, the regional offices were reorganized, and the corporate office in Little Rock underwent a change in philosophy.

13.

SERRV
Sales Exchange for Refugee Rehabilitation Vocations

Marketing of internationally made handcrafts to support the poor began in the 1950s and was administered from the Brethren Relief Center. The economic development program known as SERRV (Sales Exchange for Refugee Rehabilitation Vocations)* began as an effort to help war victims develop cottage industries to support their families when other employment was nonexistent. Today SERRV continues "to promote a sustainable way of life . . . to inspire others to SERRV. . . and to eradicate poverty, wherever it resides."

A fiftieth anniversary publication of the Brethren Service Center states that "Church of the Brethren relief workers in postwar Germany saw the need for a first step beyond crisis concerns for food and shelter among many refugees and displaced persons. A vision of economic independence inspired the relief workers to provide a means of income through the sale of the refugees' handcrafts in the U.S. The first items were sold informally at the Brethren Service Center. This later became one of several SERRV gift shops and led to the development of the wholesale and consignment sales program."[1]

---

*In 2004, SERRV's name was changed to A Greater Gift, but management returned to the name SERRV just four years later.

In a letter dated April 24, 1950, to Byron Royer, who was in Vaihingen/Enz, Germany, John Eberly expressed a heartfelt concern for the plans and outcome of the SERRV program.

The International Gift Shop may be on the way to a reality. The Eisenbises coming home from Austria brought a sizable box of the finest and assorted hand work collected from the refugee camps near Linz. Most of this will be used to set up a display at the Grand Rapids Conference. M. R. [Zigler] is considering turning over to the committee planning the Gift Shop his cuckoo clock, china business, et cetera, and even now I have been reading your well-prepared answer on these Uhren [clocks].

If all this could and can succeed on a great scale and accomplish international value and earn a million dollars for the service and peace program of the church which is now seriously threatened with the loss of official support, it would be something. It would also tempt the promoters to wonder if they are that good why they haven't gone into business for themselves.

But this thing is very likely to succeed because it has all the reasons for failure. It has the appeal of exclusiveness to the rich, the appeal of sympathy and service to the religious, and possesses intrinsic value for everyone. It will have to succeed in spite of the lack of worldly wisdom behind it.

We are interested in other items: wood carvings, music boxes, musical instruments (especially harmonicas), German doll babies, pocket knives (distinctive), and others you might recommend.

What about your refugee camps? We have much interest in the rehabilitation value of taking articles from refugees. The human interest appeal of this is big. We are open to all kinds of ideas. Don't worry yet about ethics. We are remembering them.

Sincerely yours,
John H. Eberly[2]

At first, refugees offered many handcrafted items, but eventually, BSC staff commissioned crafts people to make certain pieces and even arranged for the Brethren Service logo to appear on some items. A letter to M. R. Zigler at New Windsor from Byron Royer in Vaihingen/Enz, Germany

(Castle Kaltenstein, a village near Enz), May 15, 1950, indicated that the cuckoo clocks made by Kaiser now had the Brethren Service emblem on the leaf just below the face of the clock. Previously the Brethren Service emblem was on the pendulum, but it seemed awkward to "have the cross swinging back and forth in a somewhat unstable manner."

> Last week we received a box from Kaiser, containing three cuckoo clocks. We are personally very happy and excited about these clocks. On the leaf just below the face of the clock, they have carved a Brethren Service emblem. I was surprised at the effectiveness of this and how well it fits into the general appearance of the clock."[3]

From the same letter:

> We have a theological professor visiting Kaltenstein this week and have had a very rich fellowship with him. He is from the Evangelical Academy in Braunschweig. This academy is the same type academy as the one in Bad Boll. They bring groups of men for various periods of time to study the message of Christianity to their profession. Perhaps a group of lawyers comes at one time, then a group of doctors, farmers, businessmen, etc.
>
> This man is a personal friend of Sigmund-Schultze [founder of the Fellowship of Reconciliation and one-time pastor to Emperor William] and he suggests that we visit Schultze at the earliest opportunity. This man is very much interested in pacifism and has asked if I could spend a good bit of time with him. We will speak together tonight at some length only about Christianity and pacifism.
>
> It is fortunate that we can be confident that God can work through us even if we, His tools, may not be the most perfect. I will be anxious to write further about the result of this, but I am convinced that if we can influence some men in these academies in the direction of Christian pacifism, they will have a great influence in Germany. If this and other talks are satisfactory, perhaps we can visit this man together and possibly even visit the academy together when you return.[4]

As Byron's impressions here reveal, Brethren have found many ways to share their beliefs in pacifism and other aspects of their faith in a variety of ways worldwide.

> I find that the nearer the time comes for our returning to America the richer our experience becomes. It is strange that in Germany under the present circumstances that a man acquires standing in a community in two or three years which would require twenty to thirty years in the States. This situation brings its privileges, but at the same time demands a great amount of humility. Our greatest hope always is that we may continue to be worthy of this.[5]

Minutes of the Brethren Service Commission (BSC) meeting in June 1950 prior to Annual Conference at Grand Rapids, Michigan, report on a discussion about establishing an international gift shop at New Windsor.

> Approved a committee to investigate and bring back all details to BSC for consideration before final action is taken. Asked the committee to send a report to the chairman as soon as available. Committee: Paul W. Kinsel, chairman; Benjamin G. Bushong; and W. Newton Long.[6]

This committee met at New Windsor on July 20, 1950, to work out details and made the following recommendations:

A. That the International Gift Shop be tried on a limited basis for a period of one year.
B. That an attempt be made to secure an interested, qualified person from BVS or other volunteer to supervise and manage the shop.
C. That a committee of five persons be named to supervise the project, to whom the manager will be responsible. Suggestions for the committee are W. Newton Long, chairman; John Eberly; Ray Kyle; K. Ray Hollinger; and Samuel A. Harley.
D. That the committee shall investigate and decide a list of possible articles, cost, import duty, selling prices, etc.
E. That the purpose of the Gift Shop shall be—

1. To provide an outlet for materials produced by refugees and other folks (for purpose of rehabilitation).
2. To include items from other areas—items tending to extend international friendship and understanding.
3. Earnings, after necessary expenses have been cared for, shall go into a special fund to be used at the discretion of the BSC for the promotion of world peace.

F. That an appropriation or a loan be made by BSC to start the project by creating a revolving fund. This fund should be from $1,000 to $1,500 for the initial period of one year.
G. That the administration of the finances of the Gift Shop be handled through the business office at New Windsor, similarly to the Cut-Garment Department or Heifer Project.
H. That the I. G. S. [International Gift Shop] be located at the New Windsor Center.

Respectfully submitted by committee: Paul Kinsel, W. Newton Long, and Benj. G. Bushong[7]

A letter from W. Ray Kyle to Mrs. Ammon D. Miller, Dover, Delaware, on August 10, 1950, had an interesting twist. Mrs. Miller was offering a quilt she had made to be sold at a relief auction, but Kyle, not knowing of any relief auctions at the time, offered to place the quilt for sale in the International Gift Shop. He wrote that after the quilt was sold he would send a portion of the price to Mrs. Miller and the balance would go toward a relief project that the gift shop supported.

In the early days of the gift shop, records and shipping papers were not set up in an orderly fashion. A letter from W. Ray Kyle to Mrs. O. R. Hersch of Manassas, Virginia, details how SERRV operated.

Whenever materials are received at New Windsor from our units in Austria, Germany, Greece, or Puerto Rico, we will mark the selling price and attach it to the garment. In this price will be figured the cost of the garment (in other words the price paid to the refugee who made the item), shipping cost and duty, plus twenty percent markup. By some arrangement agreeable to all, samples of the items available for selling will be sent to you, who in turn can distribute them to the local

Women's Work groups. The women in the local congregations could place their orders for materials with you and you in turn could combine the orders and send [them] to New Windsor. We would fill the order as completely as possible, sending you a duplicate copy of the order blank listing the items included in the package. Any items in the order that we were not able to supply would be recorded in our files and when the items were received, they would be sent to you immediately. Then, probably once a month, we would bill you the list price, less ten percent which would be retained by the Women's Work of the District or as the women of your District might decide. In other words, the refugee, whom we are trying to help would receive a fair share for making the item. Of the twenty percent markup, ten percent would stay at New Windsor to cover the handling, postage, etc., costs, and the other ten percent would go to the Women's Work group making the sale.[8]

A VIABLE IMPORT BUSINESS

This was still the first year of the gift shop's life; communication and record keeping have come a long way in today's world! It is evident that the International Gift Shop (IGS) provided a major learning experience in the beginning.

In addition to improved bookkeeping, SERRV staff learned they had to set standards of quality very early in its operation. Correspondence between W. Ray Kyle and Dr. Homer L. Burke, serving at the Castañer Hospital in Puerto Rico, indicates that the Burkes sent items to New Windsor made by local artisans for the International Gift Shop in the hopes of expanding the type of handmade items for sale and to expand market options (and income) to the local people of Castañer. Feedback from the local gift shop committee concerning the "saleability" of the items was given to the Burkes in response. As the "business" grew and the quantity of imports grew, the staff of SERRV worked with artisans to obtain high quality, marketable crafts.

In the fall of 1950, Ray Kyle reported that several conferences were held at the Brethren Service Center, and the participants purchased items from the gift shop. Also, various Women's Work groups sold items, with the gift shop keeping ten percent of sales and the Women's Work group receiving ten percent. These fundraising opportunities not only provided a ministry but also gave broad exposure to the International Gift Shop, helping to make it somewhat profitable.

What began as a "suitcase" operation, in which BSC staff carried items home to the United States in their luggage, became a regular import business subject to taxes and tariffs. November 1950 minutes of the Brethren Service Commission say the commission "Approved the report of the committee to study the International Gift Shop at New Windsor, with the request that Attorney Beverly be consulted regarding the legal aspects of importing materials."[9] Soon these added costs would affect the efficiency of the program, but not enough to undo the project.

Letters in December 1950 to M. R. Zigler in Geneva, Switzerland, from Ray Kyle at New Windsor were full of concern about the high pre-priced items coming through customs and the duty required in order to receive packages. Rosemary Block, a BSC worker in the Linz, Austria, office, was directed to reduce the prices on each item and thus reduce the custom charges, so the average person would be able to purchase them and still provide a small profit for the gift shop.

In addition to import duties, customers had to pay Maryland sales tax as well, making each item even more expensive. Early in 1951 there were several letters between Ray Kyle and Hylton Harman, an attorney in Kansas, regarding the sales tax. One piece of correspondence indicates that the governor of Maryland was working to eliminate the sales tax on items imported by SERRV because of the rehabilitation nature of the program. In a letter to Harman, Kyle proposed a "barter system" if the sales tax issue could not be resolved quickly enough:

> A refugee in Austria would make a handmade tablecloth with materials furnished by BSC—Brethren Service Commission. The material (finished product) would be brought back to the States by returning service workers under the $500 free-entry allowance. Because, as I understand it, these materials are not allowed to be resold, we would take this tablecloth made by the refugee woman and advertise it in our catalogue, but instead of setting a money price, we would say that the

price of the tablecloth would be three pairs of children's shoes and a dress. . . . I believe this plan has the added advantage of making the Gift Shop an instrument for an even more personal contact, which is so important in strengthening the bonds of friendship and brotherhood.[10]

There are many letters detailing the problems and concerns of the craft import business and the beginning of the International Gift Shop. Duty into the United States by way of international parcel post was ninety percent. The high import duty was another reason for considering the "barter system." Correspondence to M. R. Zigler in Geneva in December 1950 indicates that "one package of crocheted doilies [had] an import duty of 60 cents on the dollar, and another package of linen luncheon sets with handwork had an import duty of ninety cents on the dollar." Later on in this same letter, Ray Kyle questions "why the Brethren lack interest in this project?" The International Gift Shop staff sent out about three hundred catalogs to the District Women's Work and Ladies Aid groups at Thanksgiving time, hoping the Christmas season would bring in some mail-order business. But Kyle indicated he had not received the first order, as of the date on his letter, December 21, 1950.[11]

Frustrated by the lack of interest and sales, Ray Kyle asked M. R. Zigler to write an article for *The Gospel Messenger* about SERRV and the International Gift Shop, to appear just before the mailing of the next catalog to pastors. Kyle wondered over and over again if the simple life philosophy of the Brethren would be the downfall of the International Gift Shop, which focused on nonessential items.

By 1951, the import duty problem was still a major area of concern. At the same time, the Brethren were warming up to the idea that their purchases were assisting in the rehabilitation of victims of the war. A woodcarver, who was a displaced person, had been making bookends and other hand-carved items and was beginning to make cuckoo clocks. The inside mechanism came from Switzerland, and since cuckoo clocks were not readily available, they became an item of interest in the United States, especially when they earned a small income for the maker.

A sales record book from the fall of 1951 has many pages listing items, price, crafter, place of origin, and some of the buyers' names. For example, on October 27, 1951, two knitted doilies from Germany were sold for $1.50 each; on July 21, 1952, a cuckoo clock from Germany was sold for $35; on July 1, 1953, a Bavarian doll was sold for $4.25. Brethren Volunteer Service (BVS) workers also made items during their orientation sessions at the Brethren Service Center and sold them in the gift shop. For instance, a leather belt made by a BVSer was sold for a dollar on October 3, 1951.

EXPANDING OPERATIONS

It is clear from the letters that came and went from New Windsor to SERRV's friends in the U.S., as well as to the volunteers and paid workers in Europe, that the International Gift Shop had a rocky start. Kyle said in one communication in March 1951 that "if it is to succeed, [it] will need to be dependent to a large extent on the time and efforts that John Eberly and I can give it."[12]

Consignment sales became an effective avenue of exposure for SERRV. District workers who requested a consignment item from the inventory were often willing to put up the money for shipping and then sell the items locally just to expose the SERRV program to the congregations of that district. March 1, 1951, was the date of the first consignment.

In a letter written in October of that year, Alice Rohrer of Ashland, Ohio, inquired how she could get some international gift items to sell at a women's meeting. Explaining that the catalog was currently out of date, Ray Kyle suggested that the staff send a box of assorted items to her for the display. In his letter to her, he went on to say, "There are millions of refugees who are not able to help themselves and it is for this group that regular relief shipments will continue, but there is also another smaller group of refugees who could become self-supporting if an opportunity was afforded them to use the skills which they possess."[13]

Early in the 1960s, SERRV expanded outside of the Church of the Brethren to include Church World Service and the National Council of Churches, who participated financially and promoted the aims and purposes of the program. Methodists, Lutherans, United Church of Christ, and Presbyterians here and in Europe became valuable participants, even though the administration remained with the Church of the Brethren.[14] This cooperation with other church groups opened the market to a much wider population.

William Nyce became the first full-time director of SERRV in 1964. That year sales totaled $47,448, which supported three paid employees. The small staff worked efficiently by distributing parcels of handcrafted items to church women's groups and to congregational mission studies events. In 1965, a larger, more professional "Self-Help Handicraft Parcel Catalog" was produced and sent to those who were interested.

W. Ray Kyle died from a heart attack on December 1, 1965, while attending a meeting in Washington, D.C. His legacy was astounding. In World War II, he was stationed at Oakland, California, and also served in Burma. Helen (Griffith) Kyle Carlisle told us in an interview that Ray had said, "We bombed those countries; we ought to help them rebuild." Ray was a high school graduate and liked to read; two of his favorite authors were Dietrich Bonhoeffer and Paul Tillich. At the helm of the international gift program in its earliest days, W. Ray Kyle offered a consistent, compassionate approach to this ministry. Ray also supervised the nine Church World Service centers throughout the U.S. In the January 20, 1966, *Messenger*, W. Harold Row paid tribute to him: "Ray Kyle kept his deeds a respectable distance ahead of his words. He was a prime example of quiet diplomacy, of persistent determination, of Christian compassion concretely expressed. He was creative and practical, one who held ideas whose time had come."[15]

In the 1960s, mission studies events, sponsored by the denomination and supported by the districts, were held in local congregations and/or regions. These educational events focused on different parts of the world and provided an opportunity for SERRV to offer information and sell items from the people of the featured country or region, such as Southeast Asia, India, Europe, or Puerto Rico.

SERRV also benefited from the growing number of missionaries serving in countries around the world. Often these missionaries would approach SERRV and offer to provide craft items from their host country for resale in the International Gift Shop. In fact, two-thirds of the suppliers from the late 1950s through the 1960s learned about SERRV through their contact with missionaries. The missionary would offer to connect artisans in the community with SERRV and to find a workplace for the artisans. Articles had to be priced realistically for buyers but bring enough money that about fifty percent of the price could be returned to the artisan. Part of the producer's responsibility was to have "truthfulness and integrity," maintaining consistency in quality and size of the product with the sample that was sent to the buyer.

PERSONNEL AND PROGRESS

In 1962, Betty Young became the manager of the gift shop located in the lower level of the Blue Ridge Building. She assisted William Nyce, director of wholesale and retail sales, in selecting crafts to purchase, inspecting them on arrival for quality compared with prototypes, and then setting prices. It was during this period of time that SERRV began shipping wholesale consignments to women's groups as Christmas bazaars grew in numbers and profits.

1965 SERRV Prices

	Wholesale price	Selling price
KENYA		
ebony letter opener	$ .65	$ .75
3-piece salad set, carved heads	$1.60	$1.95
THAILAND		
coconut water dipper	$ .90	$ .95

ECUADOR		
balsa letter holders	$ .80	$ .95
large cedarwood masks	$5.00	$5.25
black cedarwood Madonna	$9.00	$9.95
INDIA		
handwoven tablecloth 36x36	$2.50	$2.95
brass vase (small)	$1.15	$1.35
brass vase (large)	$3.20	$3.50

SERRV files.

Eva Christian, the wife of a Presbyterian pastor in Swarthmore, Pennsylvania, was a strong advocate of the International Gift Shop and was instrumental in having SERRV booths at many local and district meetings of the Presbyterians. She was a member of a group of SERRV employees and interested volunteers who would get together to look over handcraft items and make recommendations as to which items had customer appeal. Jewelry, wood carvings, and baskets were the most popular items sold.

In 1964, improvements were made in the procedure for handling SERRV mail orders and over-the-counter sales. A triplicate form was used to keep better track of inventory and remittances.

At the height of the relief effort (from the late 1940s through the mid-1960s), eight of the nine Church World Service centers across the United States hosted gift shops with space and staffing for the SERRV program. They were in St. Louis, Missouri; Houston, Texas; Denver, Colorado; Pasadena and Modesto, California; Vancouver, Washington; Nappanee, Indiana; and New Windsor, Maryland. As the need for relief materials diminished, the regional relief centers were closed, so by the mid-1980s only the New Windsor location was still in operation.

Subsequently, the popular International Gift Shops began appearing in other locations. M. R. Zigler wrote in a letter to Ray Kyle, November 12, 1965,

I have been thinking that we should have a [SERRV] gift shop in our "Hotel" here at the Palms (Sebring, Florida) and when I saw the gift shop here I decided to write you to see what you thought about starting one at Sebring this winter. Maybe it's not too late for Christmas. Tourists come in January, February, and March. There are some people in the Home [who] I believe would manage it in grand style and not too expensive in overhead. Tell me what you humbly believe. I like the looks of the one here. [Adding SERRV] would work well in our Hotel and Retirement Home.[16]

The October 12, 1967, issue of *Messenger* reports,

Most customers say they find the prices surprisingly low. Prices are fixed to include only the payment to the supplier, plus duty, freight, salaries, and other costs of operation of the SERRV gift shops, and a percentage to make possible the constant increase in inventory. . . .

The largest share of imports comes from Jordan, where olivewood carving shops and mother-of-pearl jewelry industries offer employment to Arab refugees. Hong Kong is the second highest in value of imports to SERRV, and India, Ecuador, Korea, Thailand, Kenya, Taiwan, and Haiti are the next largest suppliers, in that order. The rest of the imports come from twenty other countries outside the continental United States. . . .

In some cases SERRV advances capital to help an industry get started. This was true at the beginning of the elephant grass basket industry in India, which now produces thousands of baskets yearly, but which would have been an impossibility without a capital advance to prime the pump in the early stages.[17]

This same article demonstrates how the women of other cultures were able to become independent and self-sufficient through SERRV. A group of women from Picalqui, the United Andean Indian Mission in Ecuador, operated a group of cottage industries: "Most of the craft workers in the project are women who with their handwork can supplement the inadequate wage of the chief breadwinner of the family. A group of forty women regularly get together to be supplied with new materials and embroidery cotton and to bring their finished aprons to the mission worker to sell. Through this group the missionary is trying to bring a leavening influence in the community." The article reports that "the selfishness that was so evident at first is gradually being replaced by growing concern for one another. One of the women came early one day to the project house with aprons to sell; money was urgently needed to bury her son. . . . The other women in the group responded to this mother with sympathy and concern in her need, a reaction they once would not have had."[18]

In 1970, the increase in business over 1969 was $75,851 with a total cost of imported goods at $330,707.[19] The year 1971 was better yet; there were thirteen percent more imports over 1970. Suppliers from forty-eight countries were paid $376,675, an increase of $45,967 over 1970.[20]

In 1972 there was another substantial increase in SERRV imports from the fifty-one participating countries. Total cost of goods paid to the suppliers was $503,228. Duty paid to U.S. Customs was $42,862. The sales record for the years 1970 through 1974 shows a ninety percent increase over any previous five-year period.[21]

Virginia Grossnickle, hired in 1967, had a variety of jobs in the SERRV program. "Ginny" first worked as a clerk in the International Gift Shop. She assisted Betty Young in creating eye-catching displays of handcrafted items in the shop. In 1978, Virginia became supervisor of sales and customer relations, a newly established position. She spent many hours on the phone and in face-to-face conversations with customers. The annual sales in 1979 were $1.5 million with handcrafts from artisans in sixty developing countries. In 1950 SERRV was a dream, but twenty-five years later, it was a million dollar business.

In 1968, the International Gift Shop was located in the newly constructed Zigler Hall at New Windsor. This new building had a kitchen, dining room, conference rooms, and lodging for Brethren, non-Brethren, and civic groups. The Brethren Service Center was a very active place with many visitors and conferences using the new Zigler facility. Many women's groups came by bus for the day, taking tours of

A Successful Endeavor

An increase [in 1979 over 1978] of 12.9 percent in net sales brought the figures from $1,376,310 to $1,554,484, generated from resale and retail sales.

SERRV's overall expenses include approximately 73 percent for the goods (as paid to its producers) and its transportation to New Windsor and customs duty. Approximately nine percent was spent for personnel and office expenses, and promotional expenses were low at 3 percent. Consignment orders were 28 percent of SERRV's business in the late 1970s. "Consignment sales are generally service-oriented and non-profit. . . . A goal of selling at least 75 percent of the consignment order is . . . advocated."

"SERRV New Windsor and Friends," **SERRV News 1979-1980, 7.**

the facilities, shopping at the gift shop, and eating lunch in the dining room. Interest in the Center as a destination for tour groups was so high at one point that visitors had to call ahead for reservations. For a period of time in the late 1960s, SERRV also had items for sale at the Church of the Brethren General Offices in Elgin, Illinois, in combination with a bookstore that was managed by Marty Snider.

In 1972, Carl C. Beckwith became director of sales, a newly created position. He was responsible for the retail and wholesale mail order sales and coordinated the inventory and invoicing through a data processing system. Previously, Mr. Beckwith had been in charge of SERRV sales at the Church World Service Center in Modesto, California.

By 1975 the International Gift Shop had exceeded $1 million in sales. Even so, several Church World Service Centers across the United States had been closed for economic reasons. Only the New Windsor, Oakdale, and Nappanee gift shops remained open. Fortunately, there was growth elsewhere that offset the closure of these shops. An innovative marketing plan with the Southern Baptist Convention, the nation's largest denomination, was developed, supplying crafts from SERRV to sixty Baptist bookstores across the U.S. "It was in the mid-1970s that

SERRV was recognized as one of the largest Alternative Trade Organizations (ATO) in the world, three times as large as Self-Help [later changed to 10,000 Villages], a Mennonite program. The New Windsor gift shop and others, along with a nationwide ecumenical program, made the program financially successful, self-supporting, and generating a profit."[22] In 1976, the sales for SERRV at the New Windsor gift shop alone reached $350,000.

SERRV has been known as a favorite place to do volunteer work; its volunteer base is estimated at 20,000 and includes people who come from as far away as Westerville, Ohio; eastern Pennsylvania; and Virginia. It also includes workcampers who are on the New Windsor campus for a week each summer.

Bill Nyce was the director of SERRV from 1964 to 1981. Under his direction, the full-time SERRV staff grew to thirty people and sales topped $2.5 million. In 1977, Nyce gave a paper on "Alternative Marketing in the U.S.—A Case Study" at the International Workshop of Third World Producers and Alternative Marketing Organizations in Vienna, Austria (April 28-May 4). Nyce continued as director of purchasing until his retirement in April of 1986.

In the beginning SERRV did not have the staff to travel to various countries, so they relied on CWS staff in many different locations to recommend local artisans whose work was of high quality. In the 1980s, however, SERRV hired Randy Gibson, the first SERRV employee to travel the world identifying artisans and working with them to provide high quality items.

One of the perks for the administrative staff of SERRV was an occasional trip abroad to visit a supplier. In 1980, Betty Young and her husband went to Israel, where she talked with producers and saw firsthand some of the olivewood carvings and mother-of-pearl jewelry produced for SERRV. The mayor of Bethlehem and his family were the top mother-of-pearl jewelry makers. The Youngs also traveled to Greece where lace, embroidery, and brass items were produced for resale in the United States through the SERRV program.

In 1981, Wil Nolen was named director of SERRV. Wil maintained his residence in Elgin but traveled to New Windsor about twice a month, spending three days a week in the office. One of Wil's strengths was his keen sense of business and finance that kept SERRV on a solid footing. The *Carroll County Times* reported on October 21, 1981, that the annual sales for the SERRV gift shop at New Windsor alone totaled $500,000. Gifts were coming from fifty developing countries. At that time, not many of the items came from Europe, but rather from Southeast Asia, Africa, and South America. Wil left SERRV in 1983 to take another position in the Church of the Brethren.

The *Frederick News-Post*, August 12, 1982, announced the installation of new and improved carousels for the SERRV program, a device that facilitated the picking and packing of items for customer orders at an increased rate of fifty percent: "These four carousels, 38 feet long and 8 shelves high, and 6 flow racks, built to meet the demand were necessary to improve processing of orders while cutting time and space needs. Sal Cannatella, director for warehouse operations stated, 'This means that customer orders will be filled more efficiently during the pre-holiday rush.' . . . This alternative marketing organization, designed to preserve human dignity, is supplying markets to people in developing countries and high quality gifts for folks who visit the New Windsor International Gift Shop."[23]

On February 18, 1982, *Attraction*, a local paper in Carroll County, carried an article by Virginia Leache titled "A Cornucopia of Treats Spills from New Windsor Gift Shop." Leache reported that, "Worldwide recognition is given to New Windsor, a small village of 1,000 residents southwest of Westminster. Fifty to sixty country artisans produce quality handcrafts for the International Gift Shop. Mrs. Betty Young, manager, and six full-time sales people plus three part-time workers are on hand to help you purchase elephant grass wastebaskets, dolls from Zimbabwe, Korea, Thailand, Taiwan, and Sri Lanka. You will find alpaca items from Bolivia, crewel and leather pillows, teak furniture, and a nest of tables from China."[24]

In the early 1980s, a gift shop was reintroduced at the Church of the Brethren offices in Elgin, Illinois, managed by Joanne Nesler Davis for six years. Many volunteers made the work light, and as visitors came to the national offices, they were welcomed and greeted with warm assistance from clerks such as Barbara (Peters) McFadden, who worked at the SERRV shop from 1983 to 1985. The volume of shoppers, however, was low, so after consultation with the SERRV director and others at the Brethren Service Center, the store moved to another location with more public traffic not far from the Brethren offices. The store was located near a well-known restaurant called The Milk Pail, which had adjoining shops and a steady stream of customers; sales improved for a while, but the SERRV shop closed in the winter of 1988 because of declining sales.[25]

Wilbur Wright served as director of SERRV from 1983-1986. One of Wright's contributions was a special marketing project with Holy Childhood Association, a Catholic Church program in Washington, D.C. In this program, SERRV items from the Service Center at New Windsor were used as incentive prizes for children at the school. Still, by 1983, sales had dropped slightly to $1,996,328. Despite the small decline, the gift shop expanded into newly renovated facilities at New Windsor in May 1984. The larger space in the lower level of Old Main was a beautiful and appealing gift shop, managed by Betty Young. Sales began to pick up again, and by 1985, net sales for SERRV were $2,443,309.

The years 1986-1989 again saw new leadership for SERRV. Jim Forbus led the business in steady growth with sales in 1987 of $3,640,776. Mary Myers was named director in 1989 but moved on within a year, so Forbus returned as the interim director. Net sales in 1990 were $3,899,770.

About the same time that the SERRV gift shop in Oakdale, California, was closing in 1989 (the manager retired and sales volume was low), a new SERRV shop was opened in 1990 in the Interchurch Center at 475 Riverside Drive in New York City, the headquarters of the National

Council of Churches. The International Gift Shop was a welcome addition for the many workers in the building and the guests who came and went each week.

In August 1989 Bob Chase of Appleton, Wisconsin, became the new director of SERRV.[26] During his tenure the cooperative retail catalog project with the Christian Children's Fund began. The Christian Children's Fund (CCF), located in Richmond, Virginia, was interested in marketing handcrafts from around the world to enhance their child sponsorship program, much like what SERRV was doing. In their model, individuals or families "adopt" a child from any place in the world and provide funds for clothes and fees for school. Looking for more markets, SERRV staff produced a retail catalog of craft items for CCF's sponsors and customers. Proceeds from sales were split between the two organizations to their mutual benefit for about fifteen years. The cooperative program with the Christian Children's Fund ceased in early 2006.

In early 1991, Virginia Grossnickle and her husband, Byron, along with photographers Regina Holmes and Scott Custer, traveled to Nairobi, Kenya, and Mombasa to learn more about the skilled Acombba carvers who produce wood carvings, excelling especially in masks and African animals. In the area around Nairobi, beaded jewelry was being made by men and women with physical disabilities. The crafters sat at tables with balls of local clay, fashioning necklaces, bracelets, and earrings. Having no sophisticated equipment such as a kiln, the clay beads were laid out in the sun to dry. This product gave the artisans an income they would not have had otherwise.

In 1993 sales grew to $4,715,223, and a SERRV shop was opened in the Baltimore area in a new partnership with the United States committee for UNICEF. The net sales for SERRV for 1995 were $4,627,430.

From the fall of 1996 to January 2001, SERRV leased shop space in the Cranberry Mall in Westminster, Maryland. The rent was inexpensive and there was no obligation for a long-term lease. Linda Jacobson, gift shop manager at New Windsor, oversaw the mall store. Although the shop was spacious, it was located at a junction where the traffic was not as busy as hoped, and the low sales volume prompted the decision to close the store. Sales for the year 2000 totaled $5,387,331.

AN ECUMENICAL ENDEAVOR

As with several other programs that originated in the Church of the Brethren, SERRV grew to have many denominational partners and developed into an ecumenical project. At the time that Church World Service became involved, SERRV was considering the possibility of expanding or disbanding. In the end, other partners made the difference between life or death for the program. While partners saved the organization, it remained a Church of the Brethren program until March 1998 when the director, Bob Chase, petitioned the General Board to permit SERRV to break away from the Church of the Brethren. At its next meeting in October 1998, the General Board approved this request. While SERRV became an independent organization, it kept its residence at the Service Center for another several years. In 2000 the SERRV shop at New Windsor moved from Old Main to the main floor of the SERRV building. Then in 2001, Chase moved a contingent of staff to offices in Madison, Wisconsin, after the SERRV board had considered several locations for a new home. They learned that Wisconsin ranked fifth among U.S. states in sales volume of SERRV products, and Madison has been a place for pilot projects by other fair trade organizations like SERRV.[27] Presently there is a SERRV gift shop on Monroe Street in Madison, managed by Deanna Shumaker. Altogether there are fourteen salaried staff in Wisconsin.

Some SERRV staff have remained at New Windsor to carry the load of purchasing, customer service, and receiving and shipping for all the outlying SERRV shops. New Windsor staff also recruit and supervise many volunteers on a daily basis. Churches within a fifty-mile radius of the Brethren Service Center have, at one time or another, brought a carload or vanload of volunteers to price gifts that come from all over the world. There are twenty-six paid SERRV staff located at New Windsor.

Many questions surround the fair trade handcraft market. Church leaders have often wrestled with the question whether SERRV should import handcrafts from countries governed by repressive regimes. Also, are the people who purchase SERRV items motivated by a desire to change political and economic structures or to promote sustainable development? Or are they simply consumers who like the products? Is SERRV just a matter of charity, or does it equip people with skills to be self-sufficient? Does it help the poor improve their lives, and does it help buyers feel their own lives are more meaningful and interesting when they make fair trade purchases? Perhaps SERRV supporters are motivated simply by the desire to have a business of sorts and to connect with exotic cultures worlds away. Clearly people support SERRV for many and varied reasons.

Director Bob Chase responds, saying, "Perhaps it would be fair to describe SERRV as a church-owned business designed to distribute internationally sourced crafts through churches in a way that would encourage the church's commitment to international brotherhood and understanding." A SERRV report notes that

> Attempts have been made at SERRV in recent years to develop consistent producer criteria and clarify our development role. We have developed a grant fund, are more active as advocates for producers, and have tried to educate customers about development issues. . . . There are a few stakeholders involved who want to change economic or social structures, and changing structures is what, I believe, sustainable development is about.[28]

By 2005, SERRV was earning $8,563,858. The venture began as a small idea about helping victims of World War II become self-sufficient and make a livelihood. This endeavor also gave those in refugee camps a sense of purpose by providing them an income from their crafts and a better outlook for their future. It is unimaginable how many people have benefited from this program.

Shoppers who use the catalog or visit the shop at New Windsor or Madison will always be reminded of the struggle of those first artisans and volunteers as they worked to make the idea of a self-help industry a reality. Those who buy these handcrafts gain an appreciation for the beauty and special love that goes into each item. With a simple purchase, the consumer establishes a personal contact with someone in a developing country who benefits from the SERRV program.

14.

Farmer and Student Exchange Program

World War II left agriculture in Eastern Europe in a shambles. Church of the Brethren workers for Heifer Project saw enormous need for rural reconstruction, especially in Poland, so they decided to take matters into their own hands. In December 1945, they delivered the first load of heifers to Poland. Horses and more heifers were to follow, but the utter devastation of farms and the rural economy called for something more than livestock replacement. Relief workers believed something systemic and comprehensive was needed, namely agricultural education, so they created a plan to help Polish students study agriculture in the United States. It took two years to arrange for the exchange. In 1947, Thurl Metzger, Heifer Project representative in Europe, and S. A. Pieniazek, a scientist involved in the reconstruction of Polish agriculture, developed the program to bring ten Polish agricultural students to the United States to study agricultural methods for one year. Several of the Polish students went to universities, while others lived on farms across the United States. The program was operated out of the Heifer Project office at the New Windsor Service Center.

The exchange program with Poland was suspended after only one year because of growing tensions of the Cold War—and did not resume until 1957.[1] But the concept of educational exchange bubbled up elsewhere at New Windsor. John Eberly had been teaching for eighteen years and realized it was time for a career change. In mid-1948, he took a year off from his teaching job in Indiana, studied Italian, and traveled to Italy to work with Heifer Project. That July he traveled on a ship that carried mostly cattle but also some horses. Eberly, a farmer named Will Licky, and four other men took care of the animals daily. When the boat arrived in Naples, they unloaded the cattle and then went on to Carrara where the Brethren Service project was stationed. In John's words,

> It is worthwhile to give this bit of background with the Heifer Project because it leads so naturally to the high school student exchange program. After WWII, the Brethren Service Commission was much occupied with the physical and material needs caused by the war. The Church of the Brethren had made a considerable witness throughout its history of objecting to war, and to a certain extent refusing (officially it did) to participate either in the training or in the actual war. A part of the criticism that the pacifist movement received was that not enough was done to get at the causes or the roots of dealing with war, that pacifism was only a vocal or professional stand rather than an actual stand in which one ministered to the results and the cure or prevention of war. Without concrete positive action, it would only be an empty verbal witness. You have to do more than talk about what you believe, you have to do something to live it, practice it.[2]

Eberly worked in Carrara from July 1948 to February 1949 as a representative of Heifer Project and CRALOG (Council of Relief Agencies Licensed to Operate in Germany). In Italy a committee composed of local people and regional government officials received the cattle and distributed them to selected recipients. Eberly's job was to explain to the recipients where the animals came from and the terms under which they were given. He described to each family the hallmark of Heifer Project: the first offspring to be given to another family to multiply the effect of the original gift.

While Italy was ripe for reconstruction, agricultural help for Germany was slow in coming. At the end of the war, Germany could not produce enough food to feed its people, let alone the animals. By February 1949, however, Germany was more stable and could provide grain for livestock. That meant it was time for Heifer Project to ship animals to Germany. M. R. Zigler asked John Eberly to represent the project in Germany.

Eberly's office in Frankfurt was in the I. G. Farben building, the headquarters for the U.S. military occupation forces in Germany. He was approved by the Food and Agricultural Agency (FAO) of the United Nations, which meant he had the same privileges as any military person, with access to the PX, cafeteria, and barber shop. John also had a special passport called the "red passport" for this building. Herr Mittelmann, the United Nations high commissioner for refugees, and Dr. Stieve and Dr. Buhr, two agriculturalists, worked with Eberly on the committee for Heifer Project.

At the same time, M. R. Zigler was visiting refugee camps, observing the living conditions and talking with FAO personnel regarding his observations. He asked how the Brethren Service Committee might be able to work with the FAO on improving the conditions for the inhabitants of the camps.

In an interview with Ingrid Rogers, Eberly observed, "In our simple Brethren way of thinking, picture that here were young people who hadn't had much of a balanced diet for a long time and needed some good food. What could be better than to bring them to the United States and put them with a farm family?"

Ingrid asked, "So it was not so much a matter of changing the idea of the 'enemy' that U.S. people might have had after the war?" John responded, saying, "That hardly ever entered our mind. The work of Brethren Service was simple. We acted as we were, to meet needs. . . . It was our naiveté to think in terms of food and just the good will of giving people a meal who needed it. But bringing young people out of the bad environment of a refugee camp was different. . . . We were no longer dealing with cattle or bales of food stuff or pounds of clothing; we were dealing now with human beings."[3]

As John Eberly and others began to think of their work more as a rehabilitation program than a feeding or agricultural program, they began to see the need for a change in emphasis from food to culture and society, so the program shifted from an association with FAO to an affiliation with the Office of Cultural Affairs of the State Department. Trudi Gunther was the person at the Cultural Affairs office who worked with the Brethren Service Commission. She requested that fifty young people be sent from the refugee camps to American homes for one year. Eberly said, "Why, it sounded as simple as shipping heifers."[4]

At the same time that Herr Mittelmann was screening applications to find fifty youth from the refugee camps to participate in a U.S./German exchange, Byron Royer was working for the Brethren Service Commission in Stuttgart. Royer came up with an additional forty young agriculturalists who did not come from refugee camps, but who were very interested in spending time on farms in America. The youth with farm backgrounds were from the area of Württemberg and Baden. Would the Brethren Service Commission take this additional group of forty? A phone call to Harold Row in Elgin brought this response (after some discussion): "Well, we will. We'll try it." Herr Mittelmann's fifty refugees were moved to the U.S. in August, and Royer's agricultural group of forty followed in September. The U.S. military occupation forces in Germany agreed to pay the transportation for these students to the United States and home again one year later.

The youth were sixteen to eighteen years old, and no matter where they were in their education in Germany, they would attend a high school in the United States. (See Appendix 9.)

> In the meantime, host families in the United States had been selected and approved by the Brethren Service Commission office in Elgin working through regional secretaries. The task of finding families to accept these students was not too difficult since the great value of the project was apparent to all. Room and board and incidental expenses were to be provided for by the families, and in many instances church and community organizations were more than willing to help share these expense.[5]

Many activities on both sides of the ocean were making it possible for the student exchange program to become a real ministry in so many ways. John Eberly and Ruth Royer were the welcoming party at Bremerhaven when German parents and youth arrived to begin the journey to America. Of course, the parents wanted to be present to see their children off to the United States for a whole year. As lunchtime approached, John realized that some of the families had left home early, possibly without breakfast. Since he had access to the PX and cafeteria, he decided to use his privilege to feed everyone. After talking with Ruth, he determined that the whole group could not go to lunch all at once, but he could take five or six at a time. Finally, all thirty-five of the early arrivals were in the cafeteria and had plenty to eat. When the officers' wives saw this group in the officers' mess, they raised their eyebrows, but soon the information about who they were and what was happening got around; the women began to talk with the students and had a wonderful time mingling with the young people.

The twenty-five boys and twenty-five girls spent four days in Bremerhaven before sailing on the U.S. Army transport *Henry Gibbins*, getting the necessary instructions about their travel and expectations upon arrival in the United States. The Brethren Service Center served as the port of entry for these young people. BSC staff from New Windsor met the students at the piers in New York and, after a brief tour of New York City, brought the students to New Windsor. Clean beds, warm food, and a preview of what might be in store for them in the coming year filled the next several days. Most of the host families came to New Windsor to meet their exchange students. For some hosts, however, this travel was not possible and other arrangements were made for the exchange student to reach his or her final destination.

When the initial exchange proved to be so successful, Brethren Service decided to create a "stateside office" of the Student Exchange Program, housed at the Brethren Service Center.

Minutes of the Brethren Service Commission, March 1949, report:

> Approved in principle accepting the responsibility for activities in the States of fifty German farm youth of high school age for a six-month

period, with the understanding that the occupation government will pay transportation costs and maintenance would be furnished by the home to which the youth is assigned.

Also in the same minutes: "Approved setting aside in a temporary reserve $1,000 for a self-insurance plan to cover exchange students, volunteers, and caravaners."

W. Harold Row, secretary of the Brethren Service Commission, expressed these thoughts about the exchange program:

> We feel the American home factor has great value in this project as well as the educational experience that students will receive in American public schools. The distinctive thing America has that Germany should learn to know is the spirit and quality of the American home and the freedom and democracy of the American public school. Germany's impression of American family life has come principally from the movies. But these students will get a truer picture of our community and church life, and of our school and business relations. Aside from the value the students will receive, there is the good that will be realized by the host church and the family and school that have the German youth in their midst."[6]

Minutes of the Brethren Service Commission in November of 1949 report that

> The first group of forty-seven German high school students arrived in New York on September 25, 1949. Accompanying the group was Maya Stauch, who will study at Bethany, and Karsten Moritz, who is studying at the University of Chicago. Maya was the acting leader of the group and acted as "big sister" to the girls in the group and Karsten acted as "big brother" to the boys.
>
> The students were met at New York by W. Harold Row and Mr. and Mrs. John Bowman. After a short sightseeing tour in New York, the group was taken by bus to New Windsor. Here they were interviewed personally, their clothing situation was checked, a nurse checked them physically and they were prepared for their trip to their homes.

... Many sponsoring families came by car to pick them up. Others traveled by train.

    ... The last forty-one students are now scheduled to sail from Germany on October 24th.[7]

When Ralph Smeltzer left the student exchange program in June 1950, the Brethren Service Commission "Approved asking John Eberly to assume direction of the German High School Student Project in the United States as long as need exists for such supervision, provided the Heifer Project Committee agrees to release him for this assignment."[8] On June 26, 1950, W. Harold Row of the Brethren Service Commission wrote to Dan West of Heifer Project asking him to release John Eberly from the Heifer Project Committee (HPC) for an assignment with the exchange program based at the Brethren Service Center. West approved the request to release Eberly and suggested that Ben Bushong take over the Heifer Project work at New Windsor and Thurl Metzger pick up the central area of the country for HPC.

The Cultural Affairs organization moved from Frankfurt to Bonn, the new center of German government, and a man from the U.S. State Department stationed there began working toward the exchange that would happen the following year. Bonn wanted to send 300 in addition to the 90 already in place in the U.S. Other organizations, such as the American Farm Bureau, the Council of Churches in Michigan, and others in the United States, heard about this program and wanted to become involved. After some consultation, the Brethren decided they could probably place 194 of the 300 proposed.

In July 1950, a group of 194 new students were to arrive in the States. John Eberly had returned to the U.S. Heifer Project headquarters at the Brethren Service Center the previous December, so Verna Rapp took charge of the exchange program in Germany and Ralph Smeltzer worked to find host families in the United States. He was able to find only half the number of homes he needed, so John Eberly, claiming he didn't know better, stepped in temporarily to help locate host families. He took a chance and called Wilbur Mullen, a student and a friend at Manchester College, who said, "Send a bus load and I'll place them." Mullen went to the Catholic priest in Huntington, Indiana, for help in placing two or three students. The rest were placed in homes in the North Manchester area. In the meantime John organized an official send-off for the first fifty students who were returning home. He took them to Washington, D.C., Mount Vernon, and New York, including the United Nations headquarters.

At the Brethren Service Center, Ed Crill, educational director, spoke at an orientation session and answered arriving students' questions about what might be ahead for them. When the students arrived in their new homes, they saw that education in the United States was quite different than in Germany. Some saw their first football game, ate something other than potatoes and cabbage, tasted peanuts and popcorn for the first time and liked them.[9]

M. R. Zigler, stated: "On September 14, 1949 . . . the first teenagers sailed from Europe to the United States under the auspices of the occupation forces in Germany and the Church of the Brethren in an experiment that was to prove that high school exchanges were not only possible but perhaps the most productive of all exchanges in long-range intercultural values.

". . . The people involved in the United States were not amateurs in goodwill. While the program became more professional as the year passed, nothing helped more than simple goodwill in making the exchange work."[10]

At New Windsor, Brethren Service Commission staff were keeping careful track of visiting students, helping them adjust to their new surroundings and watching for possible problems. Even pastors were asked to file reports called the "Pastor's Viewpoint" about the students' emotional and mental health. Thirty-two different pastors put their signatures to the reports on the overall health of the student and the satisfaction of the host family in this experience.

The March 1950 minutes of the Brethren Service Commission gave the program a positive assessment: "The students are being well received and are fitting well into their homes, schools and communities. There are even less problems than were anticipated at the beginning of the project." However, there were difficulties in placing some students. Ralph Smeltzer was the main troubleshooter and contact person for students and host families. He visited homes, made phone calls, and wrote notes to students and families to preempt serious trouble and keep the program on a positive keel. For instance, about half of each group that arrived was Catholic, and our Brethren folks and the Catholic students did not always see eye to eye. In some situations, the program strongly encouraged German exchange students to be willing to attend the Protestant church of their host family.

Students Placed Coast to Coast in 1949

State	Number Placed
Ohio	29
Virginia	15
Pennsylvania	7
Indiana	7
Maryland	6
Michigan	6
Kansas	4
Washington	3
California	2
Nebraska	2
Iowa	2
West Virginia	2
Illinois	1
Wisconsin	1
Oklahoma	1
Oregon	1
Arizona	1

Brethren Service Commission minutes, March 1950. Brethren Historical Library and Archives, Elgin, Ill.

Smeltzer encountered some students who wanted to stay longer than one year. A file at New Windsor on the student exchange program contains fourteen letters from students asking permission to stay beyond the year agreed upon; another file revealed that more than a dozen students had applied and would receive college scholarship funds for further schooling if they stayed, so they appealed for a year's extension. Administrators of the student exchange program discussed the requests for extensions and decided "some exceptions might be made where they would be returning to dangerous situations, and that consideration be given to resettling some of their families in the United States."

Some German students still revered Hitler and encouraged other German exchange students to "take advantage as much as possible of this fraudulent church who wanted to use us for their propaganda in Germany." Fortunately, only a small number of students held this position and it did not cause a major problem.

Another problem that required constant attention was finding a sufficient number of host families. In early June 1950, the Brethren Service Commission and staff in Germany were beginning to feel the pinch of an inadequate number of Church of the Brethren host families in the U.S. to take care of the large number of students who applied and were accepted into the program. It seemed time to go to other denominational friends who might help out with a mounting problem. Harold Row wrote to Dr. Charles Boss, Jr., Robert Tesdell, and Dr. James A. Crain from the Methodist Church, United Christian Youth Movement, and Disciples of Christ respectively, stating:

> Last September and October a total of ninety German students of high school age came to America and were placed in Brethren homes. Under strong pressure from officials in Germany and from the State Department in Washington, we have agreed to take another hundred students. These students will arrive the latter part of June. Now we have almost enough families to take care of this group, though we do have a lack of families asking for boys. . . . The State Department was most anxious for us to take the responsibility for the students and said it was all right

with them if we wanted to establish an interagency committee. Still another development is the strong interest of the Austrian government for the Brethren Service Commission to work to sponsor a hundred Austrian high school students.

He went on to say, "No project that the Brethren Service Commission has sponsored in recent years has received quite as much universal acclaim as this German high school project. Therefore, we are encouraged to expand it in our own communion and to suggest other churches take up the project."[11] The other denominations accepted the challenge and agreed to place an additional one hundred students.

Programs such as this one are susceptible to great human risk, so it is amazing, perhaps, that the operation ran as smoothly as it did. However, a tragedy struck the exchange community in late 1950. *The Gospel Messenger* reported that Heinrich Schreck, living with the Ronald Workman family in Goshen, Indiana, went to visit Hans Haas, a close friend of the Schreck family, in New York State over the Christmas vacation. The two went for a walk on Christmas day in the area of the Catskill country. The boys walked out on Black Lake, where both broke through the ice and drowned. A double funeral service was held on Thursday, December 28. Heinrich Schreck's body was shipped by air to Germany. He was an only son with two sisters. His parents lived near Stuttgart in Württemberg-Baden. On New Year's Day, a memorial service was held at New Windsor, where a number of German students and their families gathered, and a similar group gathered at West Manchester, Indiana. Letters and gifts were sent to the family in Germany.[12]

Despite the problems, the program was far more positive than negative, and over and over, the testimonials reaffirmed the value of the exchange. Brethren Service Commission minutes of November 1950 claim that "The German High School Student Project has elicited more enthusiastic response from our people, and beyond our own fellowship, than any Brethren Service program in recent years."[13] In another example of the program's success, Sylvia J. Seese, chaperon of students attending Annual Conference, wrote to Verna L. Rapp, at the Student Exchange office in Frankfort, Germany, giving her impression of the twenty-five exchange students who attended Annual Conference and how the stories of their experiences were received: "They were the picture of health and happiness and the testimonies they gave were something to hear. There were tears in the eyes of quite a few of the students and families when they talked of the time when they would have to bid each other goodbye. It just did our hearts good to see them. Many people saw them and decided they would like to have a student, too. One of the girls acted as a mother in the home where the mother had died in March. The father was at Conference with his four small children and had only words of praise for his student."[14]

The exchange program was not just about education. This bridge between two cultures helped foster openness and forgiveness after a wrenching war. Glenn, a recent war veteran, lived in Indiana and attended the Roann Church of the Brethren. He was a paratrooper in the U.S. Army during the invasion of Germany and was shot down by German soldiers, injured, and taken as a prisoner of war to a Nazi prison hospital. Now, some years later, when he heard about Gerhard, a German exchange student coming to his town, he quit coming to church. As the family and congregation welcomed the student and oriented him to life in Indiana, Glenn's and Gerhard's paths often crossed and communications followed. Soon it was clear a friendship was developing between Gerhard and Glenn. On the last Sunday of Gerhard's time in the area, he spoke from the pulpit and said, among other things, "I cannot ever take up arms to fight the Americans, because I have learned to know and love the Americans." Glenn rose from his seat and came to the front of the church and gave his own personal testimony about how much it meant to him to have Gerhard there that year. Through many tears, the student and the veteran embraced each other in real reconciliation.[15]

Maury Mussellman tells the rest of the story:

Gerhard Weiser, from Weisloch in southern Germany, arrived in Indiana in November, 1949. He carried his translation dictionary at all times as he could not speak English. He joined the senior class at Roann High School and graduated valedictorian at the end of April 1950. He stayed with Galen and Patty Eiler through the school months. Then in the summer months he stayed with several different families on their farms. Gerhard had a good experience in the Eiler home and the Church of the Brethren in Roann. When he returned to Germany in October 1950, he started a youth club patterned after the Rural Youth Club he saw in Wabash County, Indiana. He met his future wife, Johanna, the daughter of the mayor of Mauer, at one of the satellite clubs. As was tradition, he moved to the hometown of his wife, where he became the burgermeister (mayor) of Mauer, a few miles from Heidelburg. He also became involved in state government (Baden-Württemberg). He was elected to the Parliament in Stuttgart. He became the minister of Agriculture, Environment, and Forestry. He served as vice president or vice-prime minister of Baden-Württemberg. Gerhard was known throughout Germany as a man of integrity and honesty. Gerhard was active in his Lutheran church. He started an exchange student program for the Eastern Block, bringing in fifty students from Russia and fifty students from other former Soviet countries. These students would spend six months in Germany and then return home. He played a major role in the uniting of East and West Germany. He has written two books and was given an honorary doctor's degree.[16]

Gerhard passed away on January 11, 2006. Two hundred people gathered at his gravesite on what would have been his seventy-fifth birthday to pay honor to a great man.[17] This is one of many success stories about the impact the student exchange program had not only on an individual but also on his country.

RE-ENTRY

Visiting students had to make many adjustments when they returned to Germany. The Brethren Service Commission, especially John Eberly, was anxious to know how re-entry went in each case. One student, John Gwildis of Stuttgart, Germany, wrote to the staff at New Windsor about his return to Germany.

Now that we are back in Germany . . . we . . . are facing our second major and very important task. That is to make our experiences and knowledge about America, the American people, their habits and customs, etc., useful to our own German people, institutions, and government. . . .

On our arrival at the Frankfort airport, an American officer made the remark, "At this moment this program has come to an end!" . . . We were discouraged quite a bit, for re-adjusting to German life was difficulty number one. None of us thought it would be so hard! But soon most of us began to overcome this situation and to act as ambassadors of goodwill. . . .

. . . Was this whole thing just a political trick in order to Americanize these youngsters? Or was it really an honest effort by the American people to bring about a better mutual understanding between our two nations? Naturally, since this project was completely new and our group was the first one to go over and come back, these questions may have been justified.

. . . We very soon found out that we couldn't just tell them our experiences (and most of them were good ones), for people got suspicious and simply wouldn't believe what we reported. . . .

Now that we have been back for about three months, it is a lot easier to deliver a speech in a meeting. The pictures and slides we brought with us were and still are most valuable to us. What words can't say, pictures will express! . . .

One of the most important and effective ways of fulfilling our second task is to live as an example for everybody. . . .

Thus, we exchange students, pioneers of the teen-age program, in spite of all the difficulties and disappointments that confronted us, are working to form a better world through better understanding and appreciation of one another. We are doing it over here, separated by the vast waters, while you are doing it over there.

John Gwildis concluded his remarks saying, "May I extend our deepest and most sincere thanks to everyone who collaborated in this program and who made this wonderful year, so rich in experiences, possible. In particular, we thank our American parents, the Brethren Service Commission and the United States State Department and, last but not least, our 'Uncle' John Eberly."[18]

The U.S. Department of State also had good things to say about the exchange program. A booklet titled "Preparation for Tomorrow: A German Boy's Year in America," published in 1951 by the State Department, tells of efforts to provide German young people with the opportunity to become good citizens by the standards of a democratic tradition (Publication 4138). It begins, "This is the story of Ernst Hermann Taucher, a likeable young German who has recently gone back to his own country after spending a year in an American family, attended the local high school, went to the church of his 'foster family,' and helped with the farm work on the Meadowbrook Farm, as the son of any farmer would." Ernst was sponsored by Louis and Jessie Lantz of the Guernsey Church of the Brethren near Monticello, Indiana.

The February 18, 1961, issue of *The Gospel Messenger*, tells of more evaluations by German students after their year in Germany:

- I gained the important experience that America is not the land of 'fairy dreams'—that besides Hollywood and divorces, the American citizen has to think about more important things, too.

- This will eliminate the many wrong concepts which people got from our war propaganda. This at last will guide our countries toward a better understanding.

- I think the most valuable thing for me is that I am a pacifist today. After staying one year in Brethren homes, it will be impossible for me to fight any more. Valuable for both countries will be that we shall work for a better understanding between our two countries by telling the Germans the truth about America. Our student program shall be indeed a peace-promoting project.[19]

To sustain the relationships made through exchange, the staff, the students, and the host families decided to gather their letters and notes into a newsletter called *ECHO*. John Eberly usually began most issues with an article about matters of adjustment and expectations from the point of view of both the family and the student. Donna Butterbaugh Lehman, secretary to John Eberly, pulled together these pieces of correspondence from hosts and students for the newsletter:

- We spend only one Christmas of our life in America. We should enjoy this Christmas as much as we can. We shall remember Christmas 1952 all our life. Let's enjoy this Christmas—and let other people enjoy us! Let's never forget how thankful we ought to be to all the nice people with whom we spend our "American year" and who make their homes ours, too, especially now at Christmas time.— *Hiltrud Loehr, a student*[20]

- Thomas [Zwick] is improving every day with his English. He has made one speech at a farm group. He did a fine job. Thomas went to Abilene, Kansas, today to see President Dwight D. Eisenhower. He said he took several pictures. We hope they will be good. — *Mrs. R. J. Meuli, Hope, Kansas*[21]

- I thought I would write you a few lines and let you know Brigitte [Ziemann] is doing fine. She is going to school and seems to be getting along fine. As for her foster family, we already think very much of her. She is anxious to please and does anything we ask her to. She and our daughter, Glenda, get along fine and enjoy each other's company very much. They are trying to dress alike and do many things that good friends and young sisters do here in America. — *Mrs. Johnnie F. Williams*[22]

- Here in Germany young people go to school to learn, while in America learning is often secondary to athletics, clubs, etc. —*Carolyn Ikenberry, American exchange student in Germany*[23]

- When people ask me how I like this or that, I mostly can answer "I really like it." But there is an exception, about which I am asked quite often: television! How do you like that? Perhaps it is nice for people, who are too tired to work, and too tired to sleep. But when the mind is well, I think the television is a thief and murderer of the good times. It doesn't give anything back or only very seldom. It is good that I don't have to see the programs, I only watch it sometimes—when I want to sit together with my foster family. —*Hanna Ramsauer, a student*[24]

145

A two-way exchange, with American students going to live in German homes was begun by the Church of the Brethren in 1955. However, the year 1956 brought change to the program when the United States government withdrew financial support, prompting the Brethren Service Commission to evaluate its next move. Since eight denominations were participating in the exchange program, BSC decided to approach the National Council of Churches and the World Council of Churches about maintaining the program. The Councils agreed, and in 1957 the International Christian Youth Exchange (ICYE) was born. Participating denominations were the Methodist Church, Disciples of Christ, Evangelical and Reformed Church, Episcopal Church, and the Church of the Brethren. Then in 1958, the Luther League of America joined the group. "The transition from a denominational to an interdenominational program was smoothly accomplished" and in 1957-58, a total of 101 youth came to America through ICYE.[25]

As international leadership changed, Rudolf Zitzmann, a German national, took over ICYE responsibilities in Germany in October 1958. The Brethren Service representatives at Kassel, Germany, continued until 1960 to make all the arrangements for selection, passage, and visitation of exchange students who were headed to America. Then Brethren Service personnel for ICYE took on the job of visiting and consulting with American students in Germany.[26]

As the program grew, ICYE students from many countries other than Germany and Austria began to participate. In 1960-1961 sixty-one students from the following countries traveled to the United States: Austria, Brazil, the Congo, Finland, France, Japan, Korea, Holland, Norway, Sweden, and Switzerland.[27] The ICYE offices remained at the Brethren Service Center for two years and then moved to the National Council of Churches offices in New York City. An international office was set up in Geneva, Switzerland, to facilitate a truly international program.[28]

15.

Refugee Resettlement

The church's original vision was to turn Blue Ridge College into a relief center that would collect and send relief supplies to victims of war around the world who were living in desperate conditions. Many people displaced from their homelands by war, however, were living in temporary camps and had no realistic hope of returning home or finding employment to support themselves outside the camps. Therefore, in addition to sending comfort to the world's needy, the Brethren Relief Center, equipped with rooms, a large kitchen, and staff, began bringing refugees to New Windsor for comfort and aid.

W. Harold Row, in an undated letter to the Service Center director, John D. Metzler, noted that "when Dan West was in the office the other day he again urged us to consider the BSC's leading out in the program for displaced persons who are being brought to this country. Recently we had a letter from a Congregational-Christian minister urging us to take the lead in this program as we have done in the heifer program. There also have come expressions of interest from other sources that we do more in the area of displaced persons." The letter goes on to ask Metzler to work out a proposal to be submitted to the fall meeting of the Brethren Service Committee.[1]

The Brethren Service Committee approved this proposal regarding displaced persons, and in 1949 Church of the Brethren families began opening their homes and hearts to people who were living in harsh conditions in refugee camps in Austria and West Germany. In 1949, Annual

Conference challenged Church of the Brethren congregations to reset-tle one thousand families. Brethren Service workers in Europe recom-mended hosting families from among the *Volksdeutsche*, people whose ancestors had left Germany for several Eastern European countries gen-erations earlier. They were often refused citizenship in their adopted countries, and, when hostilities broke out between Germany and its neighbors, they were forced to return to Germany or Austria, where they were also considered outsiders. They were truly "a people without a country."

The administrative work required to host refugees was heavy. There were forms to be filled out by the churches willing to be sponsors, hous-ing arrangements to be made, furniture to be found, employment sought, education for children, and language training to be arranged. The church geared up to meet the challenge, but when Congress amended the Dis-placed Persons Act of 1948 in June of 1950 to allow the *Volksdeutsche* into the United States, the Church of the Brethren was only able to resettle 115 families before the quota of visas available for this group was filled.[2]

The resettlement of displaced persons was not easy for many in the church to understand. In 1950 John Eberly wrote to Desmond Bittinger, editor of *The Gospel Messenger*, saying,

> I must present a very urgent case to you. Like many other things which I saw, this matter does not let me rest. After almost two years in Europe, I am now seeing much of this same problem in the D. P. [Displaced Persons] Families which come through New Windsor.
>
> We have sent missionaries to foreign countries to befriend and teach the way of brotherhood. We have preached and prayed that people might come into the Kingdom by way of the Church. Workers have gone from village to village visiting, learning the language, giving a friendly word here, and a smile there, all for the purpose of spread-ing the spirit of Christ.
>
> We have also sent workers to Europe to administer relief and re-habilitation to needy persons, victims of a terrible war. We have be-lieved that this service would bring about better understanding and good will between the people of that land and America and thereby

encourage peace. We have not yet felt that the purpose of this service was to build a church and baptize people in Europe, although many Brethren insist that that ought to be our objective. Now comes the problem or rather may I call it the opportunity.

One thousand families! Approximately 4,000 persons are coming *now* through New Windsor. We don't have to go to them. We don't have to knock at their door. We don't have to break down a lot of prejudice and build up a carefully planned missionary approach. These people come in need. They are wanting and eager for friendship, for love, for fellowship. They have lost their country and are accepting a new land. They are ready, open, and willing for Christian fellowship.

I am not saying that we see this only as an opportunity to add 4,000 members to the Church of the Brethren. I am saying that I am certain that this will happen as a result of our friendly and Christian reception given them. I know they will respond to our Christian love and Brotherhood if we demonstrate such to them. Their answer to our love will be as Ruth answered Naomi. Here is the "stranger within our gates." The Church of the Brethren is not seeing the vision and opportunity as it might. Where are the missionary-minded people and churches? Where are the service-minded people?

Eating supper at the same table with me tonight was a fine looking mother with her own mother from Latvia. This young mother has two daughters, perhaps sixteen and eighteen, with her. These four are now in New Windsor waiting for some community and church to welcome them into their midst. I asked her about the father of her daughters. He is and has been ten years a prisoner in Siberia. Here are four beautiful personalities, refined and eager to live and make a contribution to some American community. Here are four persons needing a Christian fellowship in a strange land. Somebody or some church will lose its soul if it neglects this golden opportunity, this easy opportunity to present Christian fellowship to them.

Here is a family of seven, a fine father and mother and three very well-behaved and fine appearing children. Each of the parents has his and her mother with them. The father is a photographer trained and experienced in the laboratory phase of that work. The family is a bit large and people are afraid of the responsibility in inviting them to their community. So they have been here more than three weeks accumulating a board and room bill which will be burdensome for them to pay even after they begin earning.

We have a single man with experience in the symphony orchestra having played in some Italian city. This evening he played for the group after supper. Here is one of the artists who perhaps should be saved. He needs friends. There are many communities who could have a wonderful Christian experience in helping him.

This Christian reception and nurture should begin at New Windsor. We need to face the fact together that we are not doing it. Some expert planning and follow-up as well as better care and attention for them while they have to wait here needs to be done. We are failing partly because we are understaffed and because the church isn't seeing this opportunity and isn't demanding and supporting it.

Bringing two mothers from New York, the other day, we had the experience of one woman crying and finally confessing that she was afraid that she might be taken to a work farm. I know that she was thinking of the forced labor farms of Europe. These people didn't know where we were taking them, nor what was in store for them. They have only the experience of the last ten years from which to imagine what lies before them. They need a lot of reassuring. We need one or two of the best qualified mission-minded, service-minded people in the Brotherhood to spend full time with these families while they are here at New Windsor and after they leave.

We need to interpret this opportunity to the churches. One of the Brethren most insistent that we ought to build churches in Europe came in recently for a family. He took them out to the little home he had on the farm and within a few hours the family was back at New Windsor. They had refused to stay. The answer was that he showed them a house from which a family had moved several months before and which had not been cleaned or made ready for them. Had this house been cleaned and several mothers of the community been there with a bouquet of flowers in the center of the table, a fire in the stove, and a little lunch ready, which they could have all eaten together, this family would have loved them all, gone to church with them and worked well for the farmer.

The Brethren and New Windsor are doing a creditable thing in taking 1,000 families. You are in a position to help us all realize the significance of this program through editorials and publicity in *The Gospel Messenger.* We hope to furnish you with news items from which you can select to keep this constantly before the Brotherhood.

Sincerely yours,
John H. Eberly[3]

THE KALEPS FAMILY

Not all families had the same experiences. Many of the displaced persons who were resettled were trained in professions, but their training was not accepted by the state licensing boards in the United States. One such professional was Boriss Kaleps who was resettled with his family by the Potsdam Church of the Brethren in Ohio in late 1949 or the spring of 1950. The Kaleps were housed in a small tenant house on the R. L. Honeyman farm. When the small house was struck by lightning in 1951, the Kaleps moved to West Milton where they were able to buy a small house. The family included Boriss; his mother, Anita Kaleps-Klints; his wife, Gisela (von Malotki); and their daughter, Sybille, age two. Boriss was from Latvia, and Gisela was from Eastern Germany. The first permanent jobs that Boriss and Gisela had were as custodians in the Milton-Union High School.

In 1955 the family obtained their American citizenship and welcomed their second daughter, Venita, into their family. Boriss had been educated as a lawyer in his home country, but his credentials were not recognized here in America. After working at the high school for several years, the Kaleps sold their small home in 1956 and moved to North Manchester, Indiana, where Boriss worked on the buildings and grounds crew at Manchester College and attended classes. He graduated with a bachelor of arts in 1957 and went on to accept a teaching fellowship in German at Indiana University, graduating from there with a master's degree in German and Russian language and literature in 1959. Gisela obtained her bachelor of science in education in the spring of 1958 and began teaching sixth grade.

In 1959, the family moved west to Brookings, South Dakota, where Boriss taught German and Russian at South Dakota State University. The following year he accepted a position as assistant professor at Eastern Montana College in Billings. During a sabbatical in 1962-63, the Kaleps family returned to Germany where Boriss received his doctorate in Russian studies from Heidelberg University.

Gisela continued to teach at the sixth grade level until she received a master's degree in 1967 from Eastern Montana College. With this degree she moved to the high school level where she taught German and English.

The family moved again in 1968 to Boston, Massachusetts, where Boriss was professor at Hellenic College in Brookline while Gisela taught at Norwood High School. Boriss died of cancer in 1973 at the age of fifty-seven. In 1979 Gisela returned to Hamburg, Germany, to be with her mother. She continued to teach at the Hamburg International School until her retirement in 1992. Their daughters are both college graduates. Sybille taught German and French and settled in California with her husband and family. Venita graduated from Wellesley College and returned to Hamburg with her mother, where she is working in the publishing business.[4]

As the Kaleps demonstrate, a family that has the initiative to emigrate to a new country with almost nothing to its name also has the wherewithal to become productive citizens in a strange land, especially with the assistance of caring people. Boriss did not complain about his struggles or his blue-collar employment as a high school janitor. He would smile and talk to young high school students and encourage them to study hard and to make the most of any opportunity that life presented. He and Gisela are an example of the thousands of men, women, and children who were first welcomed into U.S. communities by the Church of the Brethren and then moved on to become productive members of the wider community.

THE KALMUCKS

When the plight of the Kalmucks came to light, the International Refugee Organization (through Church World Service) asked the Church of the Brethren to assume the task of resettlement of these people. The surviving Kalmucks were a clan who had been living in Western Europe for six years and were unwanted by any western country. Originally Argentina and Paraguay had agreed to resettle them, but reneged on grounds that they "belonged in the Yellow races." At the beginning of the seventeenth century, the Kalmucks migrated from Sinkiang Province in western China north of Tibet westward toward Russia where the Volga River empties into the Caspian Sea. In the late nineteenth century, some desired to go back to their native land, but thousands perished in the desert as they attempted to return home. Scarcely one fourth of those who set out reached their native land. Those who chose to stay in Russia were soon caught up in the Russian Revolution of 1917. Many were placed in slave labor camps in Siberia. A very small minority filtered into Europe. At the end of World War II, there were only eight hundred or so men, women, and children remaining of the tens of thousands who had once been in Europe. Even though they had been in Europe for many generations, they were considered to be Asian. Therefore, the Oriental Exclusion Act of the U.S. government prohibited them from being considered for resettlement.

Oliver Stone, legal counsel for the International Refugee Organization, wrote an appeal to the Immigration and Naturalization Service (INS), stating that these people had been in Europe for some three hundred years and should be considered Europeans and not Asian. The attorney general decided on July 30, 1951, that the Kalmucks were admissible under the Displaced Persons Act.[5]

Joe B. Mow, a member of the Church of the Brethren, was working with the World Council of Churches in Munich when he received word from Church World Service that they would give "blanket assurances" for all the Kalmucks. He recruited people to assist him in tabulating the applications and assigning numbers to the names on the list to avoid confusion over the duplicates in family names. Applications were then filed by number. Joe carried the lists for submission to the Displaced Persons Commission, arriving at five minutes before midnight, July 31, the legal deadline for acceptance.[6] Next came the processing of documentation, security, and criminal checks, visas, and clearance from the Immigration and Naturalization Service.

The New Windsor Center could not accommodate the total number of Kalmucks expected, so arrangements were made for some of them to be sheltered at a vacant CPS camp, known as Seabrook Farms, at Vineland, New Jersey.[7] But for about half of the 560 Kalmucks who emigrated by April 1952, New Windsor was their first home. Many of the Kalmucks could speak three or four languages, though English was not one of them. At the time, the staff at the Service Center spoke about the solidarity of the group, yet the Kalmucks were open and willing to learn a new language and customs. Helen Kyle, who lived at the Center at the time, remembers how her young son David shared his chewing gum with the Kalmuck children and played with the children his age even though they could not speak each other's language.[8]

Since many of the Kalmucks were from rural areas and had sheep-herding skills, Don Durnbaugh and Mary Coppock from the resettlement office found work for about one hundred of them on ranches near Roswell, New Mexico. This was not a satisfactory placement, however, since they wanted to be close to the rest of their people. Joe Mow went to New Mexico in April 1952 and made arrangements for all of them to return to the eastern United States so they could be near the larger group in the Philadelphia area.[9]

RESETTLEMENT PROGRAM TAKES ROOT

By 1952 the Brethren Service Commission had placed one thousand families in rural communities and gained a reputation for strong ministry to the displaced. It's impossible to talk about the early resettlement program without mentioning staff members Ruth Early, Helena Kruger (a former refugee herself), Ben Bushong, and Jack Gelfand, who at this time was working with the Harrisburg office of the Pennsylvania State Employment Service and provided "hands on" assistance for the Kalmucks in finding employment. Helen is better known for her work with refugees in the camps in Austria, where she established a hospital by using her clever wits to obtain supplies from many different sources, including the U.S. military. Ruth worked in the resettlement office for many years and was the lead person in the resettlement of the Kalmucks.

As world events come and go, people are continually uprooted. A case in point is the exodus of people from Hungary in 1956 into the small country of Austria. Some Brethren Service workers located in Vienna were released from their service projects and reassigned to work in the transient camps or assist in the application process for resettlement of refugees. As a bilingual volunteer, R. Jan Thompson could interview Hungarians who spoke English, assisting them in filling out applications that were printed in German.

Austria was a central location for processing Hungarian refugees. From Austria, the Hungarian refugees were resettled to third countries. In the United States, they would go first to Indiantown Gap Military Reservation, where they would be processed and resettled by church agencies. The resettlement office at New Windsor was a transient camp for Indiantown Gap, temporarily housing refugees until they were permanently settled.

Refugee resettlement staff from the Brethren Service Center also worked with Cuban refugees at Fort Chafee, Arkansas, in 1979-80, and with the Southeast Asian refugees at Camp Pendleton, California, following their exodus from Vietnam. The Polish influx in the early 1980s, the Cuban exodus, arrivals of Ethiopians and Southeast Asians and more remind us of the ebb and flow of refugee populations, but also of the continuous need for churches to open their doors to people who are displaced from their homes because of war and other acts of oppression.

Recognizing the need for an ongoing ministry to people displaced from their homes, the 1982 Annual Conference passed a "Resolution of Undocumented Persons and Refugees." Excerpts from that resolution state,

For the first hundred years of [U.S.] history, anyone could come to this country to stay; immigration was unrestricted. . . .

The primary truth of faith as we consider immigrants and refugees today is that Christ has made another appearance among us, as Himself an immigrant and refugee in the person of political dissidents, the economically deprived, and foreigners on the run. We are to join them as pilgrims in search of that city yet to come, with foundations of love and justice whose architect and builder is God.[10]

It would take too much space to mention all the outstanding people who have devoted portions of their lives to assisting in the resettlement program; however, H. McKinley (Mac) Coffman and Galen Beery are two people who must be mentioned. Both were Church of the Brethren employees, but they were often "on assignment" with Church World Service or the U.S. government, working in refugee camps here in the United States and in Southeast Asia.

Others who more recently were involved in the resettlement program would include Leah Oxley, Rebecca Eduard, Donna Derr, Elizabeth McHale, Lou Cook, John DeCaria, JoAnn Gosnell Rice, Lynn Ellenberger Quay, Heidi Beckenbausch, Micki Smith, and R. Jan Thompson.

The New Windsor Service Center served as a transit center for people who were able to move out of holding camps, but did not yet have sponsorship, that is, a local church willing to provide physical, financial, and spiritual undergirding. Often the approval for resettlement had a deadline established by government, and when the date approached, Church World Service would take responsibility for the refugee, giving a "blanket assurance" to the INS that the Church of the Brethren would be responsible for the person or family, allowing them to travel to the Church World Service transit center located at the Brethren Service Center. The Church of the Brethren resettlement office had administrative oversight of the transit center as well as resettlement responsibilities for families assigned to the Church of the Brethren.

In the early 1980s, Lou Cook, a registered nurse, was on staff to provide medical assistance and other help, such as English classes and orientation to U.S. culture. Often, several people from countries in conflict would be at the transit center at the same time. Usually they viewed each other as displaced persons and not as representatives of an enemy country. There were times, however, when political discussions got a bit heated and mediation was needed between individuals.

In the early 1980s, so many people were coming to the transit center at New Windsor that the refugee office made arrangements with Camp Eder, a Church of Brethren camp just over the state line in Fairfield, Pennsylvania, to house refugees. The Center already housed over one hundred people and could not adequately handle more. The satellite camp stayed in operation until the population decreased and the remainder could be housed at New Windsor. At the time, population increases and decreases were common, caused by political upheaval that brought refugees from Vietnam, Poland, Czechoslovakia, and Romania. The Refugee Resettlement Program needed partners, such as the camp, who could be flexible and open to the ebb and flow of refugee populations.[11]

An incident around the campfire at Camp Eder shows the unexpected outcomes of a program that brings people out of crises and into contact with former enemies. That particular night, a Vietnamese refugee told how his village had been bombed by U.S. planes, his house destroyed, and all his family killed. He was the only survivor because he was working in his garden away from the house at the time of the bombing. He shared how he had hatred for the American military and for the pilot of the plane who dropped the bomb on his house. At the same campfire was a Vietnam veteran who suffered from guilt, having flown the very planes that dropped such bombs on small villages. In fact, as the evening wore on, it became clear to both men that the American veteran was the one who had flown the plane and dropped the bomb that destroyed the refugee's home and family. The refugee and the veteran were able to ask forgiveness from one another and ended the evening by hugging one another and forgiving each other for the hurts of the past.[12]

From 1949 through 2001, The Church of the Brethren, working in partnership with Church World Service, hosted more than 79,000 refugees at the New Windsor transit center as they were being resettled in the United States.[13]

It is not uncommon for staff at the Brethren Service Center to notice visitors walking around the campus, pointing to buildings and talking with children who appear to be family members, likely sharing their memories of being in transit at New Windsor years before. In the summer of 2006, a resettled refugee came back to New Windsor to visit the place where he stayed in 1984 before being resettled by the Blacksburg Church of the Brethren in Virginia. From there he moved to Los Angeles to be near other Ethiopians and was able to complete a college degree. Now he is working as a civil engineer for the state of California. Mesfin Hailu Arsedi returned to relive memories and to give his thanks to the people who welcomed him to his adopted country. Mesfin spoke with pride of his accomplishments since arriving in his new country: "I have never taken any social assistance. I went to school in Los Angeles, graduating with a degree in civil engineering from California State University Los Angeles. I worked full time and went to school full time and managed to build a family here. I was a taxpayer ever since I came to this country."[14]

This is only one of many stories that could be told by the trees and park benches at the Center if they could talk!

16.

Brethren Volunteer Service

Over the years Brethren Volunteer Service (BVS) has been enriched by people from a variety of faith backgrounds and perspectives. They have found community in the common bond of service. At the heart of BVS are the core values of the Church of the Brethren—Continuing the work of Jesus. Peacefully. Simply. Together.

—Dan McFadden[1]

For many former BVS volunteers, the Brethren Service Center is at the heart of the volunteer service experience. In the early days of the program, all training and orientation for BVS took place at the Service Center. First, however, came the "birth" of BVS itself. BVS made its debut at Annual Conference in Colorado Springs, Colorado, 1948. And like many births, there was a long gestation period leading up to it. As described in this book, the Church of the Brethren had sponsored many kinds of service work before 1948. In the 1930s, four Church of the Brethren volunteers gave aid to Spanish people during the Spanish Civil War (Dan West, Donald E. Blickenstaff, Paul Hoover Bowman, and Martha Rupel); Forest Eisenbise and Howard Sollenberger, sons of Brethren missionaries to China, began a relief program in China.

In 1942 Annual Conference considered a query from the Council of Boards that stated, "Youth of the church have been serving for a number of years in areas of human need, giving one year of their lives without compensation." The query requested "that Annual Conference approve the principle of volunteer service by members of the church." The terse decision was stated in Conference minutes: "Request granted."[2]

The volunteer service program did not materialize because it became necessary to set up Civilian Public Service (CPS) camps for men choosing an alternative to military service in World War II. It could be said, however, that CPS was a volunteer service program because the men received no compensation for their service from the U.S. government. The only remnants of a formal service program in that era are some "Volunteer Service Certificates," signed by M. R. Zigler, that were given to volunteers who spent time at the Brethren Relief Center when it first opened. (See Appendix 8.)

Upon returning from his reconstruction work in Europe in 1947, M. R. Zigler spoke to youth at Annual Conference in Orlando, Florida. The youth, moved by his words that told of the plight of the people in the war-devastated countries of Europe, started an around-the-clock prayer vigil, seeking guidance as to what the youth of the church could do to respond to such great human need. Returning home by train, four youth—Charlotte Weaver, Gerry Pence, and two others—decided the prayer vigil was too important to drop. They discussed ways the prayers could continue. Brethren camps were contacted and many agreed to be centers for youth vigils. Youth made pilgrimages to various camps to invite others to join in the prayer vigil.[3] As summer turned into fall, several young adults said they wanted to continue this ministry, which ultimately led to the concept of Peace Caravans in which young people traveled throughout the denomination calling the church to prayer and ministry for the needy in Europe.

They kept the peace vigils and the caravans going through the year. Ted Chambers, a Manchester College student from Michigan, joined the first caravan in the fall of 1947 and stayed with the program until the 1948 Annual Conference in Colorado. The youth caravaners came to Colorado Springs with great enthusiasm, energized by their year of volunteer experience and pushing for more opportunities for others.[4]

At Conference, youth prepared a questionnaire asking for reactions to the idea of establishing a volunteer program, distributing it to more than a hundred youth and young adults in attendance. Ninety-five percent of the questionnaires returned said that a volunteer program should be established by the church. Eighty-nine percent of the youth and young adults who completed the questionnaire said they would join such a program. However, chances for getting the proposal to Conference delegates that year were slim. The agenda for Conference had been approved at the start of Conference, which meant that no new items of business could be added. Dr. Calvert Ellis, moderator, was known for his strict adherence to parliamentary procedure, so the question before the youth became, How do we reopen the agenda to allow for new business? Dan West, who worked with the youth to prepare the proposal, suggested they send a representative to talk with Ellis and ask him to consider the late business item. Alma Moyers (Long) was given the daunting task of finding Brother Ellis and convincing him to make an exception to the rule, thus permitting the young people to present their idea to the delegate body. At first Dr. Ellis said, "Well, we've never done this before. Standing Committee has to pass on everything." But in the end, Dr. Ellis said he would confer with Conference officers.

The officers were William Beahm (dean of Bethany Biblical Seminary), writing clerk; Paul Robinson (pastor of the Hagerstown, Maryland, congregation and later president of the seminary), reading clerk; and Paul H. Bowman (president of Bridgewater College), moderator elect. The officers were supportive of bringing the business before the delegates. Dr. Bowman said, "We better listen to the young people."[5] Since there was no time to run the proposal by Standing Committee, Dr. Ellis decided to allow the youth to "have their day."

Dr. Ellis explained to the delegate body that the youth had a concern they wanted to share. He said, "The officers have met and we believe this is of such importance that it ought to be admitted as business." The delegates voted to consider the matter.

Skilled in communication, Ted Chambers was selected by the youth to present the proposal. Since Ted was only 4 feet 10 inches tall, Dan West secured an orange crate from a nearby grocery store, which Ted carried to the front of the delegate body where the microphone was located. Ted climbed onto the wooden crate in order to be seen and spoke into the mike. No one has a record of his speech, nor can they remember what was said, but it must have been a persuasive speech. Two other speeches were given in favor of the proposal and a vote was taken.

By a unanimous vote, the Brethren Volunteer Service program was born.[6] Once it was finally launched, the program became vital to the Church of the Brethren and to the world. Many church leaders and pastors have received their calling to ministry through BVS assignments. Others have stated that the BVS experience was life changing for the better.

The obvious home for BVS staff and the program as a whole was the Brethren Service Center. The first BVS training unit arrived at New Windsor in September 1948, three months following the approval of the program at Annual Conference. Volunteers paid for their room and board by working half a day, sorting and baling clothing and assisting with other programs that were sending relief supplies to Europe. The remainder of the day was spent in class with guest leaders, discussing topics such as theology, service ministry, and concepts of peaceful living, as well as enjoying crafts and recreation. The first few orientation sessions were three months long, but were shortened to two months when the leaders realized that the youth were primarily from the Church of the Brethren and already familiar with the basic beliefs of the church. Also, the volunteers were anxious to get to their projects and begin their service ministries.

In 1952, during the Korean "police action," BVS was approved by Selective Service for young men who wanted to do alternative service rather than enter the military. A military draft continued through the Vietnam War, ending in 1972. More than half the volunteers from 1952 to 1972 were young men eligible to complete their "draft obligation" through BVS.[7]

Although located in New Windsor, BVS volunteers were not really part of the local community. During many of the years that orientation units were located in New Windsor, the country was at war, and the concept of conscientious objection and alternative service was not always appreciated by townspeople. The young volunteers were eager to share their peace positions, but the community was not open to "being bombarded" with each new group of volunteers. What's more, many of the volunteers came with long hair and the mode of dress of the day, which some in the wider community found offensive.

Don Snider, an early director of BVS, started "Operation Knock-Knock" in the early '60s as a way to teach young people about unconditional service. He would take volunteers out into the countryside and drop them off two by two. They were to spend the day trying to give free service to someone and then find their way back to the Center. The people of Carroll County were often surprised when one or two young people approached as they worked in their yards or farm fields and asked if they could do work for them without receiving any pay.

A number of BVSers were given permanent assignments at the Brethren Service Center. They drove trucks to pick up relief supplies and took the processed goods to the piers. They cooked in the kitchen, processed relief supplies, worked as office support staff, maintenance staff, and groundskeepers. And they helped train other BVS units. They were crucial to the success of the Service Center and an important source of labor.

In 1971, as times changed, Chuck Boyer (director), Ron Hanft (training director), and Annamae Rensberger (training assistant) made a dramatic shift. They took BVS training and orientation on the road, meeting in various locations around the country. Unit #92 (July 1971) was the first BVS unit that did not meet or train at the Brethren Service Center. For some this made sense, and for others it signaled a low point for the Center since volunteers would no longer have contact with the people who were central to the church's service work.

When BVS training and orientation left the New Windsor campus, the connection between BVS and the Brethren Service Center changed. The volunteers no longer looked to the Center as a vital part of their experience. While they had valuable experiences in other locations, many never learned of the worldwide ministries of the Church of the Brethren that were located in the small community of New Windsor. It was a loss for the Center, too, which was deprived of contact with a generation of young volunteers.

As with many situations, there are advantages and disadvantages. In recent years some BVS units have returned to the Center for training and orientation, though the orientation period has been shortened to three weeks instead of three months. To foster group cohesion, the units are self-contained. They cook their own meals and work on their agenda diligently in a retreat-like setting. One day of the orientation is devoted to working in one of the Center's ministries, such as SERRV, processing, or building and grounds. Volunteers also have an opportunity to eat at least one meal in the common dining room. The emphasis is clearly on preparation for service work rather than on building community at the Center, a shift from the earliest orientation units.

Some community building goes on, however, which is evident in the marriages that have resulted between members of the same BVS units. No one knows how many young people met, courted, and eventually married someone they learned to know in BVS or through a BVS project, but it's not uncommon.

THE PEACE CORPS IS BORN

In 1960 the U.S. government under President John F. Kennedy was interested in creating a volunteer service corps. Kennedy's staff contacted Brethren Volunteer Service, asking for names and addresses of former BVSers who might advise the administration on creating a national service program. A questionnaire of twenty or more pages was sent to a random selection of BVS alumni, and the information gathered became a vital part of structuring the Peace Corps program.[8]

From the first unit of BVS, which met at New Windsor in September 1948, until the July 2006 unit, also meeting in New Windsor, approximately 7,400 volunteers have served on projects either in the United States or in a foreign country.[9]

The Brethren did more with BVS than anyone expected, even those idealistic young people. In the . . . years since the Colorado Springs action, Brethren Volunteer Service has placed . . . volunteers in projects all over the world. It has provided countless opportunities for volunteers to serve people in need and to build relationships across barriers of religion, race, language, and economic status. Equally important, it has offered challenging experiences where the volunteers can learn about themselves and grow. It has given invaluable training to several generations of Brethren leaders and has encouraged many youth to go into full-time service in the church and elsewhere. . . . [BVS continues] to be one of the most vital programs of the Church of the Brethren.[10]

BVS Directors

Ora Huston	1948-1959
Joel K. Thompson (interim)	1960
Rodney Davis	1961-1964
Wilbur Mullen	1965-1969
Charles Boyer	1970-1976
Joanne Nesler	1977-1980
Joyce Stoltzfus	1981-1987
Jan Schrock	1987-1994
Ivan Fry (interim)	1994-1995
Daniel McFadden	1995-

(Though all who held this position directed BVS, the title has varied over the years.)

BVS Training/Orientation Coordinators

Ed Crill	1948-1952
Rodney Davis	1951-1952
Dale Aukerman	1952-1953
Ivan Fry	1953-1957
Robert Mock	1958-1960
Albert Huston	1961
Don Snider	1961-1969
Ron Hanft	1969-1973
Willard Dulabaum	1974-1977
Jan Mason	1977-1979
Beverly Weaver	1979-1983
Joe Detrick	1984-1988
Debbie Eisenbise	1989-1992
Tammy Krause	1992-1994
Todd Reish	1994-1998
Sue Grubb	1998-2002
Karen Roberts	2002-2004
Genelle Wine	2004-2007
Callie Surber	2007-

BVS records, Elgin, Ill.

Blue Ridge College (from left to right: Windsor Hall, Old Main, Becker Hall). Brethren Historical Library and Archives (BHLA) collection.

Burned timbers in the attic floor of Old Main are evidence of a fire in 1860 and still visible today. Photo by R. Jan Thompson.

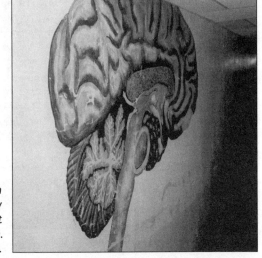

The painting of a brain on the wall in Becker Hall, ca. 1916, was only recently painted over. Presumably, it was on the wall of a science classroom. Brethren Service Center collection.

One of the two Stoner farms sold at auction, September 1944. John Jean John lived here after his father, George Bucher John, bought the farms. Photo by R. Jan Thompson.

Relief clothing is compacted for baling and then shipped from the Service Center. BHLA collection.

The myrtlewood Brethren Service cup, created in 1942, represents both reconciliation and nourishment for those in need. BHLA collection.

Shoes are sorted and repaired before being shipped overseas to people in war-torn countries. Brethren Service Center collection.

Hungry people in war-ravaged countries receive vegetable seeds so they can grow their own food. BHLA collection.

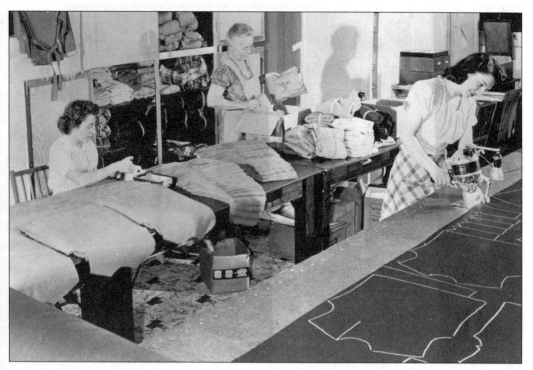

Fabric is cut at the Brethren Service Center and distributed to individuals who construct garments and return them to the Center for shipping overseas. BHLA collection.

Heifer distribution in Austria is witnessed by BVSer R. Jan Thompson on assignment in the mid-1950s. Photo by R. Jan Thompson.

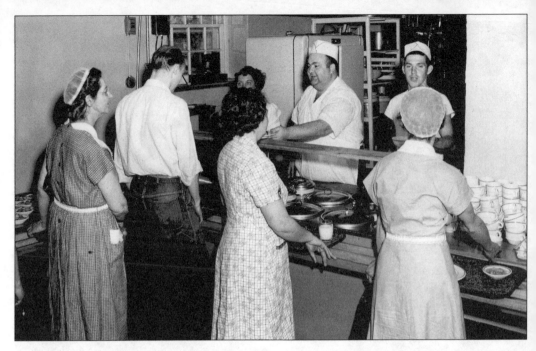

A workgroup has lunch while volunteering at the Center in 1953, not unlike the hospitality enjoyed today by those who study and volunteer there. Joel Petry (center) is the chief cook. Photo by Bill Smith. BHLA collection.

When the main floor of the gym could no longer accommodate processing of large quantities of material goods, a second floor was constructed above the gym. Brethren Service Center collection.

Velma Bowman and Virginia Grossnickle staff the SERRV shop, located in the newly built Zigler Hall in 1968. Brethren Service Center collection.

Carousels installed in 1982 increase the efficiency of storing and shipping SERRV handcrafts. Brethren Service Center collection.

The SERRV shop moved into its own building at the Brethren Service Center in 2000. Photos by Cheryl Brumbaugh-Cayford.

*Numerous volunteers help price and pack
SERRV handcrafts on a regular basis.
Photos by Cheryl Brumbaugh-Cayford.*

*Polish agriculturalists meet with Don Snider, Center staff. The first agricultural exchange was with Poland in
1947 but had a short life. The program resumed in 1957. BHLA collection.*

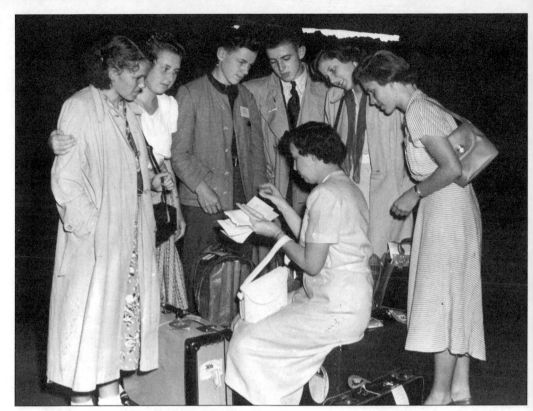

In 1951 German exchange students are welcomed by Sylvia Seese, a Brethren Service Center chaperone. Photo by Lois Rupel. BHLA collection.

An American exchange student to Austria visits with a refugee family who has been the recipient of Heifer Project. BHLA collection.

McKinley Coffman (left) and D. Miller Davis (right) welcome refugees to the Service Center in 1973 for resettlement in the U.S. Brethren Service Center collection.

R. Jan Thompson greets Mesfin Hailu Arsedi, now a successful civil engineer in California, who returned in 2006 to visit "the Center that was so nice to me when I first arrived." Photo by Roma Jo Thompson.

Medical supplies, provided by Interchurch Medical Assistance, are packed for shipping from the Brethren Service Center to countries recovering from disasters.

Aerial view of Brethren Service Center campus before Zigler Hall was built. From upper left to right: Blue Ridge Building (gym), 1914; Windsor Hall, ca. 1913; Old Main, 1848; Becker Hall (ca. 1914). BHLA collection.

Blue Ridge Building today. Photo by Cheryl Brumbaugh-Cayford.

Windsor Hall today. Photo by Cheryl Brumbaugh-Cayford.

Old Main today. Photo by Cheryl Brumbaugh-Cayford.

Becker Hall today. Photo by Cheryl Brumbaugh-Cayford.

Zigler Hall under construction, 1967. BHLA collection.

The Distribution Center (Annex), built in 1969, is across the road from the main campus. BHLA collection.

M. R. Zigler, the "pragmatic prophet."
On Earth Peace collection.

Roma Jo Thompson as director of Cooperative Disaster Child Care from 1983-1986. Messenger collection.

Children's Disaster Services

Children receive support from warm and caring trained volunteers. Brethren Service Center collection.

Roy Winter, director of the Brethren Service Center, participates in distribution of material aid following the 2005 tsunami in Indonesia. Photo by Rev. Johnny Wray, Disciples of Christ.

The "green" tool trailer. Tools are color coded for each trailer. Photo by Joan Taylor.

Jim Graybill at work in the tool trailer. Photo by Alice Graybill.

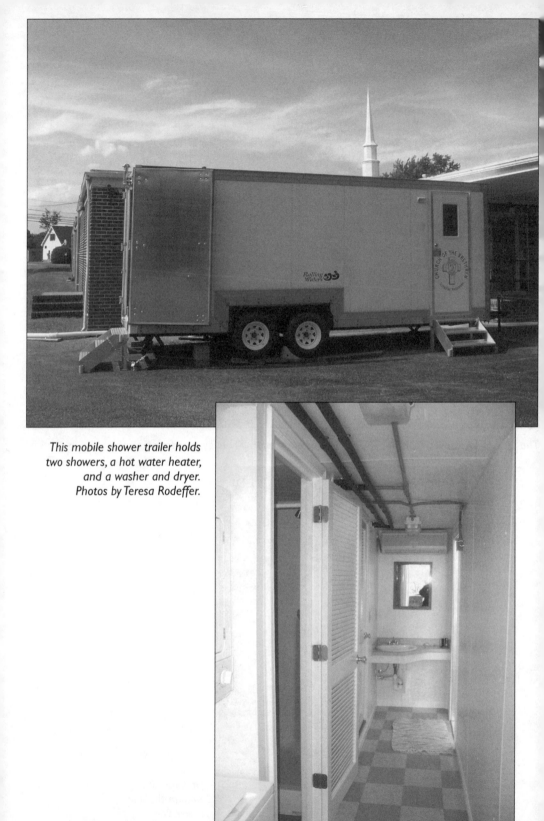

This mobile shower trailer holds two showers, a hot water heater, and a washer and dryer. Photos by Teresa Rodeffer.

Volunteers help to rebuild in Pearl River, Louisiana, after Hurricane Katrina. Photo by Amy Fishburn.

Barb Musser hangs siding in Rushford, Minnesota. Photo by Zachary Wolgemuth.

Donations arrive regularly at the Distribution Center to be processed and stored, ready to go when disaster strikes. Art Hermanson (pictured) is a long-term volunteer and host. Photos by Cheryl Brumbaugh-Cayford.

Emergency Clean-Up Buckets are in demand. Photo by Cheryl Brumbaugh-Cayford.

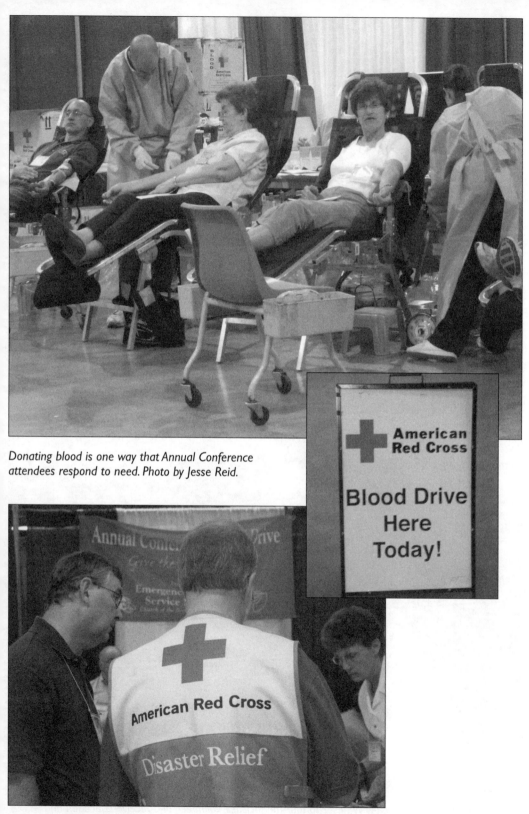

Donating blood is one way that Annual Conference attendees respond to need. Photo by Jesse Reid.

American Red Cross

Blood Drive Here Today!

American Red Cross

Disaster Relief

Photo by Jesse Reid.

Visitors of all ages travel to New Windsor to tour the facilities, volunteer, and receive education and training for making a difference in the world. Photos by Cheryl Brumbaugh-Cayford.

Russian Orthodox Church visitors in 1963 watch as Elsie Yohn demonstrates the cutting tool in the cut-garment department (from left to right: McKinley Coffman, Roy Hiteshew, W. Harold Row, Russian delegation). Brethren Service Center collection.

In the aftermath of 9/11, President George W. Bush speaks to about 300 people gathered in the Distribution Center, a distribution point for material aid to Afghan children. Photo by Walt Wiltschek.

Part IV

———— ✿ ————

Service Ministries

Photo by Martha Farahat.

17

Interchurch Medical Assistance, Inc.

Interchurch Medical Assistance, Inc., (IMA) started in New York as a small supply program for international relief run by the Women's Society of the Methodist Church, but like many of the service programs that eventually took root at the Brethren Service Center, it soon grew beyond what anyone could have imagined.

In October 1953, the *New Jersey Conference Herald*, a publication of the Methodist Church, published a story about the founding of Interchurch Medical Assistance:

> It all began with a piece of paper and an inspiration. Mrs. Charles Marker, supply secretary of the New Jersey Annual Conference Women's Society, received a list of supplies . . . [and] a brief note concerning India, which said, "If you wish to send directly to any missionary or institution under the Women's Division, you may do so under a contract which our government has with the government of India, without freight, duty or transportation costs. Our hospitals are in great need of these supplies."
>
> That was all. Not a scrap of information about the agreement, when it began, when it would end, or whom to contact.

According to her husband, the Reverend Charles Marker, in a paper titled "The Rest of the Story" that he presented to the ministers at the 1987 New Jersey Annual Conference of the Methodist Church, when "Bert" Marker received this information, she tried to verify the claims in the note with the local post office, the vice-consul of India, a Washington, D.C., contact, and the Presbyterian office in New York, but no one could help her with the accuracy of the information regarding freight, duty, and transport costs. She then went to the office of the National Council of Churches and learned that under certain conditions, the U.S. government would pay the ocean freight to ports of entry in India, and the Indian government would pay the costs from those ports to the point of distribution. "No duty, tax or other fees would be levied."

With confirmation in hand, Mrs. Marker talked with the Women's Society of Christian Service at the Princeton Methodist Church where Rev. Marker was pastor. In 1953, a woman named Dorothy Lynch, who was a member of the organization, contacted a number of chemical and pharmaceutical companies, asking for donations of medical supplies. Among the positive responses, the Lederle Company would donate vitamins, which eventually arrived in forty-eight, fifty-gallon drums and were unloaded on the front lawn of the pastor's home. Mrs. Marker and her volunteers lettered each container with names and addresses for shipping. The barrels were then loaded onto a truck and deposited at Pier F in Jersey City for shipment.

One of the many letters of appeal that Bert Marker wrote over the years went to a Mr. Larson of the American Cyanamid Company (Danbury, Connecticut) and secured supplies for Dr. E. L. Rice, United Christian Hospital, Lahore, Pakistan; Dr. Ernest Weiss, Severance Hospital, Seoul, Korea; and Dr. Harold Brewster, Christ Hospital, Kapit, Sarawak, who dreamed with Bert about a medical supply program. In a note of gratitude to American Cyanamid, Bert said, "Last year the doctors who were fortunate enough to share in the supply of sutures and aureomycin products donated by you were most grateful." She concluded her letter to Larson, saying, "May we ask your help again for the most needy areas of our work? The distribution would be under the supervision of Dr. Bruce W. Jarvis, acting medical secretary of the Methodist Board of Missions." Again the company responded positively.

Not all response was positive, however. Another company was going to donate $500,000 in medical supplies, a gift the officers of the company had approved, but in the end one executive hesitated. He worried about setting a precedent, opening the door to others who would apply for assistance. How would they handle additional requests? What complications might arise? The devastating news finally came that the whole shipment was cancelled. Bert was crushed. She prayed, pondered, and grieved for Dr. Brewster and his dream.

In 1959 Bert Marker made another start. She went to the National Council of Churches offices in New York City, where she talked with Dr. Brewster, who had returned from field work to serve as the medical secretary for the Interdivision Committee for Foreign Work of the Board of Missions of the NCC. Mrs. Marker said to Brewster, "This project will go on and should not depend on either you or me. We need to organize it and centralize it in such a way that its success will continue!" Dr. Brewster sympathized with her aims and her distress. At this meeting of the minds, a seed germinated and grew. Their dream was about to come true as Dr. Brewster shared their vision with the Protestant mission boards and agencies who were members of the NCC. These groups adopted the proposal to establish the Interchurch Medical Assistance (IMA) program in 1960.

The declaration that inaugurated the program said, "Through its member and approved agencies which have infrastructure in place overseas, I.M.A. can now provide services to four hundred hospitals and numerous clinics in more than seventy lesser developed countries. These programs of health care range from community health, primary care, clinics and rural hospitals, to sophisticated teaching hospitals. . . . What began as a ministry to India has become a ministry to the world."

The first meeting of the directors of Interchurch Medical Assistance, Inc., was held November 7, 1960, at the National Council of Churches headquarters. Officers reported at that meeting that the certificate of incorporation had been filed on October 24, 1960. According to the minutes, the following members were present at the time of the incorporation: Theodore Stevenson, United Presbyterian Church U.S.A.; R. Norris Wilson, Church World Service; Ove Nielsen, Lutheran World Relief; Harold M. Brewster, United Methodist Church; Bernard Luben, Reformed Church in America; Marlin Farnum, American Baptist Convention; and Luther Gotwald, Division of Foreign Missions, NCC. Arthur Wilde was the first administrator of IMA, with offices at the Interchurch Center in New York City.

While the administrative offices of IMA remained in New York City, Ray Kyle of the Brethren Service Center helped IMA open a warehouse in the gym at the Center in New Windsor in 1961. The facility provided ample space for storage and packing for distribution. From their offices in New York, Dr. Eugene Grubbs and Paul Maxi supervised the receiving and shipping of medical equipment.

In 1961 the member agencies were the United Methodist Church, Lutheran World Relief, United Presbyterian, Reformed Church in America, Episcopal Church, Presbyterian Church, U.S.A., Mennonite Central Committee, Adventists Welfare Service, Brethren Service Commission of the Church of the Brethren, Foreign Missionary Society of the American Baptist Convention, and the Division of Foreign Missions of the National Council of Churches. Each member agency contributed funds for operating expenses based on the percentage of contributed supplies it accepted for overseas programs.

The members of IMA agreed that the organization would not engage in public solicitation of funds. It also accepted only donated materials and supported its staff on contributions from its member organizations. They also emphasized

1. That IMA exists to assist related agencies in alleviating human suffering among the world's poorest and that the needs will exist as long as unalleviated human suffering continues.
2. That IMA is dependent upon contributions of supplies.

According to Carol Hulver, IMA assistant vice-president for administration, each partner denomination from the beginning supported the home office expenses of IMA and received a share of the donated medical supplies. For every dollar received, the program was able to purchase supplies valued at many times the purchase price. The supplies were then donated and became a write-off by the medical supply companies and pharmaceutical companies. This added to the value of stock on hand for shipping overseas.[1]

In 1965 Mrs. Marker completed her term as supply secretary of the Northeastern Jurisdiction of the United Methodist Church. At that time the Women's Division decided to discontinue the office of supply secretary, a loss that was felt deeply by many medical missionaries overseas who had depended on the Methodist Church for supplies.

According to annual audit figures, Interchurch Medical Assistance, Inc., logged donations of $16,180,168 and allocations of $12,166, 663 in 1967. In 1969-70 donations totaled $20,140,356 with allocations worth $15,175,582. Donations in 1970-71 to the program were $6,442,131 with allocations of $12,158,047. Reports show similar figures in subsequent years.

In April 1981, the Brethren Service Center truck drivers helped move the New York administrative offices of IMA to New Windsor. Dr. Grubbs and Paul Maxi also came with their families and personal belongings. From 1960 to April 1981, the recordkeeping of inventory and shipments had been recorded with pencil and paper. Soon after the move, however, Perry Hudkins, a computer consultant at the Center, and Helen Carlisle set up computerized recordkeeping for IMA. The offices were located on the north side of the main floor, in what is now known as the Blue Ridge Building.[2]

Between 1962 and 1994, several other church organizations became members of IMA: Moravian Church, American Friends Service Board, Evangelical United Brethren, Woman's Union Missionary Society of America, United Christian Mission Society (Disciples of Christ), Church World Service, Salvation Army, Christian Reformed World Relief Commission (Michigan), Assemblies of God, Friends United Meeting (Board of Missions), Ludhiana Christian Medical College Board (India), Church of Jesus Christ of Latter Day Saints, Christian Children's Fund, and International Orthodox Christian Charities.

Paul Derstine, president of IMA since 1992, speaking to member organizations about Bert Marker's vision, said, "Since Bert Marker's vision became reality, and during the twenty-five years since, I.M.A. has shipped materials with wholesale value in excess of $220,000,000 to more than 750 medical programs in 74 countries. Her vision of an ecumenical action now involves more than 30 different agencies for whom we speak to the medical industry to procure supplies and distribute to their health care activities."

THE WORK OF IMA

Basic medicines can have a great impact on poor communities around the world, and IMA has provided those basic medicines to hundreds of communities. For example, the IMA program had an opportunity to assist the country of Tanzania in 2005. Gearing up for the project, the Tanzania office of IMA expanded from a single country representative to seven personnel housed in two offices and a regional office.

The IMA Annual Report for 2005 states that "IMA entered into partnership with the Christian Social Services Commission (CSSC) and Pathfinder International to provide quality community, home-based care for people living with HIV/AIDS in five regions in Tanzania. Under the leadership of the IMA Tanzania staff, IMA connects faith-based health facilities in the target regions with the project and facilitates the procurement and distribution of home-based care kits of basic health care products, including medicines. . . . IMA also assisted in expanding the program to 20 faith-based hospitals in Tanzania and facilitated training of more than 200 health care professionals and over 150 health care students."

The 2005 Annual Report also describes a variety of other programs. The Diflucan Partnership Program (DPP), another IMA effort, was sponsored by the pharmaceutical company Pfizer and treated cryptococcal meningitis and esophageal candidiasis in those living with

HIV/AIDS who could not afford their medicines. "IMA shipped five million Diflucan tablets, serving forty-eight programs in twenty-eight countries." Tanzania was one of those countries.

A generous four-year grant to IMA from the Bill and Melinda Gates Foundation came to an end in 2005. The goal of the grant was to treat lymphatic filariasis, a parasitic disease prevalent in the countries of Burkina Faso, Ghana, India, Nigeria, and Tanzania.

When the disastrous tsunami struck South Asia in December 2004, "IMA assisted the disaster relief efforts of its member agencies by providing more than $2 million in emergency medicines and medical supplies in the form of 600 IMA medicine boxes that were shipped from the Brethren Service Center to local partners in Indonesia, Sri Lanka, Thailand, and India."

The IMA Medicine Box Plus Fund provides selected over-the-counter medical products and prescription drugs, designed to treat common illnesses in approximately 1,000 adults and children for two to three months. IMA contributors can purchase a $500 share or a partial share (in increments of $100) to support this project.

Since 1995, IMA has also facilitated an annual distribution of donated de-worming medicine to treat people in Tanzania and East Africa for the parasitic disease that causes river blindness.

Haiti and Tanzania struggle with particular diseases, such as Burkitts lymphoma, lymphatic filariasis, and elephantiasis. IMA provides technical assistance to establish programs in communities to eliminate the parasitic disease lymphatic filariasis and supports the Sacre Coeur Elephantiasis Clinic in Haiti for treatment of disabling swelling and infection due to a compromised lymphatic system in its victims.

IMA works in partnership with many other agencies. For example, the Protestant Church of Congo and IMA together administer a five-year, $25 million USAID grant to strengthen sixty health zones in the war-torn Democratic Republic of Congo. Funding from the World Bank of $11.2 million for three years supports services for an additional eleven health zones.

In November 2005, Dr. Leon Kintaudi and his wife, Beatrice, from Democratic Republic of Congo, visited with several members of the IMA staff at the Brethren Service Center in Maryland. In the *Carroll County Times* (15 November 2005), Dr. Kintaudi said, "Without the help of groups like IMA, USAID, and the World Bank, health care would be virtually nonexistent in the Congo. Getting the word out about basic health care and hygiene can be difficult in a country where few people even have radios." Dr. Kintaudi went on to say that "the Congo suffers from AIDS, malaria, and infant mortality among other problems." Using word of mouth, imprinted soccer balls, and printed cloth that can be made into clothing, Dr. Kintaudi is working to disseminate the "ten commandments of health care": family planning, vaccinations, breast feeding for the first six months of a baby's life, abstinence outside of marriage, handwashing, taking a sick child to a health clinic, and more.

The 2005 IMA "Facts and Figures" reports that "IMA provided more than $109 million in program services, purchased and donated medicines and medical products worldwide to provide basic health care for those living in poverty in under-resourced countries. IMA used less than one percent of total expenditures for administration and fundraising in 2005, consistently earning high ratings for fiscal responsibility from two charity watchdog organizations, Charity Navigator and Ministry Watch."

Agency records show that allocations have increased over the years:

Year	Donations	Allocations
1980-1981	$ 4,803,798	$ 4,147,798
1989-1990	$12,436,196	$ 9,410,752
1998-1999	$20,159,191	$ 18,896,589
2004-2005	$75,654,708	$109,440,276*

*Large increase in allocations reflects upsurge in need in 2004-2005.

The May 2006 *Update* reports: "125 IMA/Presbyterian Medicine Boxes provided by U.S. Presbyterian Women's groups sailed for Malawi on April 19 to be distributed among five Presbyterian hospitals in the country, with a total value of $330,000. The boxes will provide enough basic medicines and supplies to treat the everyday ailments of approximately 125,000 adults and children."

Who does all this shipping at the New Windsor location? Loretta Wolf, director of Service Ministries for the Center, manages a staff of five people who take care of all IMA shipments, both incoming and outgoing. Paul Derstine, president, oversees a staff of twenty people.

The employee list for the country of Tanzania is now twelve. Dr. Daniel Nyagawa is the country representative, and Mavere Tukai is regional representative.

The July 2005 member agency list includes the following: Adventist Development and Relief Agency International; American Baptist Churches USA, International Ministries; Christian Church (Disciples of Christ), Div. of Overseas Ministries; Church of the Brethren General Board; Church World Service and Witness; Episcopal Relief and Development; Lutheran World Relief; Mennonite Central Committee; Presbyterian Church (USA) International Health Ministries; United Church of Christ USA/Wider Church Ministries; United Methodist Church/General Board of Global Ministries; and Vellore Christian Medical College Board (USA), Inc.[3]

18.

Processing and Distribution of Material Aid

With what seems like providence, important forces came together to create the relief ministries at the Brethren Service Center in New Windsor. At the same time that the Church was led to establish service ministries in the 1930s and 1940s, physical space became available, partners appeared, and a volunteer labor force made it economically feasible. And while the work of the Center has changed to meet one pressing need after another, the processing and distribution of material aid has been the backbone of the program that Eldon and Cecile Burke and John and Margaret Metzler set out to organize in 1944.

While the location of the campus worked against the educational institutions in some ways, it was a perfect location for church relief ministries. Located on the East Coast near ports and administrative centers of numerous denominations, it became the nexus for a burgeoning mission of Christian service. Very early in the Center's life, the Disciples of Christ and the Congregational Church administered their relief programs through the Brethren Service Center. Soon after, Church World Service (the ecumenical service program of the National Council of Churches) chose New Windsor for one of its important homes. The rural setting also made it an ideal staging area for Heifer Project as many staff and volunteers had the farming experience to manage the program. Literally thousands of volunteers came to New Windsor for a day, a week, a month, or even a year, volunteering their time and talents to prepare and pack articles for shipment to needy countries all around the world. When volunteers needed places to eat and sleep, the Center could accommodate them in the dormitory facilities of the former college. The volunteers "paid" for their keep with their labor, keeping costs low and production high.

In the beginning, a processing fee of six cents per pound was collected with donated articles to cover the costs of processing and distributing the aid. This processing fee covered the cost of packaging materials and trucking expenses, along with the cost of sorting and bailing the items. As the cost of shipping, labor, and warehousing increased, the fee charged for processing also rose. By 2005, the cost for processing and distribution had risen to twenty-seven cents per pound. The purpose has never been to make money on this ministry, though the processing fee did provide funds for the expansion of several ministries that would be located at the Brethren Service Center.

Early Relief Volume

Often we have a hard time imagining the volume of supplies that were and continue to be processed by the distribution center. Within only two short years after the program was started, goods were shipped to thirty-one countries and contained blankets, food, seeds, hospital and medical supplies, shoes, soap, personal hygiene items, clothing, and other relief supplies.

Year	Number of items	Pounds processed	Value
1946	66,288	4,844,538	$2,749,820
1947	61,099	4,555,853	$3,378,865

Summary of Relief Shipments from New Windsor Service Center, Community Meeting Minutes, 1947. Brethren Service Center files, New Windsor, Md.

A NEW DISTRIBUTION CENTER

As the processing/distribution work became well known, other denominations and not-for-profit organizations contracted with the Brethren Service Center to process and ship their materials as well. With the addition of partners and a large volume of material, new quarters were needed to provide the excellent service for which the Center had become known, so the Distribution Center was built and occupied in 1969. This new building provided space for Interchurch Medical Assistance (IMA) as well, which had been warehousing its medicines in what is now the SERRV Building. The move to the new building made it possible to combine warehousing and shipping operations under one roof.

When W. Ray Kyle assumed the administration of the nine Church World Service Centers across the country, he encouraged a Westminster Church of the Brethren member, Dewey Little, to start work at the Center in 1963 with major responsibility for the IMA program, which was moving its headquarters from New York to New Windsor. Dewey also took on supervision of processing and shipping of clothing and other relief materials. It was during Dewey's tenure that the Distribution Center building was expanded in 1981-82 to accommodate the high volume of material aid passing through the facility. With this expansion, the clothing process was moved again from the Blue Ridge Building to the Distribution Center, consolidating all shipping from one location on campus. Then, when the second floor of the Blue Ridge Building was empty, the staff removed the makeshift second floor, returning the gym/auditorium to its original form. Loretta Wolf assumed oversight of the Distribution Center in 1983 when Dewey Little retired.

Still the warehouse was not large enough. The building was expanded in 1984, increasing the space to 70,000 square feet under one roof. This addition provided more storage for Church World Service blankets and kits as well as room for the expanded customer base that had developed over the years. It was not unusual to make a shipment of 50,000 blankets to a needy region of the world at any given time.[1]

In 1986 an article appeared in a local Carroll County newsletter that told of the work of the Service Center, which had celebrated forty years of service ministries in September of the previous year. Portions of the article spoke about the Distribution Center:

Through the Distribution Center, the Church of the Brethren provides the vital services of collecting, packaging, and distributing clothing and medical supplies for governmental agencies and other church organizations who in turn respond to disasters around the world. In 1985 the New Windsor Service Center through its Distribution Center, shipped $5,107,386.68 worth of clothing and $22,686,547.60 worth of medical supplies on behalf of 18 agencies. The Center owns three tractors, seventeen trailers, and employs four full-time drivers. In October of last year, three shipments of blankets, water tanks, generators, water purifying systems, tents, and plastic sheeting were shipped by the Center to Mexico in response to the earthquake disaster. This shipment was requested by the Office of Foreign Disaster Assistance which utilizes the services of the New Windsor Service Center as its East Coast supply warehouse.[2]

Recent Relief Volume

Year	No. of shipments	Pounds shipped	Value
1994			
Clothing, blankets, etc.	119	15,721,613	$ 7,935,009
Medical supplies	463	1,753,029	$19,049,759
1997			
Clothing, blankets, etc.	200	2,114,491	$ 6,068,890
Medical supplies	392	1,424,915	$ 11,704,183
2000			
Clothing, blankets, etc.	200	1,865,954	$ 9,756,235
Medical supplies	247	1,413,144	$12,583,226
2002			
Clothing, blankets, etc.	221	2,454,303	$12,940,794
Medical supplies	1,970	2,027,300	$ 15,000,881
2005			
Clothing, blankets, etc.	147	2,613,147	$15,427,358
Medical shipments	1,801	848,242	$ 8,806,064

Year-to-date statistics for Emergency Response Service Ministries, supplied by Loretta Wolf to authors, July 2006.

It would be impossible to list all the people and agencies who have used the services of the distribution/processing program. It is easy, however, to list those who have been long-time partners: Church World Service (CWS), American Baptists, Evangelical Convenant Church, Interchurch Medical Assistance, Johns Hopkins Program for International Education in Gynecology & Obstetrics, Lutheran World Relief, Planned Parenthood Federation of America (International), Presbyterian Church (USA), and SERRV. All of these partners have been with the program for thirty years or more.[3]

Over the past several years, the nature of the processing/distribution ministries has changed. When the program first started, the need for used clothing, or any kind of clothing, was overwhelming. At the end of World War II, people had very little to wear, and during the winter months people were literally freezing to death in Central Europe. Over the years the economy improved and local manufacturers started making fabric. Ready-to-wear clothing eventually became readily available around the world. Today the critical need for used clothing has almost disappeared. Likewise, the availability of medicines in countries around the world makes it possible for organizations to purchase medical supplies closer to the center of need, therefore, paying less for shipping. In the 1980s the number of employees in this ministry averaged twenty people. By 2006, the volume of goods being processed had changed so that the average number of employees was eleven.[4]

The same is true for relief supplies. At one time CWS stored upwards of 50,000 blankets for immediate shipment around the world as the need arose. In the last few years, the volume of blankets in storage has been reduced since manufacturers can deliver blankets quickly and directly to locations as needed. Today, at any given time, the number of blankets found in storage would be closer to 8,000-10,000.

Even the types of supplies have changed. For many years the standard CWS blanket was wool and was considered a high-quality blanket that helped shed rain as well as provide warmth. In recent years less expensive, lightweight blankets have become available that do the same thing and are more easily shipped, depending upon the region where the blankets are needed. In 2004, a total of 33,675 wool blankets and 4,600 lightweight blankets were shipped. In 2005, 47,605 wool blankets and 98,875 lightweight blankets were shipped, and in 2006, only 16,230 wool blankets were shipped while 52,525 lightweight blankets went to areas of need.[5]

It is the nature of this ministry is to be in constant flux as the world situation changes. Disaster response continues to occupy the program more than war relief, and configurations of partners come and go as new needs and services are identified. On the other hand, this ever-changing program has been well served by long-term workers and long-term volunteer groups who come on a regular basis to see that this ministry continues to serve sisters and brothers in their times of need.

It was reported in the 2004 Annual Conference booklet that "In 2003, Service Ministries staff processed 2,431 shipments to 59 countries and 45 states in the U.S. These shipments valued at $16 million totaled 1,614 tons of clothing, blankets, health kits, school kits, baby kits, plastic sheeting, water containers and medical supplies."[6]

The report for 2004 indicates that staff processed 2,134 shipments totaling 1,283 tons of clothing, blankets, health kits, school kits, baby kits and medical supplies, valued at more than $20 million to 47 countries around the world and 37 states in the U.S. These shipments were made on behalf of the partners who use this processing center.[7]

The report for 2005 is different. "In this exceptional year, Service Ministries staff facilitated 1,948 shipments totaling 1,731 tons of clothing, blankets, health kits, school kits, baby kits, and medical supplies valued at more than $24 million to 43 countries around the world and 26 states in the U.S. This is an increase of 35 percent (447 tons) over the last year." A major portion of this increase was due to the damage caused by the tsunami in South Asia. These shipments were sent on behalf of Lutheran World Relief, Church World Service, Interchurch Medical Assistance (IMA), and other relief agencies.

"Service Ministries received special recognition by many agencies [in 2005], including a commendation at the Church World Service board of directors meeting and the National Council of Churches General Assembly. In light of the extensive work in response to the tsunami, the Reformed Church of America made a $25,000 donation to support needs for additional staff and volunteers. During the first five months of the tsunami response, Service Ministries processed ten times the typical number of relief kits."[8]

These ministries could not have happened over these many years without the faithful work of people who served with very little recognition, including Dot Fritz, David Bubel, Dewey Little, Loretta Wolf, D. Miller Davis, Brenda Giles, Virginia "Tudy" Long, Rosella Reese, Sam Moledina, Jane Bankert, and Nevin Jones. The list—and the work—goes on.

19

A Place to Meet and Retreat

A NEW ZIGLER HALL

Over the years, an ample number of guestrooms, converted from college dormitory rooms, made the Service Center an attractive place for retreats and conferences, such as Mission 12, a program of the Christian Education Commission of the General Board. This program was designed to help release the potential of people to live and witness more effectively in their communities and the world. Small groups from several congregations gathered in a retreat setting for three weekends to wrestle with and discuss the meaning of faith, human relationships, personhood, and the nature and mission of the church. Some of the weekend retreats were held at the New Windsor Conference Center and demonstrated the need for additional conference facilities in the church.

For many years, BVS orientation units met at the Brethren Service Center, requiring a large number of rooms for lodging and meetings. At the same time, Conference Center programs required additional space, including an enlarged dining hall and upgraded kitchen. A Master Plans Committee for a Study of the Programs and Facilities of the New Windsor Brethren Service Center was appointed in 1964 by the Brethren Service Commission. Those on the committee were: M. Guy West, chairman; Donovan Beachley; Dale Detweiler; W. Harold Row; and John H. Eberly.

The following were among the committee's recommendations:

- The trend in our denomination is to do more training through conferences and seminars as illustrated by Mission 12 put on by the Christian Education Committee recently. New Windsor could be the Eastern Center for such purposes for all the Church of the Brethren.

- It is felt that the church should develop a greater social action program bringing together groups in welfare, government, education, business, labor, agriculture, etc., with a planned meeting for the purpose of serving these groups in discussing their problems within the environment of a Christian Center and a Christian agenda.

- Conference and training center facilities need to be further expanded. Additional and more modern accommodations and more clearly defined programs should be developed. The committee feels there is a place for the Brethren to give leadership to professional and government groups in areas of aid, and youth training, and service.[1]

The committee believed a new building would be needed if their recommendations were accepted. Committee members also acknowledged the pressing need to upgrade present facilities. Arthur Dean, architect for the denomination, had already drawn up preliminary plans for a new building at New Windsor. The Brethren Service Commission studied these plans and made major recommendations to the General Brotherhood Board. The committee recommended that the new building be started as soon as seventy-five percent of the costs could be committed. Preliminary estimates were that a building could be constructed for $200,000 without furnishings. At the same time, the relief program in Europe was undergoing some major changes, and the "Kassel Haus" in Kassel, Germany, was no longer a high priority. The Brethren Service Commission decided to sell the building to the city of Kassel and use the proceeds to support the construction of Zigler Hall. Mac Coffman was "commissioned" by BSC to negotiate with Kassel officials for a sale price. They mutually settled on $250,000, which was put to use immediately to meet the seventy-five percent of the building cost. When the sale of Kassel Haus was certain, building plans at the Service Center moved ahead quickly.

Stuller Construction Company of Taneytown was awarded the bid as general contractor.[2] No records have been found that tell when the Service Center broke ground for the new building or started construction; however, the cornerstone bears the date of 1967 and the building was dedicated on Saturday, May 25, 1968. The main speaker for the dedication was the moderator of Annual Conference that year, M. Guy West, who, interestingly, had been a member of the committee that recommended building a new building.[3]

It seems fitting that the building was named Zigler Hall after M. R. Zigler, the first executive secretary of the Brethren Service Commission, the commission that found the resources to repurchase the buildings of the defunct college in the first place and turned them into a center that became known around the world for innovation in relief and generous service. M. R. Zigler had a dream that the Church of the Brethren would have a conference center where people of different philosophies, faiths, and nationalities could come together to learn to know and accept one another and to have study and open discussion about important issues. Zigler Hall was another step in that direction.

In the end, the total cost of the building was $475,000. None of these funds came from monies given to the ministries of the church.

REMODELING OLD MAIN

After serving as a school building for ninety-five years and as a center for processing relief for twenty-five years, Old Main began to show its age. Even with periodic remodeling through the years, people began to question whether the old building had any life left. In fact, the condition of the building was becoming a danger to those who worked and lived in it. In 1968, prompted by county officials' concerns about safety, the activities that had taken place in Old Main were moved to other locations. The old building was empty for two years while its fate was debated. Some members of the General Board felt strongly that the building should be torn down and a modern office building erected on the site. Mac Coffman was director of material aid at the time and, along with community members, wanted to preserve the historic building.

In an attempt to show the board members what Old Main could become through remodeling, Coffman contacted Bill Weaver, an artist who attended the Westminster Church of the Brethren. He asked Bill to paint a picture of how the building would look at the completion of a remodeling project. With the picture in hand, Mac went to the March 1971 meeting of the General Board and presented the case for remodeling rather than demolition. His case and the picture persuaded the board to pass a recommendation for remodeling.

The General Board still had to seek the approval of the 1971 Annual Conference to be held in St. Petersburg, Florida. Conference delegates indeed gave approval for Old Main to be remodeled. On the way home from Annual Conference, the Coffman family stopped in Broadway, Virginia, to visit with former BVS volunteers Phyllis and D. Miller Davis. When Miller left his BVS assignment at New Windsor, he became associated with the Lantz building supply and construction company. Since Miller had knowledge of both the New Windsor campus and construction, Mac invited him to return to the Brethren Service Center with responsibilities to oversee the remodeling of Old Main. After some soul-searching and prayer, Phyllis and Miller Davis agreed to return and Miller became part of the staff, while Phyllis found employment as a teacher in the Carroll County school system.

"One of my first duties was to contact Ben Weese, who was an architect living in Chicago," reported Miller. Ben, a former BVSer, had been in the December 1952 unit and did his service in Europe. Returning to his hometown of Barrington, Illinois, Ben earned a degree in architecture and joined the family firm of Harry Weese and Associates. It just so happened that the firm had recently been awarded the contract to design and oversee construction of the above-ground structures for the Washington, D.C., Metro system. Accepting the invitation to re-design the interior of Old Main, Ben drew the blueprints for the re-modeling. Each time he came to Washington to check the progress of the Metro contract, he would rent a car on Friday, drive to New Windsor, confer with the staff on the weekend, and monitor the progress of the destruction/reconstruction of the building. Ben did most of his work on Old Main on a volunteer basis.[4]

After an insurance policy was obtained from Lloyds of London to cover the building and the volunteers in case of an accident, the interior of the building was torn out, except for the bearing walls. The majority of the destruction and rebuilding was done by volunteers; Paul Geesaman from Grantsville, Pennsylvania, served as the construction foreman, supervising the many volunteers who worked on the project. The work went well, except when one volunteer got a bit overzealous about tearing down the chimney. More of the chimney fell than was planned, cracking a number of original joists under the floor in room 403.[5]

The new brick fireplace in the first-floor lounge was built by Ira Good from southern Ohio. Ira, volunteering his time and travel, worked with two BVS volunteers as his tenders to "lay up" the fireplace.[6]

The classrooms on the second, third, and fourth floors were changed to guest rooms. One of the classrooms on the fourth floor was converted into a large conference room. The first floor now contained one large parlor, a conference room, and an apartment for the host. The basement was made into a gift shop for SERRV. The lower level or basement, along with the first and second floors, was opened for business in the spring of 1974.

The cost of the remodeling was covered by Center reserves. Again no money was taken from General Board funds that had been given for ministries. From the time that permission was granted to renovate Old Main in 1971 until the dedication of the remodeled building on October 23,

1977, thousands of hours, mostly provided by volunteers, were invested in the "New Old Main." The building, built in 1849, was given a new life.

By 2006 the SERRV gift shop had moved to another location, and Interchurch Medical Assistance (IMA) offices occupied the basement floor and portions of the first floor. Some areas have been renovated again to make office cubicles and smaller conference rooms. The top three floors continue to house visitors and people attending conferences and retreats, which are an ongoing ministry of the Brethren Service Center.

The care and maintenance of the beautiful grounds and historic buildings on the Brethren Service Center campus that provide hospitality for the thousands of people, visitors and volunteers alike, is due in large part to Ed Palsgrove, the current director of buildings and grounds, who has been an employee of the General Board for more than thirty years.

20

Brethren Disaster Ministries

The story of disaster response services is the story of the Church of the Brethren itself. Alexander Mack, a leader and first minister of the Church, was a wealthy miller who, according to tradition, died a poor man because he gave assistance to religious refugees who were driven out of their communities in Europe. Christopher Sauer, a friend of the early Brethren in America, spent much of his time and money working with new immigrants as they arrived in Philadelphia from Germany and Holland. He was known to have purchased herbs and medicines to heal the sick, and he housed many of them in his home until they could recuperate from their journey. The Brethren in Germantown had a "poor box" to collect money to help poor Brethren. In the mid-nineteenth century, Brethren contributed to war relief efforts after the Civil War, and near the end of the century, they were giving aid to the poor in Denmark, an early mission field for the Brethren.

In 1918 a special Annual Conference was held in Goshen, Indiana, to consider relief and reconstruction efforts following World War I. Most of its work was aimed at Armenian relief, China famine relief, and European war relief. The work of this committee was taken over by the General Mission Board in 1921. Then in 1939 the Council of Boards called on members of the Board of Christian Education and the General Mission Board to form the Peace and Relief Commission, which functioned under the name Brethren Service Committee a few months later. M. R. Zigler was named secretary of the newly formed committee. At

Annual Conference in La Verne, California, in 1941, the delegates formally changed the name to Brethren Service Committee and limited membership on the committee to members of the Church of the Brethren. Until that time the Brethren Church and German Baptist Brethren had been active participants on joint committees that worked for peace, reconciliation, and service ministries.

In 1942 the myrtlewood service cup was adopted as the symbol for the Brethren Service Committee at the Asheville, North Carolina, Annual Conference. The design for the logo depicts one hand offering another hand a cup. The hands in the artwork were drawn from the hands of C. D. Bonsack and J. E. Miller, two well-respected elders in the church.[1] The drawing represents the act of reconciliation and also the act of giving the cup of cold water or food to those in need. This logo is still used today to represent the Disaster Response Program.

Congregations, likewise, have been active in disaster response at the local level from the very beginning. Lukewarm to the idea of buying insurance from large corporations to protect their houses and barns, the Brethren instead practiced mutual aid, helping each other when disasters struck. It was well known that members of the church would rally around for a barn raising or rebuilding a house.

One of the first organized disaster responses was in the spring of 1942, when a tornado went through the city of Goshen, Indiana, causing death and heavy damage. Men in the CPS camp at Largo, Indiana, near Wabash, requested and received permission to leave the camp to assist in the immediate cleanup and repair work. Following serious flooding in Stroudsburg, Pennsylvania, in the summer of 1955, the 28th BVS training unit located at New Windsor spent the first two weeks of its training session cleaning mud out of homes affected by the flooding. In 1956, several BVS volunteers were assigned to Yuba City, California, to clean up following floods on Christmas Eve. (These were some of the first long-term stints in disaster relief.) In 1957, volunteers and materials were sent to Shelbiana, Kentucky, to aid the local community following flooding.[2]

The General Board, as a part of its statement on civil defense adopted on March 22, 1957, set forth a recommendation for individual action: "We urge our members to study carefully all Brethren plans to help the needy, such as Brethren Disaster Service. We urge the establishment of classes and other efforts to train our people for readiness to help effectively." This may have been the first official recognition of the fledgling disaster response program that was forming in the church. BVS units training at the Brethren Service Center were a ready-made workforce, and the typical outreach to victims of political disasters could just as easily incorporate aid to victims of natural disasters. Quite naturally, the Service Center staff began to take on the work of disaster response, along with other types of relief.

In the early spring of 1959, a quick thaw on the rivers in Ohio and Indiana caused ice dams to form, which backed up the water behind the icy dams. Communities on the Miami River in Ohio and on the Wabash River in Peru, Indiana, suffered from flooding. Several BVSers were sent from New Windsor with supplies and remained on location for several weeks. They were joined at the Peru location by students from Manchester College. Roma Jo and R. Jan Thompson were among those who responded from Manchester College.

EMERGENCY DISASTER FUND

By 1960, it became apparent that the church, if it was going to respond to natural disasters, would need funds to operate such a program. Transporting volunteers to the location and providing relief and building materials cost money. So the Brethren Service Commission, operating under the oversight of the General Brotherhood Board, established the Emergency Disaster Fund, to provide monies for immediate response to disasters around the world. This fund was separate from the normal operating budget of the Brethren Service Commission and was to be used only for disaster responses.

In 1962, $9,500 was spent from the newly established Emergency Disaster Fund to assist in disaster response at the international level.

These funds were channeled through the Church World Service International Disaster Response program, the service arm of the National Council of Churches.

HURRICANE CAMILLE

Hurricane Camille, one of the most powerful hurricanes of the twentieth century, came ashore along the Mississippi and Louisiana coasts in early fall of 1969. Prior to Katrina in 2005, Hurricane Camille was the hurricane that all disaster people used as a "benchmark" for destruction. The community of Pass Christian, Mississippi, received heavy damage, and the homes of many of the poorest of the poor were completely destroyed.

Joel Thompson, executive of the World Ministries Commission of the General Board, felt strongly that the Church of the Brethren should, whenever possible, respond in an ecumenical manner, so when volunteers were assigned to the project at Pass Christian, they worked under the leadership of Mennonite Disaster Services. The eleven Brethren assigned to this project were BVS truck drivers from the Brethren Service Center and others who had construction skills. Ten men were assigned to the project along with one of the wives, who was assigned the responsibility of cooking for the unit. The work took place mostly in an African-American neighborhood. Within a month, the volunteers expressed an interest in a project separate from the ecumenical effort, feeling they could do more to assist people if they were not under the administration of another group. John Thompson from Oregon, a Center truck driver working on the project, talked long and loud until he finally convinced Joel Thompson and Ken McDowell to start a separate Church of the Brethren disaster response project in Pass Christian. He was finally successful and became supervisor of the project.[3]

It is the accepted practice of government relief agencies working in disaster recovery locations to repair houses to their "pre-disaster condition." This was the level of repair that the federal government was willing to provide after Hurricane Camille, which upset many workers in

Brethren Disaster Relief, since many of the people they were helping had substandard housing to begin with. In fact, many did not have indoor plumbing prior to the disaster. Brethren had strong feelings that it was poor stewardship to rebuild houses without indoor plumbing. Being young and inventive, the volunteers found an old toilet stool and some pipe. When they knew a government official was coming to inspect the ruins of a house in order to allocate funds to rebuild, they would place the stool and plumbing in the ruins at "an appropriate location." The government inspector would see the stool in the ruins and grant additional funds for "replacement of the bathroom."[4]

When Chuck Boyer, director of BVS, was visiting the project, he sensed some tension in the group. Someone finally shared what they had been doing to trick the inspector into approving money for plumbing. Chuck had a good laugh and said, "Well, I would rather the government spend my taxes on indoor plumbing than weapons; however, I would prefer that you not do this." Chuck never asked if the stool still appeared in different locations, and the workers did not volunteer the information.[5]

One of the few tragic accidents of the disaster program happened at Pass Christian in June of 1971 when the crew went swimming in the Gulf at the end of the workday. The September issue of *Messenger* tells the story:

> By his nature, Allen Bursley was an optimist. Cheerful, eager, positive. Yet his fellow BVSers on the Pass Christian, Miss., project knew that his experiences were causing him to question assumptions and acquire a deeper faith.
>
> "We have all been wondering why his journey had to end when it did," wrote the Camille disaster project volunteers on Allen's accidental drowning June 17.
>
> The 19-year-old youth of Vermontville, Mich., was a member of the Sunfield congregation and had entered BVS in July 1970. He had been a delegate to the 1970 Annual Conference, state president of the Michigan Youth Temperance Council, and planned to prepare for the Christian ministry.

Six members of the unit were wading in deep water off the Mississippi Sound when, in starting toward shore, some of them unknowingly walked off a sandbar and were caught in deep water. Allen was known to have been a good swimmer. . . .

Hospitalized, but since recovered, was John M. Thompson, 25, of Auburn, Washington, the project director.

The tragedy prompted many letters from the community, expressing not only grief over Allen's death, but belated thanks for Brethren Service assistance given local residents in rebuilding homes damaged by Hurricane Camille in 1969. It has been the longest running BVS project in response to a disaster situation, and is expected to be concluded by the end of the year.

"Two tragedies have struck Pass Christian," wrote Jennie Armato, the city's tax clerk, "the hurricane and Allen's drowning." She could have been speaking for the community in responding: "We feel like we have lost a friend. Even those of us who did not know this young man personally feel that we knew him because of all the work these men are doing here."[6]

SAN FERNANDO VALLEY EARTHQUAKE

On February 9, 1971, the San Fernando Valley earthquake hit a twelve-square-mile area of the suburbs of Los Angeles, destroying or causing serious damage to three thousand homes. The earthquake struck at 6:01 a.m., before commuters were on the freeways and in office buildings and schools. "Within hours of the quake, Mac Coffman, director of the Service Center in New Windsor, made an onsite inspection of the earthquake damage and needs. At his recommendation Church World Service dispatched stock from the Modesto Service Center—200 blankets, 6,000 children's garments, 2,000 infants' garments, 1,500 adults' garments, and 300 pairs of shoes. These supplies were transported by Brethren Service trucks."[7]

The Church of the Brethren was present in the form of three BVSers who were immediately transferred from their assigned projects to the disaster site: Janice Gilbert, Kokomo, Indiana; Ruth Ann Rowland, Hagerstown, Maryland; and Mary Kay Snider, Bradford, Ohio. These three women worked primarily in the Spanish surname community, explaining what assistance was available for people in need and even helping residents apply for assistance if necessary. Additional BVSers were William E. Hamilton of Glendale, California, and Dale R. Seese of Delphi, Indiana. Joining them from the Modesto Service Center were Ron Duncanson and Dave Holl. BVSers assigned later were Klaus Rimpau, Voldagsen, Germany, and Chuck Eggers, a Marine from St. Croix, Minnesota. Revie and Bea Slaubaugh of Elgin, Illinois, volunteered their services as project directors and worked with Leland Nelson, pastor of the Ladera Church of the Brethren (Los Angeles); D. Conrad Burton, pastor of the Panorama City Church of the Brethren; and R. Truman Northrup, Pacific Southwest district executive. La Verne College students, excused from classes for a few days, assisted in surveying the most severely damaged areas.[8]

STORM AGNES

On June 16, 1972, Hurricane Agnes made landfall in Florida and then moved up the East Coast. By the time it reached Maryland and Pennsylvania four days later, it was downgraded to "Storm Agnes," but the rain in the storm stagnated over the northeastern coast for four days, dropping as much as 14.6 inches of water in a 24-hour period. The rain and winds brought heavy flooding and unbelievable damage. Once again Ken McDowell, Mac Coffman, and D. Miller Davis conferred about how the Church of the Brethren should respond. The federal government asked Coffman to assist them in the overall response for Maryland. Davis drove to the Atlantic Northeast (ANE) district office and, along with District Executive Harold Bomberger, conducted a survey of the northeastern section of Pennsylvania. The survey indicated that the need was greatest for a flood recovery project in the Forty Fort community, a suburb of Wilkes-Barre. A meeting of the Brethren and leaders of Mennonite Disaster Service decided that the Brethren would work on the south side of the river and the Mennonites would do the recovery work on the north side of the river.[9]

Knowing the project would extend for a long period of time, the Brethren Disaster Response program purchased a house to shelter and feed volunteers and give the project directors a base from which to operate. Davis worked at the Brethren Service Center from Monday through Friday, then drove to the project after the workday on Friday to relieve George and Wilma Million for the weekend. Driving home late Sunday night or early Monday morning, he would be in his office at New Windsor on Monday.[10]

The Brethren did such a good job organizing volunteers and repairing homes that officials of Cornell University asked the Brethren to provide on-site technical and educational opportunities for the students from their technical school. The school was a source for young, energetic, and somewhat skilled volunteers, so an agreement was made between Brethren Disaster Response and Cornell University to the advantage of both groups. From June 20, the day the storm hit Pennsylvania, through August 17, some 1,675 volunteers contributed 3,372 work days. The Forty Fort project lasted through January of the next year.[11]

Mac Coffman served as the liaison officer, coordinating the disaster response of the Brethren and the Mennonites in Maryland. Recognizing his administrative skills, the regional director of the Office of Emergency Preparedness Management of the Federal Assistance Programs, asked Mac to work with him as deputy to the federal individual assistance officer. In this position Mac was responsible for directing and coordinating efforts of federal and state agencies for the state of Maryland.[12]

Disaster response happens in one's backyard as well as in faraway places. Harold Bomberger of the Atlantic Northeast District said, "Some churches held very brief Sunday morning worship services. Members came in work clothes. After a prayer, a hymn, and a commissioning service, the 'true service' began as members picked up buckets, brushes, shovels, rags, and pumps and went out to help their neighbors along . . . 'the watery Jericho roads.' " Bomberger went on to say, "There's something of a Brethren identity in all this, something of who the Brethren are and hope to be when a neighbor is in need."[13]

DISASTER RESPONSE GAINS NATIONAL ACCEPTANCE

It was becoming clear to the denomination that disaster response was indeed part of the mission and theology of the church, so in 1973 when Annual Conference established goals for the decade, disaster response guidelines were included in these goals. District disaster coordinators were appointed and training workshops were conducted to assist these district contacts in building a grass-roots response network. The Church of the Brethren had learned that if there was to be a disaster response program, there had to be an organization and people trained in how best to respond to emergencies.

Establishment of the program came just in time. The year 1974 was known as "the year of the tornadoes." Starting in the South and moving northward, tornadoes damaged communities in Louisiana, Tennessee, Missouri, Illinois, Indiana, Ohio, and states in between. The Disaster Response program located at New Windsor called out a response team to work in Xenia, Ohio; Tennessee; and Monticello, Indiana. Local district coordinators gave oversight with input and encouragement from D. Miller Davis, who flew from New Windsor to Indiana. Local volunteers provided most of the physical labor for the immediate cleanup. Stan Noffsinger, student body president at Manchester College, asked President A. Blair Helman to excuse any student who would donate one day to assist in the cleanup effort. The request was granted. Twenty-six years later, Noffsinger would become director of the Disaster Response program and, a number of years after that, the general secretary of the Church of the Brethren General Board. Ham radio services were established for students seeking information about their families living in the affected areas. Several hundred students got involved in the response, signing up as blood donors and as response volunteers. R. Jan Thompson, assistant dean of students, and Roma Jo Thompson, a Manchester student at the time, took their three young sons out of public school so they could respond as a family. Faculty members and students helped in the cleanup around Monticello. At the request of the American Red Cross, others went to Atwood, Indiana, not far from the campus.[14] Karl Mann, the disaster coordinator for the South/Central District of Indiana, spent many days at Monticello overseeing the project. He was assisted by Pastors Ron Wine (Anderson, Indiana), Eldon Yohe (Buffalo), and Willis Maugans (Guernsey).

On the Southern Ohio front, Wilbur Mullen assumed oversight of the volunteer response. He was assisted by Byron Flory, pastor of the Beavercreek Church of the Brethren. The congregation opened the church as a project center and for housing and feeding volunteers.

BIG THOMPSON CANYON FLOOD

Ron Finney, an on-site coordinator for Disaster Response, relates the following story: "On July 31, 1976, a tremendous rainstorm dumped fourteen inches of rain into the upper regions of the Big Thompson River Canyon in Colorado in less than four hours. The storm's approach was not seen or heard by people camping in the canyon. When a state trooper by the name of Purdy heard of the storm, he drove up the canyon urging people to climb to safety. Since they had no evidence of an approaching storm, they were reluctant to leave their campsites. Soon a thirty-foot wall of water came raging downstream, destroying everything in the canyon bottom. Trooper Purdy lost his life trying to warn others of this danger."[15]

By the time the campers along the river reported hearing a loud roar, like a train coming through the valley, it was too late for many to escape. Some were able to climb the sides of the canyon to higher ground, but many were swept away by the wall of water. Homes along the path were also swept away, some with people still inside.

As soon as possible, the Western Plains District disaster coordinator, Roscoe Switzer, took the district disaster tool trailer to the project site to provide tools for the volunteers who arrived to assist in the cleanup. BVSers Dale and Alice Kreider from Annville, Pennsylvania, were named on-site directors. Ron Finney, a public school teacher and member of the Northern Colorado Church of the Brethren at Windsor, was asked to coordinate the Brethren disaster response. His school granted him one day of release time each week to do this work. In November 1976, two groups of student volunteers from McPherson College arrived to help. Thirty-one volunteers cleared debris, hauled equipment, and rebuilt and winterized homes. President Paul W. Hoffman said, "It was an opportunity to put their 'love of neighbor' beliefs into practice."[16]

Cheryl Zeiler, daughter of Herb and Eunice Zeiler, was one of the 144 people who lost their lives in this flood. Herb was the pastor of the Loveland Church of the Brethren.[17]

JOHNSTOWN FLOOD

Tuesday, July 19, 1977, seemed to be a typical day in the Johnstown, Pennsylvania, area. It was hot and humid, and the people of the community were seeking relief from the weather. No doubt some thought a gentle rain would be nice, but the weather front that moved in that day was anything but gentle. Thunder, lightning, and rain pounded the mountainous area from 9:30 p.m., until 4:30 a.m., the next day, sending down a total of eleven inches of rain. This storm would cause Johnstown to flood for the third time in one hundred years. More than seven thousand homes were completely destroyed. Thousands more were filled with mud and debris. Wendell Bohrer, pastor of the Walnut Grove Church of the Brethren in Johnstown, assumed responsibilities as coordinator of the local disaster response project, a role for which he had no previous training. When phone connections were established, Mac Coffman contacted Pastor Bohrer and promised help from the Church of the Brethren Disaster Network. Glen Sage, the disaster coordinator from the Virlina District, who had previous experience with flood recovery work in Virginia and West Virginia, would arrive by Monday, July 25, to help establish the recovery program.

The Walnut Grove Church served as the central location for assigning volunteers to the many work projects. Two other local Church of the Brethren congregations arranged for feeding and housing the volunteers. Tire Hill Church of the Brethren would ultimately house and feed more than eight hundred volunteers; another twelve hundred volunteers would be housed and fed at the Arbutus Church of the Brethren.

D. Miller Davis, in addition to his other duties at the Service Center, gave oversight to the project and helped organize the many volunteers who responded to the call for help. Following the initial cleanup of mud and debris from 6,500 homes, the long-term repair and reconstruction lasted many months.[18]

The established Disaster Network was successful in alerting the denomination about the need for volunteers to help in Johnstown, but the need for a person to serve as a full-time director of Disaster Response was apparent. In February 1978, R. Jan Thompson became the first full-time staff person employed as the director of Disaster Response and Network coordinator. His responsibility was to further develop and strengthen the established disaster network, to provide on-location oversight, and to recruit and train people who could serve as project directors.

Ongoing Work

Working with the Disaster Response Network already in place, Thompson was able to strengthen the district and local church networks, enabling a quicker and better trained response. Following serious flooding in Jackson, Mississippi, during Holy Week 1979, the Disaster Response program chartered a bus to transport volunteers to work for a week on the initial cleanup. The bus started out in southern Pennsylvania and traveled down Interstate 81, stopping at designated locations to pick up volunteers. By the time the bus reached Bristol, Tennessee, thirty volunteers were on their way to the project. Ed Cable, a Brethren Volunteer Service worker in the finance office at the Brethren Service Center, served as transportation coordinator on the bus. Although there was a sense of community for those riding on the bus, this idea did not catch on and was the only time that a chartered bus was used to transport volunteers.[19]

In spring of 1979, floods inundated Louisville, Kentucky, and some areas close to Lexington. The American Red Cross asked the Church of the Brethren to oversee some "special" volunteers in addition to the volunteers from the Church of the Brethren. A state prison in the area had asked whether a group of "honor prisoners" could work on cleanup projects in and around Louisville. The director agreed, as long as there would be "supervisors" from the prison to keep track of the inmates. A group of fifty prisoners per day worked with the Brethren volunteers for a week. Much work was accomplished with the influx of these hardworking volunteers.[20]

The Church of the Brethren Disaster Response program has been an important part of the lives of both the volunteers and the people they have served. From 1970 until 1999, more than 34,752 volunteers responded to 166 different projects. From 2000 to 2005, there were 3,552 volunteers who served on 30 different projects, and the numbers continue to increase as each year passes and with each new disaster.[21]

As the Disaster Response program developed, so did its ability to respond with the proper equipment. Early in the response program, vehicles were leased from a local dealer or from Mellinger's Ford in New

Response to the Forces of Nature

A sampling of the locations and types of disasters to which Brethren Disaster Network responded from 1978 to 2005:

Year	City	Disaster
1978	Rochester, MN	Flood
1979	Mobile, AL	Hurricane Frederick
1979	Jackson, MS	Flood
1979	Wichita Falls, TX	Tornado
1984	Mt. Olive, NC	Tornado
1985	Niles-Hubbard, OH	Tornado
1985	Onego-Riverton, WV	Flood
1986	Live Oak, CA	Flood
1986	Uniontown, PA	Flood
1986	Southeastern States	Drought

Year	City	Disaster
1990	Copahee, SC	Hurricane Hugo
1991	Santa Cruz, CA	Earthquake
1992	Franklin, LA	Hurricane Andrew
1992	Miami, FL.	Hurricane Andrew
1993	Ottumwa, IA	Flood
1993	Atchison, KS	Flood
1996	Culebra, PR	Hurricane Marilyn
1997	Orangeburg, SC	Church arson
1999	Biloxi, MS	Hurricane George
2002	Rocky Mt., NC	Hurricane Floyd
2002	Wilson, NC	Hurricane Floyd
2002	Siren, WI	Tornado
2004	Poquoson, VA	Hurricane Isabel
2004	Hallam, NE	Tornado
2005	Pensacola, FL	Hurricane Ivan
2005	Citronelle, AL	Hurricane Katrina
2005	Lucedale, MS	Hurricane Katrina
2005	Roanoke, LA	Hurricane Rita

Official records, Brethren Disaster Ministries office, New Windsor, Md., provided by Jane Yount, 2006.

Holland, Pennsylvania, which was owned by the Mellingers of the Conestoga Church of the Brethren. In the beginning, volunteers were expected to bring their own tools to the project. However, the volunteers often did not have the right tools for the work, or they had too few tools for the number of volunteers. Paul Hollinger, one of the early project directors, convinced others in the Shenandoah District that a tool trailer would be helpful on the projects. He, along with others, found an old pop-up camper, took off the canvas, and built a wooden cover for the top, along with compartments on the side for tool storage.[22] From this simple beginning in 1982, the inventory has grown to include several sets of appropriate tools that are trucked to work sites. In January 2007, equipment included four passenger vans; four pickup trucks equipped with utility beds and storage compartments; one regular pickup truck; a mobile shower trailer (containing two showers, a hot water heater, and a washer and dryer); three tool trailers, complete with hand and power tools; one medium-size, "hard shell" travel-trailer; and one flatbed trailer.[23] With this type of equipment, the program can respond professionally, providing the necessary tools for almost all disaster responses.

Several Church of the Brethren districts also have assembled tool trailers that can be used by the national office or within the district when needed. In 2007, Idaho, Western Plains, and Southeastern Districts had furnished trailers. The Illinois/Wisconsin District also has been in the process of assembling a trailer.

Directors of Disaster Ministry

R. Jan Thompson	1978–1987
Donna J. Derr	1987–1997
D. Miller Davis	1997–1999
Bob and Marianne Pittman (interim)	1999–2000
Stanley Noffsinger	2000–2003
Roy Winter	2003–2006
Zachary Wolgemuth	2006–present*

*Wolgemuth serves as associate director of Brethren Disaster Ministries, including Children's Disaster Services.

Several people deserve special mention here. Jane Yount came into the program in 1983 as secretary to the director and has continued in the office, accepting additional responsibilities over the years, including the scheduling of all volunteers going to the various projects. Jane deserves much of the credit for the ministries provided to disaster victims, even though she does not have many opportunities to go on projects herself. Glenn and Helen Kinsel have served the disaster office as volunteers from the mid-1990s to the present.

21.

Children's Disaster Services

A severe weather pattern developed over northern Texas and southern Oklahoma during Holy Week in April 1979. Tornadoes destroyed a large portion of Wichita Falls, Texas, and Lawton, Oklahoma. As the storm moved eastward, the tornadoes disappeared but the storm continued to bring heavy flooding. Jackson, Mississippi, received more than seven inches of rain in a matter of a few hours. At the request of the American Red Cross, the Church of the Brethren responded with volunteers for the initial cleanup. R. Jan Thompson, newly appointed director of Disaster Response, was on location to direct the team and to learn more about the "disaster business."

The Federal Emergency Management Agency (FEMA) had recently agreed to have all support agencies (e.g., American Red Cross, Salvation Army, Small Business Administration, family services, counseling services, and voluntary disaster response agencies, etc.) in a central location, so people could apply for assistance at one location instead of traveling all over the community to individual offices. These centers were called "Disaster Assistance Centers" (DACs) or "one-stop centers." People would stand in line for several hours, waiting to be interviewed by the various assisting agencies.

When Thompson stopped by the "one-stop center" to confer with agency representatives, he saw many people waiting in line, a large number of them with children in tow. The weather was warm, and the children were hot, tired, and whiney. When one little girl started to cry, the others joined the chorus. Parents, non-parents, and relief workers tried to sooth the children to no avail. Days later, when Thompson returned to his office at the Brethren Service Center, the memory of the scene plagued him.[1]

Knowing that the disaster response in Texas and Mississippi would continue through the summer and possibly as long as a year, Thompson began to call people to serve as project directors. He called David Doudt, a "graduate" of a project directors training course, asking him to be a director during some of his summer vacation from school. He was not available, but his wife, Karen, joined the conversation and hatched an idea with Thompson, who told her about the chaotic scene at the one-stop center. A former director of an early childhood program and now employed by the State of Indiana as an inspector of preschool programs in northern Indiana, Karen agreed to help Thompson provide alternative activities for children whose parents were busy meeting with disaster relief agencies.

Thompson wrestled with his idea and shared it with several "old-timers" in the disaster field. Some gave him encouragement to move ahead with the concept, but not everybody was supportive. "Nobody else is doing this," they said, or "Children are strong, they bounce back." Persevering, Jan and Karen talked by phone many times over the next several months and made on-site visits to disaster locations. Soon, they created a workshop training manual for working with children affected by disasters. Jan wrote the sections dealing with disaster response and trauma, while Karen wrote the sections on early childhood. Thompson's supervisor, Mac Coffman, was out of the country for three months, working in a refugee camp in the Far East and was not in direct contact with the development of this program. Moving ahead on faith that the program would be supported upon the return of his boss, Jan scheduled the first training workshop for March 1980 at the Brethren Service Center.

TRAINED AND READY TO RESPOND

Eighteen people (seventeen women and one man) enrolled in the workshop taught by Thompson and Doudt. A second workshop was held at Camp Mack, Indiana, in April of that year. And then came the first opportunity to put the plan into action. The first disaster child care team headed out in early May 1980 following a tornado touchdown in Kalamazoo, Michigan. The destruction was close to the Skyridge Church of the Brethren, so the child care team used the church for its base of operations. The volunteers slept on Red Cross cots in the basement, and the church office was used for phone calls and administrative work. The volunteers had been trained at the workshop held at Camp Mack only a few days prior to the disaster.[2] Since this was the first response, other agencies were very interested to see how the program would work.

Once the "child care center" was established and the children were settled in, it was clear that this ministry would be an asset to both children and parents in emergency situations. The Red Cross and FEMA interviewers soon learned they could process parents in about half the time that it took when children were present, interfering with their parents' concentration.[3] Furthermore, there were benefits for the children as well. They were able to use "play" to re-enact or debrief their experiences of the tornado while caring adults gave full attention to their stories.

The second response for the child care team was at Grand Island, Nebraska, where tornadoes roared through the community on the last Tuesday night of May 1980. Since there was such a large area affected, two centers had to be established. The original plan was to send trainers into the affected community to recruit local volunteers who could be trained to work with experienced child care workers. It soon became evident, however, that people from the affected community could not be effective volunteers so soon after personally experiencing a disaster. Several local volunteers took the training and tried working with the Brethren team, but they still needed to talk about the storm and were unable to give their full attention to the children. This idea of using local volunteers had to be reconsidered.

In the first year of the Disaster Child Care program (1980), teams responded to three disasters. Eighteen volunteers ministered to 1,484 children.[4] Thompson and Doudt held five training workshops that year, preparing 101 volunteers altogether. While the program had ample volunteers, it became apparent that more trainers were needed, especially since Doudt and Thompson had other full-time assignments. They designed a workshop for trainers and held the first training at Manchester College in August 1981, where twelve experienced child care volunteers were invited to be trained as instructors for the expanding program. Both volunteer and trainer workshops were of professional quality. Ruth Hersch, director of the early childhood program at La Verne College in California and a trainer for the Disaster Child Care program, arranged for the first workshop on the West Coast. Because of the good reputation of the workshop, La Verne College was willing to grant "in-service credit" for employees of early childhood programs who attended the entire training workshop.

The workshop soon became a weekend experience as well as a training class. They were conducted in local churches, church camps, and some Church of the Brethren colleges. Organizers arranged to borrow cots from the local Red Cross so participants could stay overnight in conditions similar to those they would experience at a disaster site.

To be easily identified by the other disaster organizations, volunteers wore blue and white checked smocks or shirts. Volunteers bought the fabric and made their own smocks and shirts. Some preferred the "cobblers apron" that was worn over their own clothing. There were large pockets in the apron for keeping all kinds of essential items handy.

Each trained volunteer developed his or her own "Kit of Comfort," often with assistance from a local congregation. The kit consisted of a suitcase that contained all the "props" volunteers would need to quickly establish a center for the children on location. The contents included such things as finger paints, play dough, toy cars and trucks (including emergency vehicles and Red Cross vans), books, paper supplies, paint-brushes and markers, small wash tubs, sheets of plastic, masking tape, jump rope, and puppets. Directional signs, brochures for parents, registration forms, and name tags were also included in the kit. Later a Polaroid camera and film would become a necessary tool for security reasons. Volunteers took pictures of children with their parents or guardians and kept them on file. Only the adult in the picture was permitted to take the child from the center.

The locations of the child care center were often makeshift, requiring leaders to be creative with space. For example, they turned tables on their sides to keep children from falling off a stage. At another center, leaders used bales of straw to define the area and keep children safely within its confines. One time a center was established on the driveway of a house, so when it started to rain, five children and one volunteer moved into the back of a station wagon until the rain shower passed. Many stories could be told about the creativity of the caregivers in setting up centers as they ministered to the children.

Volunteers were often called away from their homes and families for several days or weeks at a time. The Disaster Relief program designed a program called CHEF, "Churches Help Extended Families," to minister to the needs of loved ones the volunteers left behind. The program encouraged a volunteer's local congregation to become part of the disaster ministry by giving support to the family members who remained at home. This included carry-in meals, help with laundry, and chauffeuring children to school events. For some churches this provided a way for many people to become involved in disaster relief.

THE PROGRAM EXPANDS

As the program became more and more successful, Thompson found he could not continue to direct the disaster cleanup and rebuilding response and do justice to the new child care program as well. In the fall of 1982, Ruby Rhodes, executive for the World Ministries Commission, which replaced the Brethren Service Commission in the 1968 reorganization, approved the new position of a full-time director of the child care program. Roma Jo Thompson was offered a contract late on a Friday afternoon, and by Sunday afternoon, she was on location in Louisiana, setting up Disaster Child Care Centers. Since the flooding was so widespread, centers were established in four cities and staffed by eighteen trained volunteers.

Many disasters happen in locations where there are no Church of the Brethren congregations. Since it is expensive to send volunteers great distances, the director of the Disaster Child Care program extended invitations to other denominations to join in the child care ministries. The Methodists and the Presbyterians were the first of several denominations to ask for training workshops for their members. When the Aid Association for Lutherans learned of the program, they gave a financial grant to assist with administrative costs as well as supplies for the centers. With the addition of the partnerships, the name of the program was changed in 1984 to "Cooperative Disaster Child Care" in order to be more inclusive of the other organizations. A new logo and name tag were designed by Marsha Graybill Leiter.

Following tornadoes that cut across North and South Carolina in the spring of 1984, Roma Jo Thompson, director of the Disaster Child Care program, initiated a community outreach program for disaster-affected communities. A team of five experienced caregivers visited 15 public schools, 20 daycare centers, and made 24 other contacts. A meeting with county Head Start teachers had 46 of the possible 50 teachers present to learn what to expect and how to help children who were still feeling the effects of the tornadoes.[5]

In August 1984, the Marlboro County Consolidated School System in South Carolina asked Roma Jo to give workshops at professional growth meetings for teachers at the beginning of the school year. She conducted a half-day session for elementary teachers and another half-day session for high school teachers. The workshops assisted the teachers in planning curriculum related to storm distress and what to expect from students when dangerous weather patterns emerge.[6]

When producers and writers of *Sesame Street*, the TV program for children, were planning a series of programs about children and disasters, they contacted Roma Jo in the fall of 1984. She spent several days in New York sharing insights that she and volunteers had acquired from actual experience on disaster locations.

In the spring of 1987, Roma Jo resigned as director. With the resignation of the director and some hesitancy on the part of other denominations to keep providing financial support, it seemed wise to evaluate the program and discuss implications for the future. In July, following Annual Conference at Cincinnati, Ohio, ecumenical partners met to discuss the future of the Cooperative Disaster Child Care program with administrators of the Church of the Brethren. Agencies present for this discussion were the American Red Cross, Lutheran Church, Christian Reformed Church, Seventh Day Adventists, United Church of Christ, Presbyterian Church, and Church of the Brethren.

Roger Schrock, executive of the World Ministries Commission of the Church of the Brethren, conducted the meeting. Following a long discussion, the group decided "it would be best if the administration continued with the Church of the Brethren. The other agencies would continue to provide volunteers to be trained and some limited financial support and all would work in a cooperative nature." With this decision, the name was changed back to Disaster Child Care Program, Church of the Brethren. Following the meeting the representative of the American Red Cross said, "If this program were to go out of business today, the American Red Cross would have to initiate, through its volunteer organization, something to take its place."[7]

With R. Jan Thompson's resignation in July 1987, Donna Derr became director of the Disaster Response programs. Donna had served as administrative assistant of the Refugee Resettlement and Disaster Response program since 1980 and was well qualified to accept the position of director of the programs. Soon after, Lydia Walker was hired as the director of the Disaster Child Care program. She continued the ecumenical training programs and the ongoing conversation with the Canadian

Government Office of Emergency Services, which began in early 1986. Eventually the program expanded across the border into Canada where key Canadians were trained to set up a child care response program in their country.

ADAPTING TO CHANGE

Training workshops and disasters continued to happen and the program continued to make adaptations as the Red Cross and federal government moved from setting up the "one-stop center" to receiving applications via a toll-free phone number. This reduced the number of people requesting assistance in any given center, and eventually the "one-stop centers" became a part of history, to return only if phone service failed following a catastrophic disaster.

There was still a need for emergency disaster child care in some settings, however. Following several large civilian aviation disasters, the federal government established the "Federal Family Assistance Plan for Aviation Disasters" and assigned responsibility for family services to the Red Cross. This assignment included care for children. When the Red Cross asked Lydia Walker to be responsible for the care of children at aviation disaster sites, she readily agreed and the CAIR (Child care in Aviation Incident Response) team was established. The longstanding "Statement of Understanding" between the American Red Cross and the Church of the Brethren was modified November 9, 1998, to include the following:

> The Church of the Brethren Emergency Response/Service Ministries will provide trained teams of certified volunteers to provide child care in Aviation Incident Response in Red Cross Centers.
>
> Each party to this Statement of Understanding is a separate and independent organization. As such, each organization retains its own identity in providing service and for establishing its own policies."[8]

Volunteers who are involved in the CAIR program are trained and experienced in the Disaster Child Care program and have received additional training and provide unique skills needed for this response. Volunteers are assigned one or two months in the year when they are on call to respond within two to four hours of receiving notification of an aviation disaster. Following 9/11, for example, the Red Cross revised its program to include all incidents that involve mass casualties, not just aviation disasters. This program could respond to transportation disasters, incidents with weapons of mass destruction, and other mass casualty disasters within the boundaries of the United States. This expansion meant that people in the CAIR program had to undergo additional training by the Red Cross and others who were experienced in biological and radiological disasters. Training sessions were offered by the Red Cross and military personnel who were experts in biological and radiological warfare and the aftereffects of such a "disaster." In July 2003, the name was changed to Critical Response Child care (CRC) Team.

Most Disaster Child Care responders have their favorite story of a special child who "wormed her way into my heart." John Kinsel was one of ninety-eight Disaster Child Care volunteers who responded following the attack on the Twin Towers in New York City, September 11, 2001. His story is representative of the experiences of so many child care volunteers.

> In another setting, the six-year-old girl would have been sent to the principal's office. She was scampering all over the Family Assistance Center established for survivors of loved ones killed in New York's World Trade Center attack. She climbed on furniture, provoked other children, didn't keep doing one thing for more than thirty or forty seconds.
>
> Psychologist John Kinsel and his colleagues watched the girl closely enough to keep everyone safe. They were volunteers with the national Disaster Child Care organization, trained in understanding children's emotional needs after disasters. Kinsel was in New York the third and fourth weeks after the attack.
>
> What the girl needed now was a trip to the restroom. With a long line at the convenient one, Kinsel took her across the building and past the wall that was postered with memorials and missing-person notices.

Even the visiting adults tried to avoid the pictures, ribbons, flowers, and childish notes on the wall, but as the girl passed, she casually said, "Oh, there's my aunt."

"You know, that's why my mom is crying all the time," she went on. The girl said her aunt had died in one trade center and she loved her and missed her and worried so much about her mom.

This was all on the way to the bathroom and back. When they returned to the children's area, the girl sat down with paper and crayons to make a card for her mother. She kept at it for forty-five minutes. "After just getting off her chest what was really on her mind about her aunt's death, she no longer looked like she had Attention Deficit Hyperactivity Disorder." Kids grieve as surely as adults, but they do it differently.

Most volunteers listened to and talked with kids while their parents took care of paperwork or visited the attack site, but as a family therapist in his regular work, Kinsel also talked to parents and whole families. One family included his youngest client of the trip, a girl not quite six weeks old and the parents, who despaired of bringing a child into such a horrible world that had killed her grandma.

"But then they sat in the child care center," Kinsel said, "and seeing the children play and their daughter happy and cared for by strangers from across the country, they felt a renewed faith. They felt like now they were going to be able to start living their lives again. You could almost see the healing happen right there."[9]

From the first training workshop held at the Brethren Service Center, March 1980, to the end of October 2006, there were 194 workshops conducted with 3,307 people in attendance. In the same period of time, the Disaster Child Care program sent 2,550 trained child care volunteers to 185 different disasters. In that amount of time, 76,921 children have received loving ministry from these strangers in the blue and white checked smocks.[10]

Staff for Children's Disaster Services

R. Jan Thompson, founder and director
Karen Doudt, volunteer consultant, co-author of first training manual, author of "Helping Your Child Cope" (a brochure available to parents at a disaster site)
Roma Jo Thompson, director, 1983-86
Lydia Walker, director, 1987-1999
Roy Winter, director, 1999-2003
Helen Stonesifer, secretary, 1987-2003; director, 2003-July 2007
Johanna Olson, interim director, July-September 2007
Judy Bezon, director, September 2007-present
Sue Myers, secretary, 1983-86
Bill and Jeanne Chappell, BVS, 1984-86
Dick and Verna Forney, BVS, 1986-87
Glenn and Helen Kinsel, volunteers, mid-'90s to present

Children's Disaster Services office records, New Windsor, Md.

Part V

---- ⑥ ----

A Witness for Peace: Education and Advocacy

Photo by Cheryl Brumbaugh-Cayford.

22

The Conference Center

From the very beginning, the Brethren Service Center was a conference facility. The college residence halls, large spaces, and institutional kitchen made the Center the perfect place for training, processing refugees, holding conferences, staging disaster responses, and processing relief supplies. Brethren Volunteer Service training units were held at the Center four times each year for many years precisely because of the accommodations. Soon businesses, school administrators, churches, and organizations learned of the convenience and efficient service at the Center and began to hold conferences and meetings there.

In 1948, when few facilities would agree to accommodate racially mixed groups, the Brethren were willing, even eager, to host blacks and whites for events and retreats focused on race relations. A letter dated February 5, 1948, from D. D. Funderburg, director of the Brethren Service Center, to Foster Bittinger, Fort Republic, Virginia, demonstrates that the Center, if not the community of New Windsor, had an open door policy.

> We can handle fifty to eighty . . . by doubling up. We have tried to make no difference in our Center as to race. . . .
>
> You raise a question about the reaction of the village soda fountains. We are told that at least one of our fountains is very liberal. Yet, I am not sure it is one hundred percent. We are working quietly on this and we do not want to try to force the issue. We are pacifists. We can serve ice cream on the grounds here, and there would be no need for

going downtown, should we find there is not one hundred percent equality.

Funderburg goes on to say,

> It is our hope that there would be no parades or other planned efforts by the camp to demonstrate to our community what ideal race relationships would be like. We think we are making some progress with the problem and will continue our own program. It seems to me, each camper should think in terms of his own community and plan to work there.

The schedule for an interracial retreat in 1948 was typical of Brethren camp schedules. The day began with morning watch at 7 a.m., then breakfast, and classes until noon. After lunch and a rest period, participants attended forums, took part in recreation, ate supper together, worshiped at vespers, and closed the day with a campfire. The leaders of this particular retreat, June 27-July3, were Harold Row, Richard McKinney and James Kelly (from Storer College in West Virginia), T. Wayne Reiman, Bayard Rustin (Fellowship of Reconciliation), Ora Huston, Samuel Harley, Dan West, Ruth Ludwick, and Barbara White (Methodist Church), Foster Bittinger, J. Oscar Lee (Federal Council of Churches in America), and Myron Miller.[1]

There were, of course, individual Brethren who objected to a meeting of the races at the Service Center and held the view of the dominant white culture that the races should be segregated. As a church, however, the Brethren have supported race equality, even supporting integration through Annual Conference statements and assigning to denominational staff the work of improving race relations.

The Center not only promoted good race relations, it welcomed interreligious dialogue. A letter from Charlotte Weaver to D. D. Funderburg, November 1948, asked for assistance in setting up a meeting for an *ashram* (an interdenominational, interfaith, and possibly interracial retreat) at the Brethren Service Center. She laid the groundwork for this gathering, making clear that the Brethren would like to host this event at the Brethren Service Center and be part of the planning group.

An Early Effort at Integration

The brochure on the Inter-Race Camp of June 27-July 3, 1948, inviting people to a race-relations retreat at the Service Center invites you to

> "Come Apart" for awhile with God; to enrich your spiritual life; to deepen warm Christian fellowship; to form close friendships across racial lines; to study today's problems; to broaden your horizons; to relax, play, rest, worship. To be held at New Windsor, Maryland (Church World Service Center–Brethren Service Center).

Brethren Service Center files, New Windsor, Md.

In his response to an inquiry in 1948 from Bernice Bridges of the Youth Division of the National Social Welfare Assembly, D. D. Funderburg noted that housing at the Center was spartan, that beds were arranged in dormitory fashion with six to twelve people in a room. He set the cost at $2.50 per person per day for meals and lodging and described the transportation as "a train that comes to New Windsor from Baltimore, every day except Sunday." A bus was also available to Westminster.[2]

A very wide variety of groups have used the Center for meetings. The Department of Education and Research of the Congress of Industrial Organizations (CIO) came to the Conference Center in the summer of 1949. In the confirmation letter, the Conference Center promised to "have candy and ice cream on sale at times to suit your convenience." But, "We ask that there be no smoking in the buildings and no drinking of beverage alcohol on the grounds."[3]

Some groups wishing to use the Center for meetings and retreats began to feel crowded by the limited number of sleeping accommodations. Old Main had dormitory rooms on the third and fourth floors, but offices occupied the first and second floors. The Windsor Hall basement housed the kitchen and dining room; only the upper floors of Windsor had rooms for guests, with the bathrooms down the hall. Becker Hall housed staff and their families.

The General Brotherhood Board noted in its minutes in 1964 that

a) New Windsor furnishes an important service in the life of the church, which will probably increase in the years ahead.
b) New Windsor is "permanent" in the sense that it is not limited to any emergency or temporary use.
c) It is serving a very valuable ecumenical function and has the opportunity to increase in this direction.[4]

Once Zigler Hall was completed in 1968 to meet the growing need for more space, M. R. Zigler's dream for a facility and a new peace program was fulfilled. The new Zigler Building had meeting rooms in the basement and a large dining room and kitchen on the main floor to serve larger groups than was possible before. SERRV's gift shop on the first floor was just inside the main entrance. Later, a bookstore operated by On Earth Peace occupied space in the lobby. Upstairs there were meeting rooms, a lounge, and guest rooms for conference attendees.

Many groups used the Zigler Building, including school administrators, Church Women United, weekend retreat groups, and denominational gatherings. The Conference Center soon gained a reputation as "a quiet place to get things done," which became the advertising slogan of the Center.

Volunteers and some salaried employees served as hosts for the facility over the years, especially from the 1970s to the present. Elizabeth Bruckhart Miller Eller, Doris Pierce, Betty Armacost, and Trudy Mills worked as hospitality coordinators. Directors of the Conference Center have included D. D. Funderburg (the first director), D. Miller Davis, Terri Meushaw, and Joe Buss.

Stanley J. Noffsinger arrived at the Service Center in 2003 to be the director of Emergency Response/Service Ministries but was soon named director of the Brethren Service Center, which included responsibility for the Conference Center as well. When Stan was chosen as the general secretary of the denomination, Roy Winter, who had been working with the Disaster Child Care program, became director of the Brethren Service Center and Conference Center. Kathleen Campanella is now director of Partner and Public Relations.

23.

On Earth Peace

In the 1970s W. Newton Long, a Juniata College graduate, church-man, and businessman living in the Baltimore area, and a lifelong friend of M. R. Zigler, kept challenging Zigler to develop a program that would provide a spiritual and intellectual base for a program for peace. The peace program would be a companion to the service programs based at the Center in New Windsor. As an encouragement for M. R. to start such a program, Long gave him $1,000 as seed money. Zigler also discussed this idea with his good friend Charles D. Lantz, a prominent businessman and church member in Broadway, Virginia.[1]

Many years before, during World War II, General Lewis B. Hershey, director of Selective Service, and M. R. Zigler had become good friends as they worked to provide an alternative form of service for those who refused to be a part of the military. One day General Hershey asked Zigler about the different Brethren groups and why there were so many. To him it seemed the Brethren groups should spend more time "making peace among themselves." Knowing key people in five of the Brethren groups who trace their heritage to Alexander Mack and Schwarzenau, Germany, M. R. was bothered by this challenge for many years until he was finally able to bring 125 representatives from the different Brethren groups together to discuss "peacemaking." They met at Tunker House in Broadway, Virginia, on June 12-13, 1973, not only to discuss peace-making, but also to begin to think about publishing a Brethren encyclopedia. In May 1976, based on discussion at the "Brethren Churches meeting" at Broadway, some Brethren historians proposed a massive compilation of Brethren information, which would become *The Brethren Encyclopedia*. The first two volumes were completed in 1983, the third volume in 1984. The fourth volume was completed and arrived in homes in the winter of 2006.

Zigler held a second meeting of key peacemakers in the Church during the Christmas season of 1974 when, as usual, the words "Peace on earth, goodwill to all" were posted everywhere. Gathering in New Windsor in the conference facilities, M. R. called the meeting the "On Earth Peace Conference." Those who were invited included people who had served in Civilian Public Service, those who had served in the military, and those who felt that the Church of the Brethren needed to be more outspoken about the peace position of the church. This conference was the beginning of what would become the On Earth Peace Conference (later "Assembly"). A small group of people attending this conference had become resource people for Zigler. They evolved into an *ad hoc* board of directors and later the foundation for the On Earth Peace Assembly organization.

Financial support for the program became a problem, but not for the lack of money. Those who knew M. R. knew he was a determined fundraiser. He had given up driving in his later years following an accident that killed his wife, Amy, while he was driving in Sweden. He traveled by bus, train, and friends' cars to tell of his dream, seek advice, and raise funds. "The first to donate was Charles Lantz and his wife from Virginia. Within several weeks Zigler had the promise of $30,000."[2] The policy of the Annual Conference, however, was that all funds raised were to be channeled to a single, unified budget in the church. Individual programs did not do their own fundraising, mostly to avoid soliciting the same people over and over for different projects and letting good, but not so glamorous, programs fail for lack of funds. Tensions built between Zigler and a few church leaders.

In the church organizational structure, M. R. was reportable to Charles Boyer, peace consultant for the General Board staff. Chuck, who was also working on peace programming, had worked out a division of labor with M. R., separating training programs from peace education. In July 1977, M. R. wrote that, "he [Zigler] should fade out of On Earth Peace and its total planning." To his surprise, Chuck took him up on his suggestion and accepted his resignation. The OEPA board, however, did not accept the resignation and asked M. R. to stay on.[3]

On June 25, 1978, with participants and supporters gathered in Indianapolis, Indiana, for Annual Conference, On Earth Peace parted from the General Board programs and became reportable directly to Annual Conference. Then in 1981, at a special called meeting of the organization, On Earth Peace Conference was incorporated as a not-for-profit organization independent of the General Board or Annual Conference. But in 1982, On Earth Peace approached Standing Committee of the Annual Conference, asking for recognition "as an organization which is related to the Church of the Brethren with permission to solicit funds among the churches and church members for the support of its current and future programs."[4] At the same meeting OEPC changed its name to OEPA (On Earth Peace Assembly) to reflect its program of large assemblies on issues of peace.

The request was denied by Standing Committee with the admonition that the General Board and the On Earth Peace board find a way to work together "peacefully." Issues of financing were the main concern. Soliciting funds for individual projects had become a problem in the denomination and was making an impact on the general budget of the church. Annual Conference did agree, however, to appoint an oversight committee to organize an integration of OEPA into the General Board under the World Ministries Commission. OEPA would be more than "related" to the Church of the Brethren. It would be part of it. The World Ministries Commission extended this cooperative agreement for three years (1983-1986). In 1986, World Ministries renewed the agreement for five more years.

Dale V. Ulrich, president of the OEPA board at that time, spent the summer of 1982 at New Windsor assuming responsibilities for the program. In 1983, M. R. Zigler stepped down as OEPA leader and Harold D. Smith was named executive director of OEPA. Smith was a recently retired professor from the University of Maryland and had been connected to the program since its early days. In 1984, David Eberly joined the staff when he became the coordinator of the Peace Academy, a program of On Earth Peace that brought youth together for a weekend peace retreat. Tom Hurst served as director of OEPA in the early 1990s. Bob Gross and Barbara Sayler served as co-directors from 2000 to 2007. Among the volunteers who carried many responsibilities for the program over the years were Linda Logan, Ruth Early, Ida S. Howell, Hazel Peters, and David Braune.

In 1997, delegates to Annual Conference approved a major reorganization of the Church of the Brethren General Board. With this reorganization, On Earth Peace Assembly and the Association of Brethren Caregivers were granted the privilege of becoming organizations reportable directly to Annual Conference rather than to the General Board. These two organizations became "peers" of the General Board, the Brethren Benefit Trust, and Bethany Seminary, all five answering to the Annual Conference.

With this new arrangement, On Earth Peace Assembly and the other four units were permitted to solicit funding from supporters. The board and staff of OEPA were available as resource leaders to all district meetings and congregations. By 2006, the organization had grown to a staff of six and a board of fifteen who shared many gifts and much expertise across the denomination, providing workshops on peacemaking, training conflict mediators, offering a ministry of reconciliation for broken relationships between members of the church, and more. With the program expanding to cover much more than assemblies, the organization has dropped "Assembly" from its name and is known now simply as On Earth Peace. When invited the staff makes presentations at National Youth Conferences, National Older Adult Conferences, Annual Conference, and Song and Story Fest. OEP has hosted Civilian Public Service reunions, gatherings for business people, and other similar groups.

One of the ministries of On Earth Peace, and a source of income, was the Brethren World Peace Bookstore, which opened in 1980 in the lobby of Zigler Hall. In 1989, the bookstore carried more than 326 different titles, mainly on peace and reconciliation topics. Many visitors to the Center browsed the bookstore as they waited for meals. In 1988 visitors bought 3,800 books, making a significant witness for peace and reconciliation. Today, OEP sells peace resources on consignment, sending a basketful of books to conferences and events. OEP has changed the format for the weekend peace retreats, taking them "on the road" to congregations and districts, as well as offering them at the Brethren Service Center.

In the 1930s, the Mennonites, Quakers, and Brethren were dubbed the "Historic Peace Churches." Feeling, however, that the church operates from a peace position today, not just historically, Annual Conference took action recently to refer to the church as a "Living Peace Church." The witness of M. R. Zigler (the "Pragmatic Prophet") and On Earth Peace is evidence that the peace witness of the Church of the Brethren is dynamic and very much alive.

24.

A Nimble Tradition of Service

BRETHREN SERVICE FOOD PRESERVATION SYSTEM

Always alert to new ministries to serve the hungry and the powerless, the Church of the Brethren negotiated with the Ball Corporation of Muncie, Indiana, for their compact canning system. Knowing the Ball Corporation had decided to close out this portion of its company, Joel Jackson, a Ball employee and member of the Anderson Church of the Brethren, made contact with appropriate Brethren staff about the possibility of acquiring the equipment for a new service ministry.

Mac Coffman of the Service Ministry staff and Wil Nolen of the Community Development Staff met with administrators of Ball Corporation in April 1980. Ball agreed to donate $160,000 in equipment, along with the services of Mr. Jackson, to the Church of the Brethren. The canning center was installed at New Windsor in the ground level of the Blue Ridge Building. The canning system and all rights for future sale and distribution of the canning equipment and systems were given to the Church of the Brethren by Ball Corporation.

The canning system was designed for long-term community development in areas of this country and around the world where preservation of homegrown or inexpensive food can help the community overcome long-term nutritional needs. When a community or group purchased the canning equipment, the Service Center would provide training and instruction in operating the equipment. The canning operation at New Windsor that was used for training and demonstration was made available to local community groups who wanted to preserve quantities of fresh food.

Joel Jackson was "on loan" to the canning center for three months, at which time he joined the New Windsor staff.[1] Due to several factors, the canning program was not as viable as was hoped and the program ended in 1985.

ANNUAL CONFERENCE BLOOD DRIVES

In 1983, Annual Conference met in Baltimore, Maryland. As R. Jan Thompson, director of the Refugee Resettlement/Disaster Response program, was driving to Baltimore for a pre-Conference meeting, he heard a public service announcement on a local radio station in which the Red Cross was asking for blood donors. It was near the Fourth of July holiday, and the blood supplies were extremely low. When Thompson arrived at the convention center, he called the Red Cross Blood Services and asked if they would bring a mobile blood unit to the convention center if he could recruit twenty-five or more donors. All the mobile units were already scheduled, so Thompson began making arrangements for the next Annual Conference.

Thompson asked the Annual Conference manager, Doris Lasley, if it would be possible to conduct a blood drive at the 1984 Annual Conference in Carbondale, Illinois. She granted his request and the blood center in St. Louis was contacted. Since Red Cross Blood Service and Red Cross Disaster Services are separate departments, the Blood Services did not recognize the Church of the Brethren Disaster Service personnel when they called. After waiting a few weeks and receiving no return phone calls, Thompson contacted his close friend and colleague, Bob Vessey, national director of American Red Cross Disaster Services. When Thompson explained that the St. Louis Blood Services was not responding to calls, Mr. Vessey offered to make a phone call himself. Within ten minutes, the head of the Blood Services called Disaster Services to discuss the possibility of sending a mobile blood unit for a day to

Annual Conference. The Church of the Brethren's reputation for disaster response opened doors at the American Red Cross.

The first year, Conference attendees and some students from Southern Illinois University at Carbondale signed up to give blood. The response was so great that the Blood Services could not accommodate all potential donors in one day. Since there was such a critical need for blood near the Fourth of July holiday, the Red Cross staff volunteered to come back a second day, using their free time to draw from donors who could not be seen the first day. The draw for the first year was 306 units. The drive was deemed a success and another Annual Conference tradition and ministry was started, originating at the Brethren Service Center.

The largest blood draw of any Annual Conference to date was in 1987 at Annual Conference in Cincinnati, Ohio, where the drive went on for three days. A fifty-gallon drum was displayed in a central location to represent the fifty-gallon goal. The local Red Cross officials were sure that the goal was unreasonable and did not have enough supplies for a 400-unit draw. By the end of the second day, they sent a car back to the warehouse to get additional supplies. At the end of the third day, 508 units or 63½ gallons were collected. The Church of the Brethren set a record for the largest blood collection at a single location, staffed by the Cincinnati Region of the Red Cross.

From the first "draw" in 1984 through 2006, exactly 6,606 units of blood have been donated at Annual Conferences to support the local Red Cross Blood Services of communities where the Conference is located.[2]

2¢ A MEAL CLUB
In the early 1980s, the world became aware of millions of people facing starvation in Northern Somalia. The traditional, nomadic cattle herders were confined to a small geographical area along the Ethiopia-Somalia border. Historically they moved their herds when the available pasture had been grazed. Now they were restricted to a single area that was stricken with drought. The cows and camels that represented their means of survival were dying.

Church World Service, along with other humanitarian organizations, organized a relief effort to save the population. Refugee camps were established. Medical and food aid programs were initiated. Reforestation and economic development programs were begun. A stove designed to reduce the amount of wood required for cooking by ninety percent was built from locally produced sun-dried bricks and mud.

Church World Service initially pledged $10 million for the international effort. R. Jan Thompson, director of Refugee Resettlement/Disaster Response, represented the Church of the Brethren General Board on several CWS committees when the relief effort was initiated. He pledged $1 million from the Church of the Brethren toward the goal of $10 million. Other denominations marveled at the large amount of money the Brethren pledged, but they knew that if the Church of the Brethren made a commitment, it would be fulfilled.

Thompson's challenge was to make the vast needs of these refugees known in Church of the Brethren congregations and to raise the necessary funds. At another meeting the next day, Thompson talked with a CWS committee member from Texas. She told how the Presbyterian women's organization of Texas had raised money for their projects by suggesting that people contribute two cents at each of their meals.

Thompson presented a proposal for the "2¢ a Meal Club" to the World Ministries Commission at the fall General Board meeting held at New Windsor in 1983. He noted that "more people were killed by hunger in the last five years than in one hundred years of murder, war, and revolutions." If one person saved two cents per meal at twenty meals per week for one year, he could contribute $20.80 to the appeal for that year. If 10 to 100 people in 500 to 750 churches would join in this effort, the possibility of contributing up to $1,560,000 could be reached in one year. After some discussion the World Ministries Commission sent a recommendation to the General Board that the "2¢ a Meal Club" be approved, with fifty percent of the funds going to CWS Global Hunger Appeal and fifty percent for ongoing Brethren hunger programs.[3]

Howard Royer, director of interpretation for the General Board, oversaw the design of promotional materials for the club, including labels for empty soup cans that served as family piggy banks on kitchen tables across the denomination. The concept of "My 2¢ Worth" caught fire in churches, and the little collection began to add up. Church World Service, in cooperation with Catholic Charities and Lutheran World Relief, assumed responsibility for one of ten refugee camps that were established along the Juba River near the community of Lugh, in Northern Somalia. Some of the money contributed by the Church of the Brethren to the relief effort was used to send five short-term volunteers to help people in the Ali Matan refugee camp. The volunteers were Dr. John Glick, M.D.; Dr. Hal Forney, M.D.; Carolyn Hatcher, R.N.; Ruth Stump, R.N.; and Roma Jo Thompson, who taught two local women to cook for the relief workers.

Even after the goal of $1 million was met, donors wanted the club to continue to support other hunger projects. A more general program against hunger was created called the Global Food Crisis Fund, which used the 2¢-a-Meal concept as a main source of funding. Today many churches continue to collect the offerings once a month as part of Sunday morning worship.

Several years later, the Thompsons were vacationing in Canada and attended a small Presbyterian church where they noticed a tin soup can with a label that said "1¢ a meal to feed the hungry." That project had been established after World War I. Concepts are not always original, but great ideas are often "re-invented" to bring much good to the world.

CHURCH WORLD SERVICE DISASTER OFFICE

Following the Johnstown flood of 1977, religious-based disaster response agencies, including Brethren Disaster Network, agreed that people and communities would be better served through cooperation. At the local level, many denominations and faith groups wanted to assist affected areas of their communities, but there was little interaction between individual congregations or denominations. On occasion flood victims learned to "work the system," going to different churches seeking physical and financial assistance without the churches realizing the victims had already received help from other churches in the community.

After long and serious discussions, the directors of disaster response organizations suggested that Church World Service, who had experience in the international arena of disasters, be the catalyst to bring various organizations together. They believed Church World Service could be helpful at the local level in bringing different faith groups together into an "interfaith organization" that would be established to minister for the duration of the disaster response.

Church World Service tapped Wendell "Dib" Dibrell, a seasoned Red Cross disaster worker who was about to retire but was willing to assume the challenge of getting national and local organizations to work together on this new project. Dibrell chose to locate the CWS office for U.S. disasters at the Brethren Service Center rather than in New York with other Church World Service offices. It was closer to his home on the outskirts of Washington, D.C., and he would not have to move his family. The Center provided good support for office needs, and it was close to government offices, the American Red Cross, the Salvation Army, and other disaster agencies located in the Washington, D.C., area.

The New Windsor CWS office opened in the spring of 1977. Brenda Shenk Palsgrove was hired as the administrative assistant in May of that year. The office trained select people to go into a community following a disaster and meet with the religious leaders, encouraging them to form a local interfaith organization to respond to the crisis. All people affected by the disaster could come to this organization to receive fair treatment. The Red Cross and government agencies had strict guidelines to follow, but the interfaith organization would be able to minister to those who fell between the cracks and meet needs that were not met by other organizations.

Communities generally accepted the concept of organizing the religious response to disaster through a local interfaith organization. As the concept became known, Church World Service found it easier to convince local communities of the benefits of such an organization. It was such a successful model that national disaster response organizations began to work in cooperation with the local interfaith organizations, empowering local groups to make decisions about how to administer assistance.

In the fall of 1982, Dib retired a second time. At that time, the CWS disaster office moved to the National Council of Churches headquarters in New York City with the rest of the Church World Service offices.[4] When the program left New Windsor in 1982, it continued to warehouse equipment and relief materials there.

A GOLDEN JUBILEE

The Brethren Service Committee purchased Blue Ridge College on Wednesday, September 6, 1944. Six months before the purchase, volunteers began to process clothing for relief, repair shoes, make soap, cut material to be stitched together by women of many churches, and bring heifers to collection centers to be shipped to needy families. By all rights, the month for celebrating the anniversary of the Brethren Service Center is March, but the actual purchase date in September provided a proper date to celebrate the first fifty years of ministries in 1994 that have happened since acquisition of the college campus.

Thousands of volunteers and staff have worked through the Center to alleviate the suffering of sisters and brothers around the world. The many ministries that have developed over the last fifty years have changed the world, one person at a time. Some of the ministries began at the Center and moved outward around the world to help those in need. Other ministries started at some far corner of the world and brought people to the Center with only a few possessions, looking for a new start in life.

To celebrate the enormous achievements of Brethren Service, the Center sponsored a celebration for the church and the community. On Saturday, September 11, 1994, Heifer Project International, a ministry that began in these very buildings and neighboring farms, also celebrated fifty years of ministry. Sunday was the culmination of a celebrative year commemorating the ministries that have taken place over the last fifty years at the Brethren Service Center.

Donald Miller, general secretary of the General Board (1986-1996) said, "The heart and soul of the Brethren Service Center is a Christlike dedication to world peace, service, and the alleviation of human suffering. . . . May this commemorative year mark the beginning of another fifty years in which sisters and brothers of all ages and cultures are committed to a way of life that places service and self-giving at the center."[5]

The celebration was attended by many volunteers and staff who had worked at the Center sometime in the last fifty years. They came with their memories and their stories. They told how their lives had been changed by one or several incidents at the Center. Some told of being seagoing cowboys, herding cows or horses to war-devastated countries, and seeing men, women, and especially children undernourished and ill-clothed. They could never drive those images out of their minds. Others spoke of the refugees who had passed through New Windsor on their way to new homes and new lives. Still others talked of processing clothing as part of a BVS training unit and how many bales of clothing they were able to bale on a good day.

The celebration was overshadowed only by the tragic loss of Joel K. Thompson, who was to be the keynote speaker for the event. As former executive of World Ministries, Joel planned to reflect on the Service Center's fifty years of witness, but he was killed on his way to the event when U.S. Air flight 427 crashed on the approach to landing at the Pittsburgh airport. The celebration planning committee contacted his office to see if he had left a draft of his remarks on his desk or his computer, but none was found. D. Miller Davis, director of Center operations, was called up to fill the vacancy left by Joel's death.

A COOPERATIVE SPIRIT

The facilities at the Brethren Service Center have been ideal for a variety of tenant organizations that needed office space and work space but were not service ministries of the Church of the Brethren. At the same time, the Center has benefited from its association with these good neighbors. Leases have provided income for the Center and magnified the service ministries of the Church of the Brethren. For their part, renters desire this location because of its quiet, rural, retreat-like character, with easy access to the major metropolitan areas of Baltimore, Washington, and New York. They are local organizations that serve the community of New Windsor, Carroll County, or the Church of the Brethren. At one time or another, the Brethren have welcomed Meals on Wheels, Carroll County Red Cross, the office of the director of District Ministries for the Church of the Brethren, Mid-Atlantic District Offices, an office for a regional member of the stewardship team, and offices for a group of General Board employees whose headquarters are the General Board offices in Elgin, Illinois.

This variety of associations exemplifies an ability of Brethren Service to meet an array of pressing needs as they come. As needs for service ministries have changed, the Center has adapted gracefully. Human need, disasters, crises, wars, and epidemics come and go. When they come, the Brethren Service Center is ready to open its doors. When needs and emergencies go, the Center quickly retools for the next need, demonstrating a nimbleness in the Center's response to human need.

———————— ⑥ ————————

Epilogue

In the World But Not of It

Often Brethren Service agencies have found themselves working with government agencies to accomplish their service ministries. Civilian Public Service answered to Selective Service. Disaster Service Ministries have often worked with FEMA officials. Refugee resettlement has worked with U.S. Immigration. Relief supplies were shipped through government channels after World War II. Brethren relief workers worked under the auspices of CRALOG (Council of Relief Agencies Licensed to Operate in Germany). SERRV has had to operate within U. S. tax law and pay tariffs on imported goods. Even Heifer Project's seagoing cowboys were beholden to the government for providing shipping of animals. For a church movement that, in principle, remains apart from powers and principalities, Brethren have worked closely with the U.S. government in service ministries.

Despite the many connections with government agencies, Brethren Service has also remained true to itself, speaking the truth as we understand it, albeit imperfectly, and making our witness to the Prince of Peace in the face of powerful governments without giving up basic Christian principles. The result of this ability of the church to work with government without appeasement has helped both sides respect the other. The people in government who have worked with the Brethren hold the church in high regard, accepting the contributions and counsel of people such as M. R. Zigler, Harold Row, Helena Kruger, Thurl Metzger, and Anna Mow.

Two important stories of church-government association bring a fitting end to this story of the Brethren Service Center, a place that has, above anything else, fostered peace, understanding, and love of enemies. The first is an encounter between the Brethren and a perceived enemy from another part of the world, a group of Soviet religious leaders. The second is the story of the Service Center and the president of the United States, who, for some Brethren, represents principalities and powers that compete for our allegiance to Christ and the church. Both stories characterize the mission of the Brethren Service Center in a way that few other stories can.

CHURCH OF THE BRETHREN AND THE RUSSIAN ORTHODOX CHURCH EXCHANGE VISITS

During the 1960s and into the mid-1970s, the United States was involved in a civil war between North and South Vietnam in what many historians describe as an extension of the Cold War between Russia and the United States. Russia was assisting the North Vietnamese army by supplying tools of war, and the United States was giving support to the South Vietnamese army by sending thousands of soldiers and massive amounts of military equipment. This war was not popular with many people in the United States, especially young people on college campuses, in part because Selective Service was drafting young men to fight the war. Thousands of young Americans were killed in the conflict.

During this troubled time between two super powers, W. Harold Row and other leaders of the Church of the Brethren and leaders of the Russian Orthodox Church arranged for visits by church leaders in each other's countries. There were two visits in each country. The Soviet church leaders visited in the United States from August 24 through September 4, 1963, and again November 11 through December 1, 1967. The Church of the Brethren church leaders visited in the Soviet Union in October 1963 and again in July 1966.

According to Howard Royer, "The visit [in August/September 1963] was the result of mutual striving of both churches for brotherly cooperation in strengthening the ecumenical spirit and in serving for the good of mankind. It was realized as a result of preliminary talks between representatives of both churches."[1]

During their visits the Russian Orthodox delegation visited several religious and educational centers as well as several congregations and the Church of the Brethren General Board offices. On both visits the delegation visited the Brethren Service Center in New Windsor, Maryland. For most people these reciprocal visits were deemed to be a helpful step in fostering a better understanding between the two church bodies. "In this brotherly fellowship, both groups recognized the living force and meaning of the words of the Apostle Paul about the equality of all before God: 'Here there cannot be Greek and Jew, circumcised and uncircumcised, barbarian, Scythian, slave, free man, but Christ is all, and in all (Col. 3:11).' "[2]

Not everybody was happy about this exchange between church leaders from the two countries. One of the most outspoken and active critics was the Reverend Carl McIntire, president of the International Council of Christian Churches. McIntire wrote editorials to the local newspapers stating his opposition to the visits. He also organized local groups to protest any of the local meetings that were held in any given community. The protests at the Brethren Service Center were held at the edge of the campus, just beyond the property line. Since the visit of 1963 was in August, the protestors were standing along the road in the hot sun. Elizabeth "Betts" Bruckhart, hospitality coordinator, saw the protestors standing in the blistering heat and, in the spirit of the Brethren Service Center, thought that an act of kindness would be to offer "a cup of cold water" to those who were in disagreement with the visit. Along with some of the volunteers at the Center, she filled pitchers with cold water, took cups out to the picket line and offered the "cup of cold water" to those who were opposed to the visit. The opponents accepted the water but were not convinced to end their protest.

During the 1967 visit, Rev. McIntire was again present at New Windsor during the protest. The leader of the Soviet delegation, Metropolitan

Nikodim, suggested to some Church of the Brethren leaders that he would like to talk with the people on the picket line. He also wanted to try to engage Rev. McIntire in a discussion of the reasons for the visits and to understand why McIntire was so opposed to Christians undertaking peaceful dialogue. McIntire was unwilling to engage in any conversation and resorted to calling the Russian guests unkind names.[3]

The experiences of the Russians at the Brethren Service Center are an indication of the strong feelings Americans had against such visits. In reporting on the impact of the international visits, Howard Royer said, "Time will be needed to measure the international and ecumenical effects of the exchange. What [the visits] meant to individuals and congregations and host communities can be more readily cited."[4]

The report went on to describe a specific situation at Mt. Morris, Illinois, where the community debated the Soviet/American exchange. One incident demonstrates the impact this visit had on the lives of at least a few people. A group of teenage boys from a neighboring town came to the church to protest, in their own style, the presence of the Soviets. They were prompted in part by the protest campaign of critics who purchased a full-page, anti-exchange newspaper ad created by a person from Rockford. They were especially influenced, however, by the report that morning of the tragic death of a brother of one of the boys. He had been killed in Vietnam. So had the brother of another boy in the group some months earlier.

While Merle Hendricks, moderator of the church, fielded questions at the fellowship meal and addressed them to the Orthodox panel, his wife approached the boys in an adjacent hallway and began talking with them. She could identify with their sorrow; a year earlier she and her husband had lost their beloved son, Don, in Vietnam.

In time Mrs. Hendricks and the boys had joined the audience at the forum. At 7:30 the casually dressed fellows entered the sanctuary for the worship service at which Metropolitan Nikodim was to speak. Following the service the boys waited their turn to greet the Russians, after which they embraced Mrs. Hendricks and left.

What had turned them from their earlier intentions? "I said to them that they could stand up and protest here and eventually go to Vietnam and fight, but that neither of these would resolve the basic problems of today's world," Mrs. Hendricks recounted. "What is really needed to overcome enmity," she said to the boys, "is for persons like you to be big enough to accept these visitors, to hear them out, and to put into practice the love which the Christian faith teaches."

Later Mrs. Hendricks remarked, "The boys listened attentively throughout the service. I was never prouder to walk down the aisle after a church service with anyone than I was to walk beside these boys."[5]

PRESIDENT GEORGE W. BUSH VISITS THE SERVICE CENTER

In the aftermath of the September 11, 2001, attacks on New York and Washington, the Brethren learned that President George W. Bush and First Lady Laura Bush would be paying a visit to the Brethren Service Center on December 8, 2001. There were mixed feelings about the visit, perhaps because of a resistance on the part of Brethren to be seen as the servants of government. Brethren wanted to be sure that the president's visit would symbolize our service *with* government rather than *to* government.

George and Laura Bush were the first sitting president and first lady to visit the Center. School children of Carroll County and school children all over the United States responded to President Bush's challenge to raise money for supplies for school children in Afghanistan. Many of these supplies were to be shipped by the Carroll County Red Cross through the Distribution Center of the Brethren Service Center.

A visit by a president does not happen on the spur of the moment, and for several days prior to the visit, the head of the Secret Service detail and the director of the Brethren Service Center were in meetings to plan the travel route, security, and all that goes with such a visit. After much discussion and compromise, an agreement was reached about the events of the day. A good old-fashioned handshake completed the agreements.

The president and first lady arrived by helicopter, landing on the soccer field at the New Windsor Middle School, and traveled in a fifteen-vehicle motorcade to the Service Center. Speaking in front of stacks of cardboard boxes, New Windsor seventh-grader Kristen Thompson introduced the president. Kristen was selected by school principal Thomas Eckenrode to introduce the honored guests after she and her friends raised more than $200 for America's Fund for Afghan Children, which the president was promoting.

The first shipment of goods for Afghan children included more than 1,500 oversized and winterized tents, 1,685 winter jackets, and 10,000 gift boxes for children, stuffed with hats, gloves, school supplies, and even candy and toys. "Coming here makes me so proud of America and our young people," Bush said. "We have given the Afghan children something to smile about, because America's children are kind. That's a lot of effort by a lot of youngsters."

Nearly three hundred people were invited to be present in the warehouse to hear the president speak. Many of the invited guests were students—elementary, middle school, and high school students from Virginia and Washington, D.C., as well as from Carroll County.[6]

Some people came that day, however, to protest Bush administration policies. In spite of a previous agreement between the director of the Center, Stan Noffsinger, and the head of the Secret Service detail that protestors would be able to stand along the route of the motorcade, the head of the Secret Service detail took it upon himself to have the protestors moved out of the area to another area where the president would not see the protestors or their signs. By the time Noffsinger learned of this break in their agreement, it was too late to correct the situation. Following the visit, Noffsinger received many phone calls, e-mails, and letters from friends and supporters of the ministries at the Center, questioning his reasons for moving protestors away from the motorcade route. He explained that he had not been consulted about the decision to move them and that he would not have agreed to such an action, though his explanation didn't satisfy everyone.[7] The visit to the Center by a sitting president was good for recognition of the Center in the local media. It was not as good for many who felt administrators of the Center had "sold out" to politics.

New Windsor council member Neal Roop stood along the street to watch the motorcade go by. He said in passing he wished he could have been in the select group that met with the president inside the Distribution Center. He may have said it best when he said, "Well, Washington calls the shots, not New Windsor on this one."[8] The Brethren Service Center was not calling the shots that day, but the ministry of service for more than fifty years has been a higher, more enduring calling, one that harnesses the power of love to change the world. Even superpower presidents can't do that.

Appendix I

———————— ⑥ ————————

Tidewater Portland Cement Company Contract

IT IS AGREED, That the Tidewater Portland Cement Company will purchase the property of the Blue Ridge College, at Union Bridge (consisting of all the land and improvements thereon owned by the College) for the sum of THIRTY THOUSAND ($30,000.) DOLLARS; terms of payment to be Thirty-five Hundred ($3500.) Dollars on July 8, 1912; Thirty-five Hundred ($3500.) Dollars on August 8, 1912; Thirty-five Hundred ($3500.) Dollars on September 8, 1912; Ten Thousand ($10,000.) Dollars on July 6, 1913; the title to said property to be good and marketable and free of all encumbrances; possession to be given August 8, 1912, upon the making of the second payment. Interest on the deferred payments not to run until August 8, 1912.

Notes for the deferred payments to be delivered on August 8, 1912, and a formal Contract of Sale to be entered into on July 8, 1912, evidencing the interests of the respective parties.

This Agreement does not contemplate the purchase of the property recently devised to the Blue Ridge College by the late Jacob Stoner.

May 21st 1912   TIDEWATER PORTLAND CEMENT COMPANY
                           By   _____ Atty.
                           Blue Ridge College

                           By   W. M. Wine
                           A. P. Snader, Trustees

Blue Ridge College Collection (BCSC-3), Special Collections and Archives, Alexander Mack Memorial Library, Bridgewater College, Bridgewater, Va.

Appendix 2

———— ⑥ ————

Joint Committee Meeting, Winchester, Virginia.

TO THE TRUSTEES OF BLUE RIDGE AND
BRIDGEWATER-DALEVILLE COLLEGES:

Your joint committee met in room 202 at the George Washington Hotel, Winchester, Virginia, at 11:30 a.m., on Wednesday, January 23, 1929, to confer on the problem of the relationship of our two schools. After a careful study of this problem we herewith submit our recommendations.

First: That the territory of Blue Ridge and Bridgewater-Daleville Colleges be merged into one educational unit; that the Maryland districts be granted representation on the Bridgewater-Daleville Board on an equal basis with the districts which now comprise the Bridgewater-Daleville territory, and that Blue Ridge College be granted the privilege of electing to their board representatives from the Bridgewater-Daleville territory if in their judgment it seems advisable.

Second: That the schools of this combination be separate and independent in their business and financial operations, and that in matters of policy and program the trustee boards function as they now do except for mutual advice and friendly cooperation.

Third: That financial campaigns which may be undertaken to strengthen these institutions be made as cooperative movements upon some basis to be agreed upon by the respective boards.

Fourth: That college students of freshman and sophomore rank be expected to attend their respective schools except in special cases which shall be adjusted by mutual agreement; that all students of junior and senior rank be provided for at Bridgewater; and that the college curriculum for the freshman and sophomore years be coordinated in the best possible way for the benefit of the Junior College graduates who may continue their college education at Bridgewater.

Fifth: That the records of former Blue Ridge students holding credit of junior and senior grade be transferred to Bridgewater for permanent preservation and future certification by Bridgewater; that Bridgewater recognize the college degrees conferred by Blue Ridge College, certify their credits, and admit them to all alumni privileges; and that the college graduates of Blue Ridge interested in having their degrees standardized be granted the privilege, thru summer study at Bridgewater, of qualifying for a Bridgewater degree.

Sixth: That a committee of three be appointed by action of the trustees for the purpose of handling executive and administrative problems. Your committee suggests that this committee be the President of Blue Ridge College, and the President and Dean of Bridgewater College.

Blue Ridge College Collection (BCSC-3), Special Collections and Archives, Alexander Mack Memorial Library, Bridgewater College.

Appendix 3

———————— ⑥ ————————

BLUE RIDGE COLLEGE

(JUNIOR COLLEGE)

ITS AIM . . .

The development of the young folks of both sexes, physically, mentally and morally, under the best Christian influences, amid wholesome and pleasing surroundings.

Future of the College

In its reorganization the trustees have endeavored to place the College on a sound basis in the field of education and provide an education that is recognized as standard. The two-year plan will permit it to render efficient service in developing men and women by close contact and supervision and offering an opportunity to develop initiative and independence of thought and action early in the college course.

Courses Offered

As a Junior College the following courses are emphasized:
1. The first two years of regular liberal arts course of the college whose completion admits the student to the junior year of other colleges of the State. Students must select their major and minor studies.

2. A. The two-year pre-professional course which fit the student for study of medicine, law or dentistry.

B. Two-year courses in commercial subjects as the secretarial, or bookkeeping and accounting courses and the first two years of the course in business administration. Students who have taken the commercial high school course may complete these courses in one year.

C. Courses in music and art which may he completed in two years, if the student has had some training before taking up these courses. The college has always strongly emphasized music and has maintained an excellent record in this field.

3. A two-year completion course. This is a new field in providing an education for those who wish just two years of college work, as many students drop out of college at the end of the second year. This course allows a wide selection of subjects to meet the needs and interests of those who enroll in it. It supplements the preparation given by the high schools and bridges the gap between its completion and taking up of the active duties of life. The work is of college grade but does not provide for the continuation of the college course beyond the two years. The fact that the junior college offers just two years of college work makes it possible to emphasize this field of activity to good advantage.

Buildings and Campus

The college with its well-kept and comfortable buildings, beautiful campus and attractive scenery offers a home-like environment to students. The mountains to the west of the College are an inspiration to study and the quietness of the place makes it possible to pursue work without distractions.

Extra-Curricular Activities

Extra-curricular activities include Chapel, Sunday School, Church, Y.M. and Y.W.C.A., Literary Society, Glee Club, Athletic schedules in the major and minor sports. A good lyceum course brings the students the best talent of the day. Opportunities are offered to all students to get practical work.

Blue Ridge College Bulletin, *Vol. XVII, No. 2, June 1929.*

Appendix 4

———————— ✿ ————————

Thirty-seventh Annual Commencement from Blue Ridge College while under the administration of the Church of the Brethren.

The graduates were:

Evelyn Celestine Barnes	New Windsor, Md.
Edythe Elizabeth Bowman	New Windsor, Md.
J. Paul Bowman	Union Bridge, Md.
Alice Katherine Beard	Westminster, Md.
Roger Leonard Crum	Frederick, Md.
Diana Sharretts Curley	Monkton, Md.
William Clyde Durrett	Baltimore, Md.
Edgar Frederic Faulkner	Lansdowne, Md.
George Watson Fluharty	Preston, Md.
Norman Franklin Ford	Frederick, Md.
Mary Edith Gumm	Showell, Md.
Doris Ruth Harrison	Baltimore, Md.
Miriam Elnore Holsinger	Ridgely, Md.
Anna Marie Hull	Westminster, Md.
Marshall Albert Morningstar	New Windsor, Md.
Ruth Frances Parlett	Baltimore, Md.
Harry Lee Porter, Jr.	Oakland, Md.
Annabelle Lee Price	Salisbury, Md.
Doris Merrick Prout	Owings, Md.
Ray David Riley	Emmitsburg, Md.
Ross Alberta Wagoner	Mt. Airy, Md.
Doris Virginia Woodie	Hagerstown, Md.
Marshall Albert Woodie	Hagerstown, Md.

Dr. James E. Lough, New York, delivered the commencement address speaking on "Education for the Moderm World." (Carroll County Times, *May 1937*)

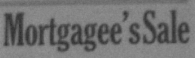

Mortgagee's Sale

of property known as the

Blue Ridge College Property

at

New Windsor, Maryland

Saturday Sept. 4

Blue Ridge College Property

"**Old Main**"

Girls' Dormitory

Boys' Dormitory

Gymnasium and Auditorium

THEODORE F. BROWN
Attorney named in mortgage

Brown and Shipley, Solicitors

Sterling Blackston, Auctioneer

Sale Postponed

The Public Sale of the

Blue Ridge College Property

at New Windsor, Maryland, heretofore advertised to take place on September 4, 1943, has been

POSTPONED

Carroll County Times *[Westminster, Md.]* 13, 20, 27 *August 1943, Historical Society of Carroll County, Westminster, Md.*

Carroll County Times *[Westminster, Md.]* 3 September 1943, Historical Society of Carroll County, Westminster, Md.*

TRUSTEES SALE

BLUE RIDGE COLLEGE

3 Valuable Houses, 2 Building Lots, 2 Large Farms and Personal Property

At New Windsor in Carroll County, Md. 7 miles west of Westminster, on

SEPTEMBER 6th, 7th, 8th and 9th, 1944

Sales will begin each day at 10 A. M.

ALL REAL ESTATE WILL BE OFFERED FOR SALE ON SEPTEMBER 6th, 1944

BLUE RIDGE COLLEGE

DWELLING HOUSE

DWELLING HOUSE

DWELLING HOUSE

BUILDING LOTS

F. NEAL PARKE, Attorney
S. BLACKSTEN, EARL HOFF, Auctioneers

FARM

FARM

PERSONAL PROPERTY

THEODORE F. BROWN, IVAN L. HOFF
Trustees and Attorneys at Law with offices in Westminster, Md.

Carroll County Times [*Westminster, Md.*] *11 August 1944, Historical Society of Carroll County, Westminster, Md.*

Appendix 7

———————— ⑥ ————————

Official Minutes of Brethren Service Committee of the Church of the Brethren, Elgin, Illinois, Nov. 1944.

THE BRETHREN SERVICE COMMITTEE AND THE BLUE RIDGE COLLEGE PLANT

General Statement:

The Brethren Service Committee purchased the Blue Ridge College plant at public auction on September 6, 1944. The purchase was made on the basis of substantial gifts from a group of Brethren of Eastern and Middle Maryland and a loan from Bridgewater College. The cost was $31,300.00.

The interest of the Brethren Service Committee in this property grows out of certain functions assigned to the Committee of the La Verne Conference of 1940 for which it has inadequate facilities.

The Committee has been encouraged to assume the responsibility involved in this purchase by the action of the District Conference of Eastern Maryland of 1944, authorizing the transfer of this property to the Service Committee for its work. The General Education Board took similar action at McPherson, Kansas in 1943 transferring such interest as it may have in the assets of Blue Ridge College to the Service Committee, in cooperation with Bridgewater College. The Huntingdon Conference of 1944 gave approval to this action.

Organization:

1. The name of the center at New Windsor shall be _____.

2. The center is the property of the Brethren Service Committee and the projects and program of the Center are under the direction of that Committee. A local committee on administration shall be created consisting of two representatives from the Brethren Service Committee and three from the local church districts of the East. The Executive Secretary and the chairman of the Brethren Service Committee shall be ex-officio members. The committee shall represent the Brethren Service Committee in the business and financial administration of the Center and general oversight of the activities as approved by the Brethren Service Committee.

There shall also be created an advisory council nominated by the committee on administration and approved by the Brethren Service Committee. This council shall be representative of the interests and groups of the church related to the service which the center undertakes to perform and shall function in an advisory capacity to the administrative committee.

General Objectives:

The general objectives of the center shall be in harmony with the purposes of the Brethren Service Center as defined by the La Verne Conference of 1940 and shall be administered in harmony with the policies approved from time to time by the Brethren Service Committee.

Immediate Projects of the Center:

1. The center shall serve as relief headquarters for the brotherhood, housing the clothing and food projects and the workers connected with the same.
2. The center shall serve as an assembling station for "heifers for relief" in preparation for shipment from the port of Baltimore or other eastern ports.
3. The center shall serve as a training station for relief and other church workers where short courses of specialized training for such work may be given.
4. The center shall serve temporarily as a soil conservation camp under C. P. S., housing about 50 men.
5. The center shall be made available for other brotherhood agencies in the promotion of this work. It is believed that the center may serve our educational interests in some measure. In this case, the general direction of projects shall reside in the college of the region and the General Education Board.

Future Projects:

The Brethren Service Committee recognizes that its program of service will be radically changed in the post-war period. The following proposals, however, are regarded as possible functions for the New Windsor center which offer a high degree of stability:

1. Relief program
2. Rural rehabilitation
3. Human relationships
4. Educational pioneering
5. Brethren casualties
6. Brethren Retreat for study and research
7. Other possible function—orphanage services, alcoholics rehabilitation, retreat for Missionaries.

Financial administration:

The center shall be operated as a unit within itself. Its business and financial operations shall be independent of the projects carried on at the center and shall be operated on a self-supporting and self-liquidating basis.

The following schedule of income and expenses is suggested:

Income

Rental of space to clothing center:

Gymnasium	$75.00 per month	$ 800.00
Windsor Hall	100.00 per month	1,200.00
Rental of six apartments to workers and their families @ $36.00 per month		2,592.00
Board and room for 40 CPS men at $30.00 per month—estimated income		6,000.00
	Total estimated income	$10,592.00

Expenses

Interest of loan at 4%	$ 1,000.00
Wages of caretaker and cook	2,400.00
Upkeep and repairs	1,500.00
Fuel, light and water	2,000.00
Total expense	$10,592.00

"This schedule anticipates voluntary labor, voluntary food and community cooperation in the current operations of the center." *(BSC Minutes, November 1944, Elgin, Ill.)*

———————— ⑥ ————————

Volunteer Service Certificate

This is to certify that _Wayne F. Buckle_

has completed _one year_ of work on a volunteer basis for the

BRETHREN SERVICE COMMITTEE
CHURCH OF THE BRETHREN
Elgin, Illinois

as _Manager of Relief Center_ in _New Windsor, Maryland_

from _January 1, 1945_ to _January 1, 1946_

"Inasmuch as ye have done it unto one of the least of these, my brethren, ye have done it unto me."

The committee wishes to express appreciation for the unselfish spirit of love and concern which prompted this service. May you receive God's blessing!

July 30, 1946
Date

M. R. Zigler
Executive Secretary B.S.C.

Volunteer Service Certificate

This is to certify that _Wilma Buckle_

has completed _one year_ of work on a volunteer basis for the

BRETHREN SERVICE COMMITTEE
CHURCH OF THE BRETHREN
Elgin, Illinois

as _Assistant at Relief Center_ in _New Windsor, Maryland_

from _January 1, 1945_ to _January 1, 1946_

"Inasmuch as ye have done it unto one of the least of these, my brethren, ye have done it unto me."

The committee wishes to express appreciation for the unselfish spirit of love and concern which prompted this service. May you receive God's blessing!

July 30, 1946
Date

M. R. Zigler
Executive Secretary B.S.C.

Appendix 9

———————— ⑥ ————————

General Brotherhood Board
BRETHREN SERVICE COMMISSION
22 South State Street
Elgin, Illinois

The Brethren Service Commission, the relief agency of the Church of the Brethren, in cooperation with the Cultural Affairs Branch of the American Government, has brought to the United States 90 German high school boys and girls for a year in urban and rural Brethren homes, attending high school, and participating in rural youth activities of the community in which they are located. There has been so much interest in this project that we are sponsoring another 100 of these German youth. In order that clearances may be made for these students to come to the United States, it is necessary that we have a certification from the principal or superintendent of the school in which the youth will be enrolled.

****

We hereby make application for a German high school boy / girl (Draw circle around one desired) to live as one of our family and attend high school. We understand the purpose of this project and will do our best to help develop understanding between German and American youth and to give these German youth a sensible picture of good American, Christian living.

Sponsoring family: _____ Children: _____
Address: _____ Ages: _____
Telephone: _____ _____
_____

State whether this is rural or urban situation, occupation of father and other information which will help us assign to your family a student of similar interests:

Could you take either boy or girl, in case we do not have your choice? Yes___ No___

Signed: _____   Congregation: _____
       Pastor
Address: _____   Date: _____

****

I hereby certify that I shall be happy to cooperate with the Brethren Service Commission of the Church of the Brethren in its Student Exchange Project by assuring that one of these German youth will be enrolled in the _____high school of _____ for the coming year as a regular high school student upon his / her arrival in the United States.

Signed: _____
       Principal or Superintendent
Address: _____

****

Date:_____   Countersigned: _____
       Secretary,
       Brethren Service Commission

Part I. The White Building on the Hill

1. Calvert College, 1848–1870

1. Nathan H. Baile, excerpts from diary, 1913, Historical Society of Carroll County, Westminster, Md.; "Dr. Edward C. Bixler Tells the History of Blue Ridge College from 1839-1937," *Democratic Advocate* [Westminster, Md.] 16 July 1937; Julia Cairns, personal interview, 2 August 2001.

2. "Dr. Edward C. Bixler Tells the History."

3. Edward Crill, comp., "History of Blue Ridge College," 1948, unpublished manuscript, Historical Society of Carroll County, Westminster, Md.

4. Cairns.

5. Cairns; Baile diary.

6. Nancy M. Warner, Ralph B. Levering, Margaret T. Woltz, *Carroll County, Maryland: A History 1837-1976*, Carroll County Bicentennial Committee, 1976, 149-150.

7. Baile diary.

8. Mr. Baker's creditors were Josiah Hibberd, James Erhard, Solomon S. Ecker, Levi Snader, David Smelser, Jos Stouffer, Elhanan Stouffer, and L. P. Slingluff.

9. Baile diary.

2. New Windsor College

1. Edward Crill, comp., "History of Blue Ridge College," 1948, unpublished manuscript, Historical Society of Carroll County, Westminster, Md.

2. Bryce Workman, "College on the Hill," 2006 (working draft), New Windsor Historical Society, New Windsor, Md.

3. New Windsor College Year Book 1893-94; Crill, "History of Blue Ridge College."

4. Jay Graybeal, *Carroll County Times* [Westminster, Md.] 9 December 1996.

5. According to Nathan Baile's diary, the men from the Baltimore Presbytery were Robert H. Smith, Theodore Miller, Mr. Fester, Mr. Reed, Mr. McDonald, George H. Birnie, Dr. Ramsdell, Nathan H. Baile.

6. *Democratic Advocate Supplement* [Westminster, Md.] 13 October 1910.

3. Blue Ridge College

1. J. Maurice Henry, *History of the Church of the Brethren in Maryland* (Elgin, Ill.: Brethren Publishing House, 1936) 383-387.

2. Henry 383-387.

3. Jay Graybeal, *Carroll County Times* [Westminster, Md.] 6 May 2001.

4. Maryland Collegiate Institute, College Brochure 1905-06, Julia Cairns collection, New Windsor Historical Society, New Windsor, Md.

5. Maryland Collegiate Institute, College Brochure 1905-06.

6. Francis Fry Wayland, *Bridgewater College, The First Hundred Years 1880-1980* (Bridgewater College, Va., 1993) 248.

7. Wayland 246

8. Wayland 246-47.

9. Julia Cairns, personal interview, 2 August 2001.

10. Blue Ridge College Permanent Endowment subscription certificate. Found in Court Case No. 7500 record, see note 11.

11. *The Union Bridge Banking and Trust Company v. The Blue Ridge College and Others*, No. 7500 Equity, Circuit Court for Carroll County (Md.), 23 August 1943, 13, State Archives, Annapolis, Md. (hereafter referred to as No. 7500).

12. S. Z. Sharp, *The Educational History of the Church of the Brethren* (Elgin, Ill.: Brethren Publishing House, 1923) 247.

13. Henry 386; "J. Maurice Henry," *The Brethren Encyclopedia*, Vol. 1 (Philadelphia, Pa. and Oak Brook, Ill.: The Brethren Encyclopedia Inc., 1983) 598.

14. Eastern Maryland District Conference Minutes, April 24-25, 1923, 14.

15. Jacob F. Replogle, "Look to the Hills: A Study of the Early Beginnings of Brethren Church Camping in Maryland," Bridgewater, Va., 1982, Mid-Atlantic District Office, New Windsor Md. Only fifty copies were produced at the author's personal expense.

16. Henry 386.

17. Dr. Robert L. Kelly, "Evaluation of Blue Ridge College 1932-33," Association of American Colleges, 111 Fifth Ave., New York City, N.Y., Blue Ridge College Collection (BCSC-3), Special Collections and Archives, Alexander Mack Memorial Library, Bridgewater College.

18. Kelly.

19. No. 7500.

20. No. 7500.

21. Paul Haynes Bowman, *Brethren Education in the Southeast* (Elgin, Ill.: Brethren Press, 1955) 236.

22. Bowman 236.

4. Outside Investors in Blue Ridge College

1. *The Union Bridge Banking and Trust Company v. The Blue Ridge College and Others*, No. 7500 Equity, Circuit Court for Carroll County (Md.), 23 August 1943, 11, State Archives, Annapolis, Md. (hereafter referred to as No. 7500).

2. No. 7500, 17.

3. Paul Haynes Bowman, *Brethren Education in the Southeast* (Elgin, Ill.: Brethren Press, 1955) 239.

4. No. 7500, 17.

5. "Blue Ridge College Opens September 20th Under New Organization" 9 (newspaper clipping), n.d., Julia Cairns collection, New Windsor Historical Society, New Windsor Md.

6. Book 96: 18-20; Book 168: 97-98; Book 171: 207-209 and 521-523. Real Estate Record Books, Carroll County Court House, Westminster, Md.

7. Blue Ridge College "Reflector," March 1937: 1, Blue Ridge College Collection (BSCS-3), Special Collections and Archives, Alexander Mack Memorial Library, Bridgewater College.

8. "Reflector" 1.

9. *Baltimore Sun* [Baltimore, Md.], 27 August 1937.

10. *Hanover Evening Sun* [Hanover, Pa.], 26 August 1937.

11. *Baltimore Sun*, 27 August 1937.

12. *Hanover Evening Sun*, 26 August 1937.

13. *Hanover Evening Sun*, 26 August 1937.

14. *Pilot* [Union Bridge, Md.], 24 September 1937.

15. Book 867: 547, Recorded Deeds, Carroll County Court House, Westminster, Md.

16. Julia Cairns, personal interview, 2 August 2001.

17. "Blue Ridge College Bulletin," Centennial Year 1839-1939, Vol. XXVII, No. 1, April 1939, Julia Cairns collection, New Windsor Historical Society, New Windsor, Md.

18. Enos Heisey, personal interview, 24 July 2001.

19. Mr. and Mrs. Harry B. Cook of Baltimore established a scholarship fund in memory of Mrs. Cook's sister, Annabelle Walker Pardew. Laura J. Graddick of Forsythe, Georgia, established a fund for worthy students. "Miss Graddick was one of Blue Ridge's oldest living alumni and made this contribution in honor of her fiftieth year since graduation from Blue Ridge College." Still another endowment was established by Mr. and Mrs. Howard Roop of New Windsor for an annual speaking contest called the Julia Ann Roop Public Speaking Contest in honor of their daughter Julia Ann Roop Cairns, a student in the class of 1931-32. A fourth fund was given by Stanley E. Rogers in honor of his parents, Mr. and Mrs. S. E. Rogers, for prizes to be given for an essay contest in physics. ("Blue Ridge College Opens September 20th [1939] Under New Organization" (newspaper clipping), n.d., Julia Cairns collection, New Windsor Historical Society, New Windsor, Md.)

20. *Carroll County Times* [Westminster, Md.] 16 February 1940.

21. *Carroll County Times.*

5. Effects of World War II on Blue Ridge College

1. *Carroll County Times* [Westminster, Md.] 3 May 1940.

2. *Pilot* [Union Bridge, Md.] 20 February 1942.

3. *Carroll County Times* 11 July 1941.

4. *Carroll County Times* 4 September 1942.

5. *Pilot* [Union Bridge, Md.] 20 February 1942.

6. *Democratic Advocate* [Westminster, Md.] 19 March 1943.

7. *Carroll County Times* 31 July 1942.

8. *The Blue Ridge College v. The Eastern Maryland District Meeting of the Church of the Brethren*, No. 7406 Equity, Circuit Court for Carroll County (Md.), 30 September 1942 (hereafter referred to as No. 7406); *The Union Bridge Banking and Trust Company v. The Blue Ridge College and Others*, No. 7500 Equity, Circuit Court for Carroll County (Md.), 23 August 1943, 23, State Archives, Annapolis, Md.

9. No. 7406.

10. No. 7406.

11. George J. Touwsma, letter to Jacob F. Replogle, director of Reuel B. Pritchett Museum, Bridgewater College, n.d., Blue Ridge College Collection (BCSC-3), Special Collections and Archives, Alexander Mack Memorial Library, Bridgewater College.

6. Blue Ridge College Closes Its Doors

1. *Carroll County Times* [Westminster, Md.] 12 November 1943.

2. *The Union Bridge Banking and Trust Company v. The Blue Ridge College and Others*, No. 7500 Equity, Circuit Court for Carroll County (Md.), 23 August 1943, 17, State Archives, Annapolis, Md. (hereafter referred to as No. 7500).

3. No. 7500, 18.

4. No. 7500, 21.

5. No. 7500, 21.

6. No. 7500, 22.

7. Annie Stoner's Will, Liber U.P.B. No. 14, folio 215, Carroll County Court House (Westminster, Md.).

8. No. 7500, 36.

9. *The Eastern Maryland District Meeting, etc., v. The Union Bridge Banking and Trust Co., a body corporate.* Homer E. Cooper; Raymond P. Jefferis, Jr., John P. Marbarger and Donald M. Pace, No. 73, October 1944, Court of Appeals of Maryland.

10. *Hanover Evening Sun* [Hanover, Pa.] 15 January 1945.

11. Julia Cairns, personal interview, 2 August 2001.

12. Harry and Verda Mae Peters, personal interview, 20 June 2001.

13. CPS fellows and volunteers, Brethren Retirement Community, Greenville, Oh., personal interview, 30 August 2001.

14. Listed among other outstanding accounts owed by Blue Ridge College in Court Case No. 7500 Equity. Dated May 13, 1944, and signed by Erscre G. Benedict, clerk, Village of New Windsor, Md.

Part II: War Relief

7. A Ministry of Service

1. Roger E. Sappington, *Brethren Social Policy: 1908-1958* (Elgin, Ill.: Brethren Press, 1961) 48-51.

2. Anetta Mow, "Call for Clothing for Spain," *The Gospel Messenger*, 14 January 1939: 25.

3. Anetta C. Mow, "Clothing in Christ's Name," *The Gospel Messenger*, 30 December 1944: 10.

4. Mow, "Clothing in Christ's Name," 10.

5. Mow, "Clothing in Christ's Name," 10.

6. Kenneth I. Morse, "New Windsor Center" (Elgin, Ill.: Brethren Press, 1979) 46.

7. *The Union Bridge Banking and Trust Company v. The Blue Ridge College and Others*, No. 7500 Equity, Circuit Court for Carroll County (Md.), 23 August 1943, 503, State Archives, Annapolis, Md.

8. Marion Noll, personal interview (CPS fellows and volunteers, Brethren Retirement Community, Greenville, Ohio), 30 August 2001.

9. "Brethren Service News," *The Gospel Messenger*, 23 September 1944: 21.

10. Virginia Crim, personal interview (CPS fellows and volunteers, Brethren Retirement Community, Greenville, Ohio), 30 August 2001.

11. "Clothing for Greece," *The Gospel Messenger*, 9 April 1944: 10.

12. "Brethren Service News," *The Gospel Messenger*, 25 November 1944: 11.

8. Fulfilling a Dream: Creation of a Relief Center

1. Official Minutes of the Brethren Service Committee of the Church of the Brethren, May 1944, 63-64. Brethren Historical Library and Archives (BHLA), Elgin, Ill.

2. Elders' Meeting Minutes, Eastern Maryland District, New Windsor Md., 23 August 1944, S. R. Wright, clerk, BHLA, Elgin, Ill.

3. Official Minutes of the Brethren Service Committee of the Church of the Brethren, August 1944. BHLA, Elgin Ill.

4. John Jean John, personal interview, summer 2005. John Jean John is the grandson and son of the surveyors.

5. *The Union Bridge Banking and Trust Company v. The Blue Ridge College and Others*, No. 7500 Equity, Circuit Court for Carroll County (Md.), 23 August 1943, 501, State Archives, Annapolis, Md.

6. Paul Haynes Bowman, *Brethren Education in the Southeast* (Elgin, Ill.: Brethren Press 1955) 242.

7. J. Kenneth Kreider, *A Cup of Cold Water: The Story of Brethren Service* (Elgin, Ill.: Brethren Press, 2001) 82; Donald F. Durnbaugh, *Pragmatic Prophet: The Life of Michael Robert Zigler* (Elgin, Ill.: Brethren Press, 1989) 148.

8. "The Brethren Service Committee and the Blue Ridge College Plant," Official Minutes of the Brethren Service Commission, Elgin, Ill., November 1944, Addenda, 11, BHLA.

9. John.

10. J. Vern Fairchilds, Jr., letter to the authors, 21 August 2001.

9. Establishing a Permanent Place for Service

1. *Carroll County Times* [Westminster, Md.] 15 September 1944.

2. *Pilot* [Union Bridge, Md.] 15 September 1944.

3. "Brethren Relief Center," *The Gospel Messenger*, 7 October 1944: 10.

4. Charles C. Sutton, letter to the authors, 18 December 2001.

5. Harry and Verda Mae Peters, personal interview, 20 June 2001.

6. Virginia Crim, personal interview (CPS fellows and volunteers, Brethren Retirement Community, Greenville, Ohio), 30 August 2001.

7. Sutton.

8. *Carroll County Times* [Westminster, Md.] 22 September 1944.

9. Harry and Verda Mae Peters.

10. Gilbert and Marjorie Walbridge, personal interview, 18 July 2001.

11. CPS fellows and volunteers, Brethren Retirement Community, Greenville, Ohio, personal interview, 30 August 2001.

12. CPS fellows and volunteers.

13. "Current Relief Needs," *The Gospel Messenger*, 28 October 1944: 19.

14. Byron and Virginia Grossnickle, personal interview, 18 July 2006.

15. Sutton.

16. Wayne and Wilma Buckle, personal interview, 18 July 2001.

17. CPS fellows and volunteers.

18. CPS fellows and volunteers.

19. "Brethren Service News," *The Gospel Messenger*, 25 November 1944: 11.

20. Blanche Spalding, personal interview, 27 June 2006.

21. "Brethren Relief Center," *The Gospel Messenger*, 7 October 1944: 10.

22. "Brethren Service News," *The Gospel Messenger*, 25 November 1944: 11.

23. Wayne and Wilma Buckle; "Brethren Service News," *The Gospel Messenger*, 1 September 1945: 10.

24. Enos and Jane Heisey, personal interview, 24 July 2001.

25. "For Brethren Relief Program," *The Gospel Messenger*, 15 April 1944: 20.

26. J. Kenneth Kreider, *A Cup of Cold Water: The Story of Brethren Service* (Elgin, Ill.: Brethren Press 2001) 84.

27. Carroll County Public Library reference desk, Westminster, Md.

28. Minutes of the 159th Recorded Annual Conference of the Church of the Brethren, North Manchester, Indiana, 1945 (Elgin, Ill.: Brethren Press, 1945) 67.

29. Minutes of the 160th Recorded Annual Conference of the Church of the Brethren, Wenatchee, Washington, June 11-16, 1946 (Elgin, Ill.: Brethren Press, 1946) 33.

30. Summary of relief shipments from New Windsor, Md., 1946-1947, staff meeting minutes, n.d.

10. Partnership with Church World Service

1. Ronald E. Stenning, *Church World Service: Fifty Years of Help and Hope* (New

York: Friendship Press, 1996) 3.

2. Stenning 3.

3. Stenning 2.

4. Stenning 3.

5. Stenning 3.

6. CPS fellows and volunteers, Brethren Retirement Community, Greenville, Ohio, personal interview, 30 August 2001.

7. Kenneth I. Morse, "New Windsor Center" (Elgin, Ill.: Brethren Press, 1979) 46.

8. "Clothing for Greece," *The Gospel Messenger*, 8 April 1944: 10.

9. John D. Metzler, Sr., "Fiftieth Anniversary of Brethren Service Center," 1994.

10. Bimmy Little, personal interview, 2 August 2005.

11. Stenning 87.

Part III. Post-War Relief Ministries

11. CROP

1. Ronald E. Stenning, *Church World Service: Fifty Years of Help and Hope* (New York: Friendship Press, 1996) 4.

2. Stenning 6.

3. Stenning 41.

4. Stenning 54-55.

12. Heifer Project

1. "Heifer Project International," *The Brethren Encyclopedia*, Vol. 1 (Philadelphia, Pa., and Oak Brook, Ill.: The Brethren Encyclopedia, Inc., 1983) 594.

2. Roger and Olive Roop, "Recollections of Heifer Project Days," December 1985, Union Bridge, Md.

3. Roop.

4. Roop.

5. "UNRRA and the Dunkers," *The Gospel Messenger*, 1 September 1945: 10. First appeared in Time magazine, July 23, 1945, and reprinted by permission.

6. Fran Nyce, personal interview, 27 July 2001.

7. John H. Eberly, interview by Ingrid Rogers, January 1985, North Manchester, Ind., personal collection of the authors.

8. Community Meeting Minutes, Brethren Service Relief Center, 7 September 1948.

9. "From Relief to Development: The Evolving Mission of Heifer Project International, Inc.," Clio Research Associates, University of Arkansas (Little Rock), a class research project, History 7391: Public History Seminar, 18, 25, 35, 43.

13. SERRV

1. Calendar, Fiftieth Anniversary of the New Windsor Service Center, 1994.

2. John H. Eberly, letter to Byron Royer, 24 April 1950, Brethren Service Center files.

3. Byron Royer, letter to M. R. Zigler, 15 May, 1950, Brethren Service Center files.

4. Royer.

5. Royer.

6. "New Windsor," Brethren Service Commission Minutes, June 1950, 4j, 9, Brethren Historical Library and Archives (BHLA), Elgin, Ill.

7. "Report on International Gift Shop at New Windsor," Brethren Service Commission Minutes, November 1950, Exhibit Q, 43, BHLA.

8. W. Ray Kyle, letter to Mrs. O. R. Hersch, n.d., Brethren Service Center files.

9. Brethren Service Commission Minutes, November 1950.

10. W. Ray Kyle, letter to W. Hylton Harman, lawyer, 951, Brethren Service Center files.

11. W. Ray Kyle, letter to M. R. Zigler, 21 December 1950, Brethren Service Center files.

12. W. Ray Kyle, letter to Russell Eisenbise, 2 March 1951.

13. W. Ray Kyle, letter to Mrs. Alice Rohrer, October 1951, Brethren Service Center files.

14. Virginia Grossnickel, *History of SERRV*, 1983 (unpublished), SERRV files.

15. "The Quiet Diplomat," *The Gospel Messenger*, 20 January 1966: 14.

16. M. R. Zigler, letter to W. Ray Kyle, 12 November 1965, Brethren Service Center files.

17. Frances Nyce, "A Chance to Help Themselves," *Messenger*, 12 October 1967: 2-4.

18. Nyce 4-5.

19. "SERRV Imports Increase," *SERRV News*, Spring 1971: 5.

20. *SERRV News*, Spring 1972.

21. Grossnickle.

22. Grossnickle.

23. *Frederick Post*, 12 August 1982.

24. Virginia Leache, "A Cornucopia of Treats Spills from New Windsor Gift Shop," *Attraction* [Carroll County, Md.], 18 February 1982.

25. Barbara McFadden Royer, personal conversation, October 2006.

26. "Outlook," *Messenger*, August 1989: 8.

27. "SERRV announces move to Wisconsin," *Messenger*, March 2001: 8; SERRV files.

28. Bob Chase, SERRV report, n.d.

14. Farmer and Student Exchange Program

1. J. Kenneth Kreider, *A Cup of Cold Water: The Story of Brethren Service* (Elgin, Ill.: Brethren Press, 2001) 181.

2. John H. Eberly, interview by Ingrid Rogers, January 1985, North Manchester, Ind., personal collection of the authors.

3. Eberly.

4. Eberly.

5. Marian Buckle, ed., "German High School Students Arrive," *The Gospel Messenger*, 12 November 1949: 18-19.

6. Buckle 19.

7. "German High School Student Project," Brethren Service Commission Minutes, November 1949, Exhibit C, 15, Brethren Historical Library and Archives (BHLA), Elgin, Ill.

8. Brethren Service Commission Minutes, June 1950, BHLA.

9. Buckle 19.

10. Donald F. Durnbaugh, ed., *To Serve the Present Age: The Brethren Service Story* (Elgin, Ill.: Brethren Press, 1975) 205.

11. Harold Row, Brethren Service Commission letter to Ecumenical Friends, June 1950, BHLA.

12. John H. Eberly, "German High School Student Tragedy," *The Gospel Messenger*, 10 February 1951: 19.

13. "General Report on Brethren Service Program," Brethren Service Commission Minutes, November 1950, Exhibit A, 15, BHLA.

14. Sylvia Seese, letter to Verna Rapp, 21 June 1950, Brethren Service Center files.

15. William Eberly, letter to authors describing John H. Eberly's work, summer 2006.

16. Maury Mussellman, "A Personal Story—Gerhard Weiser," private papers sent to the authors September 2006.

17. Mussellman.

18. John Gwildis, "Two Messages from Returned German Students," ed., Lorell Weiss, *The Gospel Messenger*, 3 February 1951: 18-19.

19. Ruth Davidson, "And an Idea Became a Reality," *The Gospel Messenger*, 18 February 1961: 20.

20. Donna Lehman, *ECHO*, December 1952, Vol. 4, No. 16: 1, BHLA.

21. Donna Lehman, *ECHO*, November 1953, Vol. 5, No. 20: 7, BHLA.

22. Donna Lehman, *ECHO*, October 1953, Vol. 5, No. 19: 7, BHLA.

23. Donna Lehman, *ECHO*, February 1954, Vol. 5, No. 22: 6, BHLA.

24. Donna Lehman, *ECHO*, February 1954, Vol. 5, No. 22: 5, BHLA.

25. Davidson 21.

26. Davidson 21.

27. Davidson 21.

28. Durnbaugh 207.

15. Refugee Resettlement

1. W. Harold Row, letter to John D. Metzler, n.d., but found among other letters dated 1946 and 1947, Brethren Service Center files.

2. J. Kenneth Kreider, *Cup of Cold Water: The Story of Brethren Service* (Elgin, Ill.: Brethren Press, 2001) 103.

3. John H. Eberly, letter to Desmond Bittinger, 23 April 1950, personal collection of the authors.

4. Gisela M. Kaleps (Hamburg, Germany), letter to the authors, September 2006.

5. Joseph B. Mow, letter to Mrs. Abuschilaou, 4 November 1992, Brethren Historical Library and Archives (BHLA), Elgin, Ill.; Ruth E. Early, "The Kalmucks: Strangers No More," *Messenger*, May 1977: 26-29.

6. Mow.

7. "When East Meets West," Baltimore *Sun* (Sunday magazine), 24 February 1952.

8. Helen Kyle Carlisle, personal interview, 21 July 2005.

9. Mow.

10. "A Statement Addressing the Concern of Undocumented Persons and Refugees in the United States," business item No. 11 (Conference action: paper adopted), 1982 Annual Conference Minutes (Elgin, Ill.: Brethren Press, 1982) 435-440.

11. Donna Derr, phone interview, 22 July 2006.

12. Oral tradition, told by camp personnel and refugee resettlement staff. No written record found to verify this story.

13. Kathleen Campanella, letter to Kalmuk Association in celebration of the fiftieth anniversary of their arrival at Brethren Service Center, New Windsor, Md.,

n.d. Note that figure of 79,000 includes all those who passed through the transit center.

14. Mesfin Hailu Arsedi, personal conversation with the authors at the Brethren Service Center, 11 August 2006.

16. Brethren Volunteer Service

1. James H. Lehman, *Living the Story, 50 Years of Brethren Volunteer Service* (Elgin, Ill.: Church of the Brethren General Board, 1998), foreword by Dan McFadden.

2. Lehman 1.

3. Lehman 2.

4. Lehman 2-3.

5. Lehman 4.

6. Lehman 4.

7. Lehman 9.

8. Personal experience of the authors.

9. Information supplied by the Brethren Volunteer Service office, Elgin Ill., October 2006.

10. Lehman 16.

Part IV. Service Ministries

17. Interchurch Medical Assistance, Inc.

1. Carol Hulver, personal interview, 24 July 2006.

2. Hulver.

3. Hulver.

18. Processing and Distribution of Material Aid

1. The authors were privileged to be on the receiving end of relief supplies sent from New Windsor. One shipment of 50,000 Church World Service blankets was received by the Sudan Council of Churches in 1990, when R. Jan Thompson worked for that organization. The blankets were distributed to displaced persons from Southern Sudan who were living in makeshift housing in the northern portion of Sudan, close to the capital city, Khartoum. Roma Jo Thompson assisted in the distribution of health kits, school kits, sewing kits, and baby layettes in two refugee camps in Kenya in 1991. Distributing the kits and witnessing the appreciation of the recipients completed the circle for Roma Jo who had encouraged church groups to assemble such kits when she was a CWS/CROP director in the Mid-Atlantic Region.

2. "Carroll County Overview for Business and Industry," Vol. 6, No. 1, March 1986, Carroll County Economic Development Commission, Westminster, Md.

3. Partner/Client Summary, provided by Loretta Wolf to authors, July 2006.

4. Loretta Wolf, phone interview, 15 February 2007.

5. Loretta Wolf, e-mail correspondence, 15 February 2007.

6. Service Ministries report, 218th Annual Conference Booklet, Charleston, West Virginia, July 3-7, 2004, 81.

7. Service Ministries report, 219th Annual Conference Booklet, Peoria, Illinois, July 2-6, 2005, 75.

8. Service Ministries report, 220th Annual Conference Booklet, Des Moines, Iowa, July 1-5, 2006, 78-79.

19. A Place to Meet and Retreat

1. The Report of the Meeting of the Master Plans Committee for a Study of the Programs and Facilities of the New Windsor Brethren Service Center, May 1-2, 1964, Brethren Historical Library and Archives (BHLA), Elgin, Ill.

2. D. Miller Davis, personal interview, 18 July 2006.

3. "Center to Dedicate, M. R. Zigler Hall," *The Gospel Messenger*, 9 May 1968: 15.

4. Davis.

5. Davis.

6. H. McKinley Coffman, personal interview, 14 August 2006.

20. Brethren Disaster Ministries

1. A. H. Brandt, [editorial], *The Gospel Messenger*, 8 March 1941: 1.

2. R. Jan Thompson, "History of the Church of the Brethren Disaster Response" (unpublished), 1980. Brethren Disaster Ministries office, New Windsor, Md.

3. Charles Boyer, phone interview, 17 August 2006.

4. Boyer.

5. Boyer.

6. "Pass Christian BVSer Dies in Swim Accident," *Messenger*, 1 September 1971: 7.

7. "Brethren Respond to Earthquake, *Messenger*, 1 April 1971: 2-3.

8. "Brethren Respond to Earthquake," 3.

9. D. Miller Davis, personal interview, 18 July 2006.

10. Davis.

11. " 'They love us in Wilkes-Barre,' McDowell says," *Messenger*, 1 November 1972: 6; "Brethren Response to Hurricane Lauded," *Messenger*, 15 November 1972: 3-5.

12. "Brethren Response to Hurricane Lauded," 4.

13. "Brethren Response to Hurricane Lauded," 4.

14. Personal experience of the authors and family; *Wabash Plain Dealer* [Wabash, Ind.], 8 April 1974.

15. Ron Finney, personal reflections, August 2006.

16. "McPherson Responds to Big Thompson," *Messenger*, March 1977: 6.

17. Finney.

18. Wendell Bohrer, *Johnstown, a Story of Tragedy and Love* (Elgin, Ill.: Brethren Press, 1978) 36-37.

19. Personal experience of the author.

20. Personal experience of the author.

21. Official records from Brethren Disaster Ministries office, provided by Jane Yount, 2006.

22. Personal experience of the author.

23. Zachary Wolgemuth, e-mail correspondence, 26 January 2007.

21. Children's Disaster Services

1. Personal experience of the author.

2. Personal experience of the author.

3. Verbal reports from Red Cross and FEMA caseworkers, Kalamazoo, Mich., 1980.

4. Official records, Children's Disaster Services office, New Windsor, Md.

5. R. Jan Thompson, "Annual Report—Refugee/Disaster Program, 1984," submitted to World Ministries Commission, General Board, January 1985, personal files of R. Jan Thompson.

6. Thompson.

7. R. Jan Thompson, staff report to J. Roger Schrock, 29 July 1987, personal files of R. Jan Thompson.

8. CAIR Training Manual, 1998, Children's Disaster Services office, New Windsor, Md.

9. Kevin Lamb, "Local Psychologist Helps Grieving Children," *Dayton Daily News* [Dayton, Oh.] 22 January 2002.

10. Official records, Children's Disaster Services office, New Windsor, Md.

Part V. A Witness for Peace: Education and Advocacy

22. The Conference Center

1. The Inter-Race Church Camp of June 27-July 3, 1948, brochure, Brethren Service Center files, New Windsor, Md.

2. D. D. Funderburg, letter to Bernice Bridges, director, Youth Division-National Social Welfare Assembly, Inc., 21 December 1948.

3. D. D. Funderburg, letter to George Guernsey, 12 May 1949.

4. The Report of the Meeting of the Master Plans Committee for a Study of the Programs and Facilities of the New Windsor Brethren Service Center, May 1-2, 1964, 1, Brethren Historical Library and Archives (BHLA), Elgin, Ill.

23. On Earth Peace

1. Donald F. Durnbaugh, *Pragmatic Prophet: The Life of Michael Robert Zigler* (Elgin, Ill.: Brethren Press, 1989) 276.

2. Durnbaugh 276.

3. Durnbaugh 284.

4. Durnbaugh 286.

24. A Nimble Tradition of Service

1. "New Program Provides Food Canning Centers," *Messenger*, July 1980: 6.

2. Data collected from Annual Conference "Wrap-up Journals," Annual Report files, Brethren Historical Library and Archives (BHLA), Elgin, Ill., and Brethren Disaster Ministries files, New Windsor, Md.

3. "Global Food Crisis Appeal," World Ministries Commission Minutes, October 1983, 5-6, BHLA.

4. Brenda Palsgrove, personal interview, summer 2006.

5. "New Windsor Hails 50th," Agenda, Newsletter for Church of the Brethren Congregational Leaders, November 1993:1.

Epilogue: In the World But Not of It

1. "A Joint Communiqué," *The Gospel Messenger*, 5 October 1963: 14.

2. "A Joint Communiqué," 14.

3. Lamar Gibble, personal conversation, 2 February 2007.

4. Howard Royer, "The Russians: Reflections on the Exchange (Special Report)," *Messenger*, 18 January 1968, 20.

5. Royer 20.

6. *Carroll County Times* [Westminster, Md.], 9 December 2001: 1.
7. Stanley Noffsinger, personal conversations, summer 2002.
8. *Carroll County Times* [Westminster, Md.], 9 December 2001: 1.

Note: some index entries include references to the unpaginated photo section (*p.s.*).